The
Living Theatre
of Medieval
Art

THE LIVING THEATRE
of MEDIEVAL 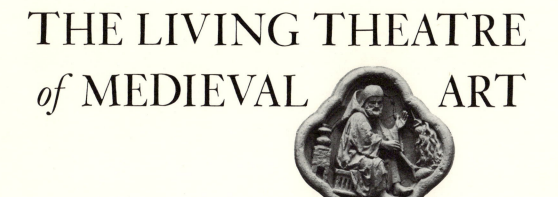 ART

BY HENRY KRAUS

FOREWORD BY HARRY BOBER

University of Pennsylvania Press

PHILADELPHIA

First Pennsylvania Paperback edition 1972
Library of Congress catalog card number: 67-24004
ISBN 0-8122-1056-5
Manufactured in the United States of America

To Dorothy

CONTENTS

FOREWORD BY HARRY BOBER   *xiii*

PREFACE   *xix*

I The Eight Invisible Reliefs at Notre-Dame   *3*

II The Social Factor   *22*

III Eve and Mary: Conflicting Images of Medieval Woman   *41*

IV The New Classes as Donors and as Subjects   *63*

V The Popular Impact   *100*

VI The Church Fights Heresy:
With Flame, With Sword—and With Art   *119*

VII Anti-Semitism in Medieval Art   *139*

VIII Iconoclasm and Its Rationalizations   *163*

IX The Medieval Artist and the Building Boom   *183*

CHRONOLOGY   *211*

LIST OF MONUMENTS   *219*

NOTES   *223*

INDEX   *239*

ILLUSTRATIONS

1 The Martyrs' Portal, Notre-Dame de Paris   2
2 "Life of the Students" series, Notre-Dame de Paris   10
3 The Prodigal Son window, Bourges cathedral   11
4 "Life of the Students" series, Notre-Dame de Paris   14
5 "Honorable Amends," former convent of Grands-Augustins, Paris   19
6 Church of Sainte-Foy, Conques-en-Rouergue   27
7 The ambulatory, abbey church, Saint-Denis   27
8 Sick rising from their beds, abbey church, Saint-Benoît-sur-Loire   29
9 Louis VII offering the church to St. Vincent, church of Avenas   34
10 Theophilus and the Devil, abbey church, Souillac   34
11 A seignior giving property to church, former church of Mervilliers   35
12 Money-coining scene, church of Saint-Pierre, Souvigny   37
13 A judicial duel, abbey church, Saint-Benoît-sur-Loire   37
14 The Flight into Egypt, abbey church, Saint-Benoît-sur-Loire   37
15 Bishop Odo, The Bayeux Tapestry   38
16 The Vice of Unchastity, Chartreuse-du-Val-de-Bénédiction, Villeneuve-les-Avignon   43
17 The Vice of Unchastity, Autun cathedral   43
18 Eve and the serpent, Reims cathedral   43
19 Potiphar's wife, Chartres cathedral   43
20 The Vice of Unchastity, church of Sainte-Croix, Bordeaux   44
21 Adam and Eve driven from Paradise, Notre-Dame-du-Port, Clermont-Ferrand   44
22 The Nativity, Chartres cathedral   49
23 Noah's family, Bourges cathedral   51
24 Hosea and the Harlot, Amiens cathedral   51
25 Esther and Ahasuerus, Chartres cathedral   51
26 Judith covering her head with ashes, Chartres cathedral   51
27 Judith with head of Holofernes, church of La Madeleine, Vézelay   52
28 The Massacre of the Innocents, Chartres cathedral   52
29 The Prodigal Son window, Bourges cathedral   52
30 The Creation of Adam, Chartres cathedral   54
31 The Rising Dead, Amiens cathedral   54
32 The Original Sin, Reims cathedral   54
33 The Tempter and the Foolish Virgin, Strasbourg cathedral   56
34 Mother and child, church of La Madeleine, Vézelay   57

35 Herod and Salome, former cloister of the monastery of Saint-
    Étienne, Toulouse   57
36 David and Goliath, church of La Madeleine, Vézelay   65
37 The Temptation of St. Anthony, church of La Madeleine, Vézelay 65
38 Death of Dives, church of Saint-Pierre, Moissac   68
39 Merchant Furriers' "signature," Chartres cathedral   73
40 Watercarriers' "signature," Chartres cathedral   73
41 Shoemakers' "signature," Chartres cathedral   74
42 Fishmongers' "signature," Chartres cathedral   75
43 Butchers' "signature," Chartres cathedral   76
44 Sculptors' "signature," Chartres cathedral   77
45 The Noah window, Chartres cathedral   78
46 The St. Lubin window, Chartres cathedral   78
47 Trucker on wine-delivery route, Chartres cathedral   79
48 Tavernkeepers' "signature," Chartres cathedral   80
49 Tavernkeeper and a traveler, Chartres cathedral   80
50 The donor Gaufridus and his family, Chartres cathedral   81
51 The donor Matheus, Tours cathedral   83
52 Matheus' wife, Dionisia, Tours cathedral   83
53 Drapers' lancet, church of Notre-Dame, Semur-en-Auxois   84
54 Christ Crowned with Thorns, Strasbourg cathedral   86
55 The Judgment Day window, Strasbourg cathedral   87
56 Woad merchants, Amiens cathedral   88
57 Salmon fishery, church of Sainte-Marie, Oloron-Sainte-Marie   88
58 The dishonest draper, Reims cathedral   89
59 The dishonest draper pledges his amendment, Reims cathedral   89
60 Bagpipe player, The "House of Musicians," Reims   92
61 The Lion, Villard de Honnecourt's Sketchbook   92
62 Ekkehard and Uta, donors, Naumburg cathedral   95
63 Isabelle d'Aragon, Musée des Monuments Français, Paris   96
64 Jeremiah, church of Saint-Pierre, Moissac   96
65 St. John the Baptist, Chartres cathedral   97
66 Adam, Notre-Dame de Paris   98
67 Aristotle, Chartres cathedral   98
68 Sculptured oxen on tower, Laon cathedral   101
69 Woman combing wool, Chartres cathedral   101
70 Worker crushed under pillar, abbey church, Saint-Gilles   101
71 The Vice of Ingratitude, Amiens cathedral   101
72 The First Family, Chartres cathedral   102
73 The Labors of the Months: November, abbey church, Saint-Denis   103
74 The Labors of the Months: August, Strasbourg cathedral   103
75 The Labors of the Months: September, Parma cathedral baptistry 104

76 Honey-gathering scene, church of La Madeleine, Vézelay   *104*
77 The Labors of the Months: May, Amiens cathedral   *104*
78 The Months and their zodiacal signs, Amiens cathedral   *107*
79 Lazarus and Dives, church of Saint-Pierre, Moissac   *110*
80 Animal fabliau, abbey church, Saint-Benoît-sur-Loire   *113*
81 The Virtue of Courage, Notre-Dame de Paris   *116*
82 The Vice of Cowardice, Notre-Dame de Paris   *116*
83 The Vice of Discord, Amiens cathedral   *117*
84 The "Democracy of the Damned," Reims cathedral   *118*
85 The cathedral-fortress, Albi cathedral   *121*
86 Interior view, Jacobins church, Toulouse   *123*
87 The Labors of the Months: December, church of Saint-Pierre,
   Souvigny   *126*
88 Job and the angel, former convent of La Daurade, Toulouse   *127*
89 Job and the Devil, Chartres cathedral   *127*
90 The Entry into Jerusalem, abbey church, Saint-Gilles   *129*
91 Mary the Egyptian, former abbey church of Alspach   *130*
92 The Judgment Day window, Bourges cathedral   *132-133*
93 Melchizedek and Abraham, Reims cathedral   *134*
94 The Battle of Toulouse, church of Saint-Nazaire, Carcassonne   *135*
95 The Judgment Day tympanum, abbey church, Beaulieu-sur-Dordogne *141*
96 Detail of Judgment Day tympanum, abbey church, Beaulieu-sur-
   Dordogne   *141*
97 Ham and Noah, Bourges cathedral   *142*
98 St. Paul and Christianity's "mystic mill," church of La Madeleine,
   Vézelay   *145*
99 The Synagogue, Troyes cathedral   *151*
100 The Synagogue, Strasbourg cathedral   *151*
101 Christ with Ecclesia and Synagoga, former church of Sainte-Larme
   de Sélincourt   *152*
102 Detail of the Crucifixion tympanum, abbey church, Saint-Gilles *152*
103 Payment of Judas, abbey church, Saint-Gilles   *152*
104 Detail of the Entry into Jerusalem, abbey church, Saint-Gilles *153*
105 St. Peter and Malchus, abbey church, Saint-Gilles   *153*
106 The Taking of Christ, abbey church, Saint-Gilles   *154*
107 Detail of Carrying the Cross, Strasbourg cathedral   *154*
108 Theophilus and the Devil, Notre-Dame de Paris   *156*
109 The Stoning of St. Stephen, Rouen cathedral   *157*
110 Detail of the Crucifixion window, Poitiers cathedral   *158*
111 Detail of the Virgin's funeral procession, Notre-Dame de Paris *158*
112 Miracle of the Jewish boy convert: He prepares to take Communion,
   upper choir triforium, Le Mans cathedral   *160*

113 Miracle of the Jewish boy convert: He is thrown into a furnace,
     upper choir triforium, Le Mans cathedral   *161*
114 Miracle of the Jewish boy convert: He is saved by Mary, upper
     choir triforium, Le Mans cathedral   *161*
115 God appears to Abraham, abbey church, Saint-Savin-sur-Gartempe   *165*
116 The Nativity, Chartres cathedral   *166*
117 The Third Tone of Plain Song, former abbey church of Cluny   *173*
118 Statue of Sainte Foy, church of Sainte-Foy, Conques-en-Rouergue   *173*
119 Abbot Suger, abbey church, Saint-Denis   *178*
120 Christ in Majesty tympanum, church of Saint-Pierre, Moissac   *184*
121 Self-portrait of the architect, Villard de Honnecourt's Sketchbook   *187*
122 St. John the Baptist's envoy, church of La Madeleine, Vézelay   *189*
123 Detail of the Annunciation to the Shepherds, church of Notre-Dame-
     de-la-Coudre, Parthenay   *189*
124 The Damned, Arles cathedral   *189*
125 "Gislebertus hoc fecit," Autun cathedral   *190*
126 One of the Damned, Autun cathedral   *191*
127 Reclining Eve, Autun cathedral   *192*
128 The Fourth Tone of Plain Song, Autun cathedral   *193*
129 The Assumption of Mary, Autun cathedral   *193*
130 Simon the Magician, Autun cathedral   *193*
131 The Vice of Unchastity, church of Tavant   *195*
132 Man dancing, church of Tavant   *195*
133 The Annunciation, church of Saint-Eusice, Selles-sur-Cher   *196*
134 The Creation of Adam, Chartres cathedral   *196*
135 Hugues Libergier, former church of Saint-Nicaise, Reims   *201*

MAP

France in the Twelfth and Thirteenth Centuries   *xxii*

PICTURE CREDITS: *Archives Photographiques*—1, 2, 3, 4, 6, 7, 11, 22, 29, 30, 31, 38, 51, 52, 54, 55, 56, 64, 67, 78, 79, 83, 86, 89, 92, 95, 99, 103, 109, 112, 113, 114, 115, 116, 117, 118, 119, 120, 131, 132; *Dorothy Kraus*—5; *Marburg Bildarchiv*—8, 9, 10, 13, 14, 15, 17, 18, 19, 20, 21, 23, 24, 27, 33, 34, 35, 36, 57, 59, 60, 61, 62, 63, 65, 66, 68, 70, 71, 73, 74, 76, 77, 84, 85, 87, 88, 90, 93, 96, 97, 98, 100, 101, 102, 104, 105, 106, 107, 121, 122, 123, 124, 125, 126, 127, 129, 133, 135; *Henry Cohen*—12, 25, 26, 39, 40, 41, 42, 43, 44, 45, 46, 47, 48, 49, 50, 69, 72, 108, 111, 134; *Daspet*—16; *Dr. Mark Yanover*— 28, 81, 82; *Compagnie des Arts Photomécaniques*—32; *Éditions "Mélie"*—37; *Combier*—53, 80, 128; *Roger Viollet*—58; *Omniafoto Torino*—75; *Musée d'Unterlinden*—91; *Éditions d'Art "Jordy"*—94; *Franceschi*—130.

FOREWORD

AFTER READING the first typescript pages of this book, I was completely caught up in its contagious enthusiasm and lively illumination. Now that I find myself writing its foreword, I would rather invite the reader to skip these preliminaries and proceed directly to the stage of Henry Kraus' "Theatre" and its offerings. Despite my doubts as to the need for any sponsor of this book, I have undertaken to paint, in this foreword, a "backdrop" for Henry Kraus' stage since the study of the Middle Ages is so relatively young in the history of art. The foreword may help orient the reader in an understanding of how we have come to see and study medieval art as we do. It may help in the appreciation of Henry Kraus' approach to the subject. At the end, I have said a few words about the author himself by way of warm endorsement of his work and contributions.

Enthusiasm for medieval art has never been at a higher pitch or more universal than it is today. We are fully at the opposite pole of a cycle which began when the Middle Ages was first named and defined as a historical entity by writers and artists of fifteenth-century Italy. To them we owe the formulation of a tripartite framework, still current, which aligns and distinguishes Classical Antiquity, the Middle Ages, and the Renaissance. But it is almost forgotten that the perspective of the Renaissance historians was oriented from a thoroughly prejudicial viewpoint. They took as absolute the premise that classical art was perfectly good and true, and it was therefore the aim of the Italian artist to recreate an art along classical principles emulating Greek and Roman models. A restoration was needed, they explained, because the true line of art had been extinguished by "the barbarous Goths" during the era after the fall of Rome and remained lost to the world until its rebirth in fourteenth- and fifteenth-century Italy. The Middle Ages, then, was not so much defined as a period in which art assumed a distinctive and different form but rather the period of total artistic failure dubbed "Gothic" or "The Dark Ages." In this concept of the Middle Ages was a reverse creation since it allowed only for a medieval art without form and void, when darkness was upon the face of the earth.

The inevitable cycle of changing taste could, at first, barely turn against the resistance of this inauspicious beginning. The derogatory view was taken as a matter of evident course for over four hundred years. Only in the later eighteenth century would writers more openly admit that they found interest and charm, if not beauty, at least in those later medieval works to which we now restrict the term Gothic.

By the early nineteenth century the new cause was vigorously espoused by the Romantic writers and artists. Under the standard of Gothic art they launched their first great assaults on the neoclassicism prevalent in the academies. Against the blackened image of a Christian medieval culture wrought by hordes of ignorant barbarians, Chateaubriand drafted a telling defense of the *Génie du christianisme, ou beautés de la religion chrétienne,* in 1802. Against the rationalistic order of classical thought and culture was set the intuitive concept of genius—the genius of medieval Christianity which inspired a brilliant civilization and art. In the surviving works of the Middle Ages the Romantic enthusiasts were not long in discovering that Gothic art was beautiful and that there was a unique Christian genius in the thematic content of cathedral sculpture programs.

Victor Hugo recreated a Gothic Paris and its great cathedral in his *Notre-Dame de Paris* of 1831 and illuminated the way for generations of medieval scholarship when he wrote: "In the Middle Ages there was no thought conceived by mankind which he did not write in stone." The book and its passions inspired a dedicated following in whose circle medieval art took its first shape as the historical discipline which it now pursues. In 1845, Adolphe-Napoléon Didron published a study of Christian iconography dedicated to Victor Hugo in a letter which opened: "In *Notre-Dame de Paris* you have constructed, in several weeks, the cathedral of the Middle Ages. For my part, I would spend my entire life in carving and painting it. Engage me, sublime architect, as one of your most devoted workmen even if not the most skilled."

Didron's particular contribution was the proposal that the vast range of subjects in the sculptures of Chartres actually matched the plan and content of the *Speculum majus* by Vincent de Beauvais, the most erudite and comprehensive encyclopedia of the Middle Ages. Chartres became the "encyclopedia in stone" and the *Speculum* the key and guide to the study of Gothic sculpture. "As the statues and effigies with which our churches are decorated are all arranged according to the system of Vincent de Beauvais," Didron undertook "to adhere closely to that arrangement" in his treatise. Even though he was not to complete but a small part of this undertaking, Didron had laid down a line whose link to the present is direct, if ramified.

For most of the nineteenth century and for every student of medieval imagery, the identification of persons, scenes, and stories (iconography) became a major preoccupation. To know what is depicted seems an elementary requirement for the study of any period of art but no other period compares with the Middle Ages for the quantity, extent, and complexity of subjects and themes which were incorporated in images. In this enormous repertoire were included subjects from the Bible, Psalter, and other liturgical books; the histories, chronicles, and lives of the saints; theological, exegetic, and homiletic treatises; works of literature, instruction, and science; dogmatic concepts, the arts, crafts, labors, and daily life. Victor Hugo had expressed it well.

In the face of all the burgeoning studies of medieval art Barbier de Montault, Didron's pupil and collaborator, could still write in 1890 that "iconography, like the science which it represents, is a recent term in our language." But the century was to close with a brilliant recapitulation of its whole accomplishment in the famous book by Émile Mâle, *L'Art religieux du XIIIe siècle en France: Étude sur l'iconographie du moyen âge et sur ses sources d'inspiration*, which appeared in 1898.

All the grand lines of the century are here: Chateaubriand's "genius of Christianity," Hugo's "thoughts written in stone," and Didron's "sculptured encyclopedia of the cathedral." Mâle saw in the cathedral not only "the genius of all Christendom . . . but also the genius of France." Indeed, the cathedral was without doubt "the greatest achievement of France" in the domain of art. With Mâle, the aborted exposition of Vincent de Beauvais and Gothic sculptures by Didron was beautifully realized in a book actually composed in four divisions to mirror those of the Gothic *Speculum*. Émile Mâle's *summa* of the century of scholarship past was projected into the century to follow. Unrivaled by any other single work of its kind, his book has had its insistent impact through successive editions appearing at least once in every decade to the present day.

Gothic art was, for the iconographers, the supreme manifestation of the medieval mind. It was the single great peak toward which the entire Middle Ages vaguely groped until, in the twelfth century, a gradual upward slope began to rise.

The case was much the same for the formal appreciation of medieval art. Gothic sculpture above all, and to the exclusion of the earlier styles, was extolled for its supreme beauty no less than for its great intelligence. But there is an extraordinary aspect to this exaltation of Gothic form. In all the praise of Gothic form runs a strong and unmistakable tracer element of the classical esthetic. The excellence of a statue was explained in terms of truth to nature, canons of proportion, and verisimilitude of expression. Walter Pater's highest accolade for the *Beau Dieu* of Amiens, in an essay of 1894, entitles the sculptor to be called "a Greek" and the sculpture "almost classically proportioned." There was as yet no esthetic in formal criticism which might admit Romanesque and earlier imagery into the sphere of praiseworthy art. Walter Pater may also have begun to wonder about the sculptured capitals at Vézelay ("Irresistibly they rivet attention"). But the glimmering is dimmed by his explanation that they are "full of wild promise in their coarse execution, cruel, you might say, in the realization of human form and features."

Only recently have our eyes been opened to the discovery of a positive and distinctive formal genius in Romanesque imagery and this was made possible by the radical movements in late nineteenth- and early twentieth-century painting. Impressionism, Fauvism, Cubism, Expressionism, and other abstract movements shattered the last defenses of the classical rationale of truth to nature and literally intelligible subjects. Taste and theory, close on the heels of practice, presently articulated the new esthetic of "pure" and "significant" form. The floodgates were now fully open to the flow of all pre-, non-, and anti-classical art into the literature and history of art, the museums, collections, and universal acceptance. Romanesque art, like primitive sculpture, became a legitimized ancestor of modernism. Its formal inventiveness in abstract terms became the object of marvel; its contortions and distortions precious demonstrations of the expressionistic virtuosity of an anti-naturalistic esthetic. Even the cruder of early Christian sculptures were interpreted as heralding the first admirable steps in the direction of the most essential mission of medieval art—the formal embodiment of an anti-materialistic and transcendental faith. Something of the novelty of this approach and the freshness of its surprising revelations may still be gleaned in Charles Rufus Morey's *Medieval Art* as late as 1942. For instance, in his discussion of the eleventh-century bronze Crucifix in Werden, he notes that the artist "does not hesitate to distort material form in order to deliver more directly, the feeling [of his theme] thus engendered. The affinity with ultra-modern sculpture is astonishing."

Now more than half a millennium since the Renaissance painted that first historical portrait of the Middle Ages in broad black slashing strokes medieval art in its entirety has been finally brought into the light of acclamation. There remains no period of medieval art which is not the object of study by some and of admiration by many. Historical, formal, and iconographic studies are being published at a rate which strains the limits of our capacity to keep pace with them. Iconographic studies alone flourish in a domain admittedly outside the realm of reading, in the form of dictionaries, lexicons, encyclopedias, and indices that comprise our enormous reference apparatus. The more strictly professional investigations in this field yield more studies than ever, serving the "closed circuit" audience of its scholarly adherents.

It is as if a great centrifugal force had been generated by all these labors and had driven its most dedicated partisans from the true center of their field to its remotest periphery. In spite of this there is an ever-growing public ever more avid for medieval art and for them there has been no lack of new facilities. Wherever and whenever possible, museums all over the world have been showing magnificent exhibitions of medieval art remarkably well displayed and explained, drawing endless and insatiable throngs. Publishers also have responded to this interest and brought forth an enormous array of fine picture books ranging over the entire realm of medieval art and its various aspects.

One important link has been all but lacking, namely, readable books by competent scholars, willing and able to bring together the results of our new knowledge and understanding of medieval art and to interpret it within the whole fabric of medieval life and thought as Henry Kraus has done here.

Henry Kraus is a self-taught historian of art whose work had been that of a journalist in another field. His conversion began some ten years ago during European residence in connection with his employment. It was in this period that he found himself devoting every free moment to visiting and study of the medieval churches of France. He acquired a firsthand knowledge of the monuments which might be the envy of many a scholar but even this was not sufficient for him and he turned to intensive reading of history and interpretation of the buildings and their art. Most important of all, he had begun to ask questions about medieval art which proved to be questions not yet satisfactorily answered or not even asked before.

Some of his findings have already been published in learned journals and have assured him a welcome place as a historian of medieval art. Probably because of his nonacademic training in this pursuit he is able to see the field in its greatest and most vital breadth. Where the academic scholar might, for example, have been content with the discovery of a new interpretation for the eight "invisible" reliefs at Notre-Dame, Henry Kraus has been able to present the solution as part of the whole setting of university life in thirteenth-century Paris. Whether working from a single monument to its ramifications in the relevant social context, or from major social themes to their documentation in works of art, he has traced the broad picture of living circumstances and problems in the Middle Ages, to create a vivid documentary picture of the period and its art.

Institute of Fine Arts   Harry Bober
New York University

PREFACE

WHILE I ACKNOWLEDGE that this book has a special viewpoint and that the work looking toward it was strongly oriented, nevertheless I do not regard myself as a "specialist," and it was with considerable surprise, if not shock, that I heard myself so designated recently by Professor Louis Grodecki when he was introducing me to a colleague: "Monsieur Kraus s'intéresse à la sociologie de l'art médiéval."*

What is involved, undoubtedly, is the subjective motivation of my interest. I myself still do not recognize any distance between my feeling for this art and my work with it. What attracts me to it is its beauty and throbbing richness. I have had a love affair with it for decades, ever since my first visit to Europe as a student, in fact, when I was supposed to be "interested" in mathematics or literature or psychology. Anything but medieval art, about which I knew absolutely nothing.

Once discovered, however, the "coup de foudre" was inevitable. I know that this experience is so common that it is not necessary to explain it. The "sociological" emphasis is more particular, I realize, but all I can say about it is that it, too, began to surface very early, in the form of a nagging question: "What group of circumstances conspired to create this marvelous art?" and especially the answer, saying something like: "There must have been some extraordinary strength and excitement in the social order of that time!"

The present book is not about that. That is taken for granted in it. Others do not have to agree with this primary postulate. All that is necessary is that they accept as worthwhile the study of how the social background may have helped to model medieval art. While most historians would hardly be willing to engage in such a project themselves, they do, I believe, recognize, if often only implicitly, that its premises are legitimate. Even the remarkable Émile Mâle, while assertedly so hostile to the social approach, at times added brilliant insights of that order to his extraordinary iconographic demonstrations.

I do not intend to engage here in the unpleasant game of arguing about priorities. I do feel, and strongly, that all art historians should give serious consideration to the social context of the period they are studying. But it is ridiculous to think that failure to do so necessarily invalidates their work. All efforts to illuminate the obscure corners of medieval art are potentially helpful. All contribute to our knowledge, all enhance our appreciation. But whereas there are numerous works stressing patristic writings and church annals, upper-class

*"Mr. Kraus is interested in the sociology of medieval art."

xix

activities and conflicts, esthetics, technics, cataloguing and dating, schools, developmental cycles, the studies concerned with the social currents in medieval art are comparatively rare. This book is an attempt to help fill that gap.

Professor Bober has alluded to the widespread interest in medieval art. I believe that knowing something of the social milieu is particularly to the point for the amateur. Any sense of strangeness, of inaccessibility, will be found to dissolve quite readily on this basis. For the Middle Ages is not nearly as distant as often imagined. Not only have human motivations changed little but a number of the patterns of our own social organization were already foreshadowed by the twelfth or thirteenth century.

Indeed, the reader may, with only minor transpositions, imagine that he is studying a contemporary situation when reading about the struggle for academic freedom at Paris University, in 1229 (and the role this played in the production of a remarkable series of reliefs at Notre-Dame); or about the development of the emergent middle class as a new group of donors to church art; or about the stresses brought to bear upon that art by religious nonconformism. He will find the discussion of anti-Semitism in medieval art as up to date as the debates of the recent Ecumenical Council; equally topical are the changes in approach toward the leading feminine personalities in Christian art that are traceable during the period in question, paralleling a significant shift in woman's social position at that time.

Most surprising to him, perhaps, will be the discovery of the early artist as an independent personality, similar in important ways to his modern counterpart. So much has been heard about medieval church art having been totally controlled from above that it is generally assumed that the artist himself was lost in it. But this is no more true than that medieval man is absent from the plastic narratives of the Savior and the Virgin, of Saints and Apostles, with which old churches are peopled. Moreover, no matter how closely the medieval artist may have felt assimilated to the content of the works commissioned by his ecclesiastic employers, at times a cleavage in outlook did occur, into which his qualifying insertions (however minor, at first) were made. At other times, it was the persuasiveness of his creative ideas that was at the source of accepted innovation.

My choice of the twelfth and thirteenth centuries as the scope of this book was based primarily on personal preference. But at the same time it has remained my firm conviction that Western European art of this period attained a pinnacle rarely even approached in man's creative history. That this was also an era of profoundly important social and political changes in the West, bearing especially on the industrious classes, impressed me as the basic substratum, the inevitable accompaniment of this creative outpouring. The limitation of the book to France was dictated by the realization that, while analogous in some fundamentals, the Western countries were so dissimilar in others that grouping them together would lead to too great complexity and diffuseness.

When I got to work, I was amazed to discover the great amount of available material illustrating the social impact on medieval French art. However, this material is widely scattered or it lies buried in sources that fail to develop its full significance. The average reader would have neither the time nor the interest to mine out this treasure. This I have tried to do for him. But experiences of a richer vein abound for the alert amateur who is willing to go a bit further. With a little patience and some collateral reading, he can expand his enjoyment greatly and make more rewarding his excursions by way of art into that medieval realm which in so many ways helped prepare the modern world we live in.

Paris, France   H. K.

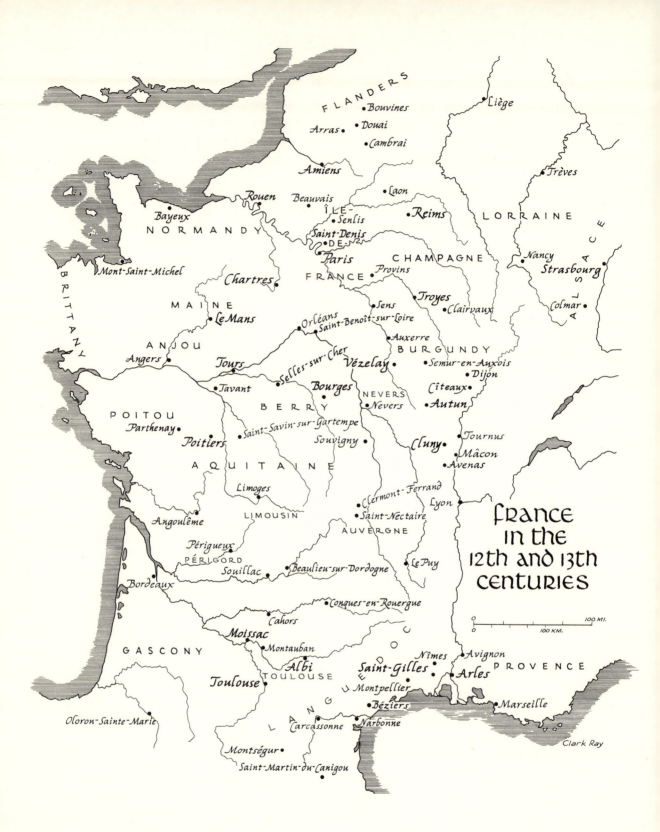

FLANDERS
• Bouvines
Arras • • Douai
• Cambrai
Liège

• Trèves

Amiens

Rouen • Beauvais • Laon
Bayeux ÎLE- • Reims
NORMANDY Senlis LORRAINE
Saint-Denis
DE- Nancy
Mont-Saint-Michel Paris Strasbourg
FRANCE CHAMPAGNE

Chartres Provins Colmar
MAINE Sens Troyes
Le Mans • Clairvaux
Orléans
Saint-Benoît-sur-Loire Auxerre
ANJOU Selles-sur-Cher Vézelay BURGUNDY
Angers Tours Bourges Semur-en-Auxois
Javant NEVERS Dijon
POITOU BERRY Nevers Cîteaux
Parthenay Saint-Savin-sur-Gartempe Autun
Poitiers Souvigny Cluny Tournus
AQUITAINE Mâcon
Avenas

Limoges
Clermont-Ferrand Lyon
Angoulême LIMOUSIN Saint-Nectaire
AUVERGNE
Périgueux
PÉRIGORD Le Puy
Souillac Beaulieu-sur-Dordogne

Bordeaux FRANCE
IN THE
12TH AND 13TH
CENTURIES
Conques-en-Rouergue

Cahors
GASCONY Moissac
Montauban Nîmes Avignon
Albi Saint-Gilles PROVENCE
Toulouse TOULOUSE Arles
Montpellier
Oloron-Sainte-Marie Béziers Marseille
Carcassonne Narbonne
Clark Ray
Montségur
Saint-Martin-du-Canigou

BRITTANY
ALSACE
LANGUEDOC

100 MI.
100 KM.

The
Living Theatre
of Medieval
Art

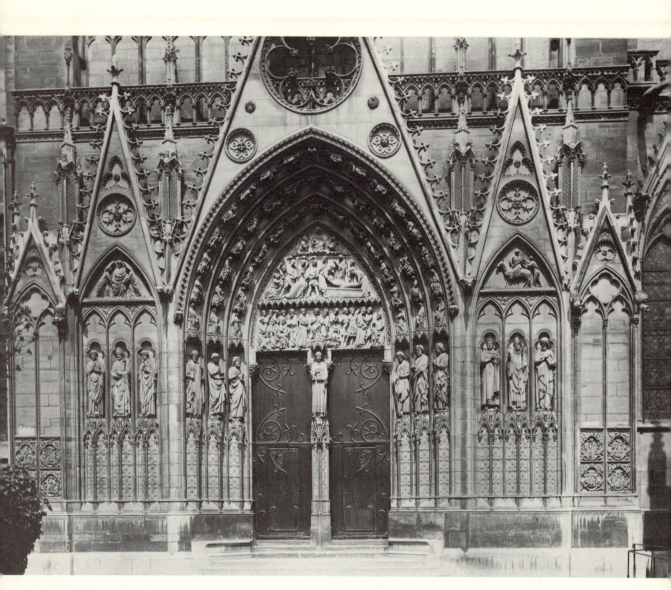

1. *Notre-Dame de Paris*. Exterior of the south transept, the Martyrs' Portal (13th century). The two pairs of four reliefs discussed in the following chapter are in the lowest register and at the extreme ends, left and right. The very tiny Latin script that runs across the façade, below, names the architect, Jean de Chelles.

CHAPTER I
THE EIGHT INVISIBLE RELIEFS
AT NOTRE-DAME

A̲t̲ ̲n̲o̲t̲r̲e̲-̲d̲a̲m̲e̲ ̲d̲e̲ ̲p̲a̲r̲i̲s̲ there is a thirteenth-century portal embellished by some remarkable sculpture that has been shut off from public view for a long time [Pl. 1]. In fact, it is difficult to say just when it was accessible. One author as far back as 1862 reported that the area outside the cathedral's south transept had already been closed off for "many years."[1] And since the great archiepiscopal palace was located here until its destruction during the uprising of February 1831, only those having to do with archdiocesan affairs, or other special visitors, could be expected to have penetrated into the court of entry before that date.

It might be hazardous to suggest that this isolation could be the cause of the persistence of Notre-Dame's thorniest riddle: the meaning of the eight bas-reliefs on the outer lateral faces of the Martyrs' Portal. They were, after all, available for study by scholars, who in the first half of the nineteenth century engaged in lively conjectures about them. One suggested that they represented some unnamed miracle of the Virgin, another that they were episodes—though unexplained—from the life of St. Stephen, to whom the major portion of the portal's tympanum is devoted. Then, in 1869, a study was published in the *Annales Archéologiques*[2] that presented a sharp break with this line of interpretation.

The appearance of Comte Félix de Verneilh's article in that important journal took place under rather curious circumstances. Verneilh had, it was revealed, written it about fifteen years earlier, but publication was held up because the editor, Adolphe-Napoléon Didron, considered it too farfetched. When it finally did appear, both author and editor were dead. The prolonged withholding of publication was the more surprising in light of the author's outstanding reputation as a scholar. Though he died a comparatively young man (forty-five), he had already made his mark with highly original works on the Byzantine influence on French architecture and the history of medieval enamel.

3

His fresh approach to old problems had several times before brought him into conflict with hallowed viewpoints, as when he maintained that Limoges work owed much to earlier German models. Verneilh was surprised to be charged with lack of patriotism on this account, replying, almost naïvely: "There is only one archeology; every country cannot have its own."[3]

His exposition of the Notre-Dame reliefs early came to have the reference mark, "Life of the Students," a title over which a light mist of frivolity seems to hover. Yet his analysis was based on the most substantial of moral grounds— that the sculpture was meant to support a broad reform of student life—a didactic purpose entirely in keeping with church art. This was translated into terms of opposing "good" and "bad" students, in Verneilh's account, the former to be seen studying and attending lectures, giving alms and demonstrating filial devotion whereas the latter were shown in the company of loose women and brawling, for which they were known to have been repeatedly punished in the thirteenth century.

But Verneilh's interpretation did not have a spectacular success with scholars. When, in 1898, Émile Mâle published his authoritative *L'art religieux du XIIIe siècle en France,* he rejected it out of hand and continued to advert to the "life of a saint as yet unidentified."[4] The eminent art historian seemed to be calling for a continued search in this direction. However, a scrutiny of the literature up to date has revealed only one attempt at such an explanation. This was by a German writer, Adele Fischel, who, in 1930, purported to see in the scenes incidents from the lives of Bonaventura and Thomas Aquinas, both of whom were students at Paris University during the period in question. But her demonstration was hardly convincing. Repeatedly disregarding the age, sex, costume, and actions of the participants as well as simple probability, she sought to impose a few actual or imagined episodes from these saints' lives upon the quatrefoils. This method could have been applied to almost anyone else of mark living in the thirteenth century.[5]

Verneilh's interpretation has in the long run prevailed. While some authors still refer to the meaning of the reliefs as "obscure"[6] or qualify an allusion to the "life of the students" with a "reputed,"[7] all have ceased to suggest other possible explanations. In fact, they seem to have dropped any further interest in the subject. It is surprising that even the late Marcel Aubert, who wrote half a dozen works on Notre-Dame, never devoted more than a few sentences in any of them to these unique reliefs. If they had indeed been concerned with the life of some saint, studies would undoubtedly have been undertaken regarding them. But medieval art specialists evidently find a purely secular subject much less worthy of their efforts.*

*One well-known scholar, queried by the author, commented: "But this student-life idea is only a legend!"

Émile Mâle thought so little of Verneilh's study, he put his reference to it into a footnote. But aside from that, he gave what appeared to be a solid demonstration of the infrequent occurrence of topical subjects in church art. Scholars had cleared away a great mass of apocryphal traditions linking religious works with historic events or individuals, he explained. Even the most famous lay figures such as Clovis or Charlemagne were sparsely represented and then only because they "symbolized some great victory of the Christian Church." This exclusion, the author added, had been possible because of the deep piety of the time which had moved lay rulers to shy away from occupying hallowed space. Accordingly, if there was "no place for Alexander or for Caesar" on a church portal, why should some silly, squalling students find a welcome there?[8]

Nevertheless, the art student or amateur who examines the eight reliefs at the south transept portal of Notre-Dame today will probably find it difficult to understand how any disagreement could ever have existed about their interpretation. These are unquestionably people involved in lay situations, very concretely and purposively described. All ritualistic-liturgical acts or postures, so exhaustively studied for the Middle Ages, are missing; there are no halos or other symbols of sainthood, no miracles, no martyrdom. That some of the actions of the masters and students here may not be readily interpreted does not negate their ultimate identity. Recognizing the quality of the participants in an artistic monument need not necessarily furnish its key.

It seemed pertinent therefore, in pursuing the meaning of these sculptures, to ask what the masters and students at Paris University might have been doing in the years prior to their making (1260–1270) that could cast some light upon them. None of the authors consulted was anything but cursory on this score. In his footnote, Mâle referred cryptically to some challenge to the bishop's authority over the University while Aubert alluded hardly more circumstantially to "a passionate struggle in which pope and king intervened. . . ."[9] And reading Verneilh's article raised more questions on this score than it resolved.

The first thing one discovers when exploring the background to these allusions is the very first event of importance in the order of chronology: the birth of the University of Paris itself in the early stages of the contest. There is something strangely timeless about the conflict as it comes down to us. Contemporary authors might almost be referring to a present-day union-management controversy and the modern reader hardly finds it surprising to learn that "*Universitas*" meant "Association," a term habitually used also for the mutually protective organizations formed by medieval barrelmakers and drapers, masons and goldsmiths.

In the case of the "*Universitas Magistrorum et Scolarium,*" paradoxically, it was the bishop's control over Paris' schools that was specifically aimed at.

Challenges of this nature were directed at various times against his power to grant or withhold licenses to teach, his right to administer justice over masters and students, and other equally important prerogatives. The unexpected element in these situations was that the pope usually took the side of the University against the bishop or his chancellor: in 1208 or 1209 for the first recorded time, and again in 1212 and in 1215. In the process the masters won effective control over the academic structure.

One is tempted to conclude from all this a degree of foresight in the papal judgment, which was not, however, the motivating factor. This was to be found rather in the need of the pope for firm allies in his protracted fight for political power and for a Church free of domination by lay rulers. The battle of investitures was by no means finally won and many prelates still retained primary loyalties elsewhere. The monastic orders, answerable directly to Rome, had proved a more reliable prop, and it was hoped that the universities would play a similar role.

The bishop of Paris did not take these successive blows with the best of grace. Continuing to invoke feudal-seigniorial powers over masters and students, he punished recalcitrants with fines and imprisonment. The conflict reached its apex in 1219 when he issued mass excommunications, charging the masters with "conspiracy." And once more the pope stepped into the wrangle, called all concerned to Rome, lifted the ban and again imposed a settlement.

There exists a remarkable set of documents witnessing the reaction of the bishop's side to this decision, in the form of sermons by the Chancellor of Notre-Dame, Philippe de Grève. The bishop's officer in charge of schools suggested that the pope ought to depose him if he would not permit him to use effective measures against the mutineering masters. They were always holding meetings, he charged, "to treat . . . of the affairs of the community," to plot and conspire, "to deliberate, to legislate, to draw up rules."[10]

The young students meanwhile, encouraged by their masters, the churchman added, abandoned theology for all kinds of will-o'-the-wisps: the sciences, philosophy. (By the mid-thirteenth century there were many more scholars at Paris University studying the so-called "liberal arts" than religion.) This opposition to the "new subjects" doubtless played a part in the controversy. But the major issue remained the bishop's desire to retain control over the University. Early in the century this concern had begun to be expressed when the bishop tried to keep all classes "between the two bridges," that is, on the Île de la Cité. But the trend, which Pierre Abélard had initiated among masters and scholars almost a hundred years before, had by this time become irreversible: that of abandoning the cathedral's blunted towers, crossing over from the Island and setting out, by way of Sainte-Geneviève's hill, on the arduous climb to academic and intellectual freedom.[11]

The Church, which had crushed Abélard for his audacious ideas, was eventually to find some of them invaluable. Just so were Aristotle's works banned again and again by papal decree, only to be proudly vaunted, in 1229, by the Dominican founders of Toulouse University, who had learned to appreciate the help of the great Greek thinker in organizing their arguments against the Catharist heretics of Southwest France![12] And it was a Dominican, Albertus Magnus, who a few years later in his courses at Paris University launched the fateful effort to integrate Aristotelianism within Catholicism, which his great disciple, Thomas Aquinas, was to carry forward into the second half of the thirteenth century, this time with the blessings of Rome. But many Church conservatives remained unconvinced by this major effort to freshen up Catholic thought and St. Thomas' doctrine was banned at Paris University as late as 1277, by Bishop Étienne Tempier, as it was at Oxford.[13]

Philippe de Grève's famous description of student excesses at Paris University was probably not greatly exaggerated, though it could hardly have applied to more than a small minority. "They meet at night," he sermonized, "armed, breaking into homes, taking possession of young girls, carrying off married women, forcing them to submit to the most criminal outrages, wounding and killing their husbands, and of the wife of one, alas, making the prey of all, as was seen just this past year. . . ."[14] A certain amount of delinquency was understandable, considering the youth of many students (they started as early as fourteen), and the fact that they lived without supervision, in squalid rooms of the crowded, noisy Latin Quarter.

Periodically, during Lent especially, when abstinence sharpened tempers, Paris was the setting of explosive "town-versus-gown" disturbances. Students were given short shrift by the royal constabulary, who were often joined by a posse of tradesmen and artisans. There are many reports of unbridled violence used against them. On one occasion, in 1200, when the bishop of Liège was among those killed, King Philippe-Auguste was obliged to grant the masters and students important privileges. The major concession was the recognition of their status as clerics, which placed them under the milder provisions of ecclesiastic justice. Also figuring prominently in the grant were obligations placed upon the city's bourgeois, who were required to come to the defense of academicians when attacked and were ordered not to turn their heads on such occasions "so as not to have to arrest the guilty or to bear witness against them."[15] All of these points have critical importance for an understanding of the reliefs, as we shall soon see.

Violations of the king's decree of 1200 by his constabulary continued to occur intermittently nevertheless. An especially outrageous incident which took place in 1229 had fateful consequences for the evolution of the University. It happened during Lent that year, too, that some students, having been drubbed by a tavernkeeper and his friends, returned with reinforcements and wrecked the inn. Headstrong Blanche of Castile, who held the regency during the minority of her son, Louis IX (St. Louis), impetuously ordered her archers out under command of the royal provost.* By all accounts the punishment they inflicted was most brutal. Many innocent students were killed, hundreds thrown into the Seine. The University professors closed the schools in protest but the queen-regent turned down their demand that the guilty parties be punished. Even the bishop, who would have handed out wholesale excommunications for some slight affront to an obscure cleric, refrained from taking action on this frightful occasion, no doubt welcoming the shattering setback delivered to his feared rivals.

The masters and students responded spectacularly, declaring a strike and proceeding en masse to abandon Paris for other universities, going to Orléans, Angers, Toulouse, even Cambridge and Oxford. Their withdrawal lasted two whole years, ending only upon the urgent and repeated interventions of Pope Gregory IX. The Paris masters were finally called to Rome and, armed with a cluster of bulls including the *Bulla Parens Scientiarum*, their Magna Carta, they made a triumphant reentry into Paris, in early 1231. Among the various concessions gained by the professors was the formal recognition of their right to strike as well as to adopt statutes necessary to their association and to exclude from it those refusing to abide by them. Also, the bishop's disciplinary (police) powers over students were sharply curtailed.[16]

All seemed well. However, a development that had taken place during the masters' absence from Paris was destined eventually to cause a resurgence of discord, this time opposing the University to the new monastic orders. The early relationship of the University with the friars had been excellent and many masters and students joined the Franciscans or Dominicans in the first burst of the friars' ebullient growth. However, during the "great dispersion" of 1229–1231, upon the request of the bishop, the friars had opened their conventual classes to secular scholars, which were found to be doing a blazing business when the striking masters and students returned to Paris.

This intrusion was deeply resented. A major point made against the friars by the masters was the unfair competition their classes constituted since, being amply supported by charity, the orders did not have to charge the students fees while the seculars made their livelihood from them. Many of the scholars were sons of poor peasants and were so destitute that they had to be licensed to beg for their subsistence. They found the friars' classes unavoidably attractive on this score.

The University masters had tried to keep a balance among the coveted chairs in theology occupied by the regulars (monks) and themselves. This was rendered difficult by the mendicants' strong recruiting among the masters since when one of the latter joined an order he would retain his chair. The matter

---

*The chief royal official of Paris, who combined broad administrative, judicial, and police powers.

was basic to independent control of the University. The friars, under strict discipline of their superiors, could hardly be regarded as free agents. It was in this context that the University, in 1252, refused to recommend a Cistercian for licensing. The case eventually passed to Rome where the pope, in flagrant violation of the *Bulla Parens Scientiarum*, ordered the chancellor to accredit the new professor over the heads of the University masters.

This dispute was complicated by another incident of violence against students by the royal constabulary. The masters once more shut their classes down, asking the friars to do the same. They refused. The masters then demanded that the friars take an oath to abide by all University decisions. But the monks, holding that this would conflict with their vows, again refused. The masters replied by expelling them and forbidding students to attend their classes.

When the friars obtained a papal bull decreeing their reinstatement, the University decided to send a delegation to Rome. This was done apparently on the urging of important members of the French hierarchy who had themselves begun to be alarmed at the friars' rapid growth. Added to the traditional rivalry—often far from fraternal—between the secular and regular clergy was the unbridled ambition of the new orders who had begun to assume more and more functions of the seculars: confession, offices for the dead, even collection of tithes. The delegation of Paris masters won important concessions from Innocent III. But his untimely death and replacement by the Cardinal-Protector of the Franciscans reopened the whole question.

Alexander IV proved a tough and uncompromising antagonist to Paris University, whose case thereafter was a losing one. Disastrous breaks began to occur in the masters' ranks. This included all but one of the four-man delegation that had gone to Rome. All the papal furor was released against this courageous master, Guillaume de Saint-Amour, who compounded his insurgency with the publication of a savage denunciation of the mendicants, whom he associated with the Anti-Christ. Alexander pursued Guillaume to the end, driving him from his University chair and into exile.[17]

This was 1257, the year, it so happens, that work on the south portal of Notre-Dame was begun, as can be read in the charming old Latin inscription that runs across its base. Carving of the eight reliefs was started shortly thereafter. So it appears only reasonable to assume that the fever and turbulence of these events were vividly present to those who worked out their iconographic program. In fact, the quarrel continued to simmer long after the defeat of the masters, which one papal bull after another (there were forty in all issued during this crisis) failed to put to rest. The great popular trouvère Rutebeuf devoted many searing verses to the conflict and twenty years after its denouement the century's most renowned poet, Jean de Meung, still recalled with bitterness the cruel injustice done to Guillaume de Saint-Amour.

> May I never take bread or wine
> If he had not in his verity
> The accord of the University
> And of all the people generally. . . .[18]

Could it have been this background that Émile Mâle found too "insignificant" to have influenced the making of the eight reliefs? And we have not yet come the the end of it. But before we continue along this route it might be well to see how what we already have may help our understanding of the sculpture.

To avoid confusion no reference will be made to Verneilh's specific comments, which are often in need of basic revision. Hence, the following remarks are limited to what are considered the correct explanations of the quatrefoils. However, these interpretations are not meant to be categorical. At times, admittedly, they are mere conjectures.

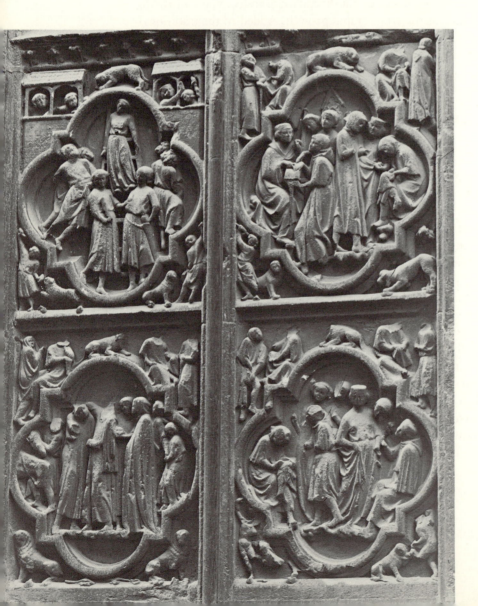

2 (opposite page). *Notre-Dame de Paris*. The Martyrs' Portal (13th century). Series representing the "Life of the Students." The four reliefs at the left. Lower left, departure for Paris; lower right, in the bishop's court; upper left, punishment on the ladder; upper right, in Notre-Dame sanctuary.

3. *Bourges Cathedral*. The Prodigal Son stained-glass window (13th century). He is greeted by harlots who embrace him and crown him with flowers.

In the first set of four at the left [Pl. 2], the lower left-hand scene (a medieval sequence is usually read from left to right and from below up) is seen as a student's departure from home. The groom has the horses ready (wealthy students brought their servants with them to Paris), and both he and his young master are spurred for the journey. The father embraces his son while the mother, flanked by her other children, fondly seconds her husband's gesture with her eyes. The oldest daughter (or fiancée) holds a package affectionately in both hands—food for the trip. It is the kind of intimate family-farewell scene that seems timeless, its pantomime unmistakable.

The father's parting counsel is apparently disregarded, however, and what happens to the young man in Paris as a result is pictured in numerous contemporary representations of the Prodigal Son, in stained-glass windows, such as those at Chartres, Bourges, and other churches, as well as in carvings: The giddy young fellow is greeted by two Parisian harlots, who bathe, dress, and regale him before stripping him of his inheritance at the gaming table [Pl. 3]. Our reliefs have skipped these colorful details. Allowing the viewer's imagination to fill in the gap, they go straight to the unhappy consequences of the student's folly. By the time we come to the second relief, the worst has already happened and we are, it would appear, inside the bishop's court.* The student at the left is testifying agitatedly. A clerk takes down his deposition. The student is evidently accusing the young woman behind him of some reprehensible act for she is balling her fist in rage. But her uncoifed head may be a telltale sign—certainly no lady of the better classes would be seen thus in public.

We are, it seems, in the midst of what the French call an "instruction" procedure, where witnesses on the two sides are confronted and probable guilt is decided. In actual fact the bishop's right of "instruction" in situations where

*Which was located in his palace, directly across from the Martyrs' Portal and these carvings.

any of his wards were charged with serious crimes was, after many challenges, specifically recognized by Philippe-Auguste, in a broad charter that the king granted Paris' prelate, in 1222. This arrangement represented a prerogative of great protective significance. In our eight reliefs it serves as a symbol for the many privileges that students as well as other clerics enjoyed as dependents of the episcopacy.

But such privileges carried responsibilities! And the scholars by their excesses endangered these precious rights, inviting abuses by the royal constabulary and others. This solemn warning was sounded over and over by many voices friendly to the scholars, among which was that of Robert de Sorbon himself.[19] And what the student stood to lose was very important, by medieval standards. Besides the already mentioned protection from arbitrary arrest and commitment to the terrifying royal prison at the Châtelet, these immunities also entailed freedom from all feudal taxes and services, including the military obligation. The student, moreover, was protected against rent gougers and was permitted to give lessons on Sundays and holidays, which might bring a badly needed addition to his limp pocketbook. In return for these benefits he had to make comparatively slight engagements. He did not even have to take minor orders or wear the tonsure, though often he did, for the protection it gave him, if for no other reason. Also, he could probably marry, though not if he meant to enter the Church, which many students planned to do, in any case, since it supplied almost the only route in the rigid feudal system by which an intelligent young man from the poor classes could rise.[20]

What we see in the other half of the court scene is what appears to be a corroboration of the student's testimony by another witness. The fact that she is a member of Paris' wealthy middle class, as evidenced by her elegant clothes and by the deference paid her by the presiding ecclesiastic-magistrate, could be meant to illustrate another shielding feature of Philippe-Auguste's basic charter of 1222. This provision specifically required the burghers to testify in court if they saw students mistreated in any way. As for the accused young woman in the scene, she too was to have her hour at the bar. But it is to be assumed that her evidence will be discredited, as was that of another fallen sister of her time, whose case appears in an early record and who admitted inventing a charge of rape against some clients because she was dissatisfied with their fee![21]

Such perjury was sternly punished in the Middle Ages, and so it seems to be in this case, as we note in the next quatrefoil, at the upper left in our photograph. For, insofar as the attrition of time allows for identification, the young woman on the ladder is the same person as appears in the court scene below. The placard she carries on her chest once bore the letters: "P. FA/US. S," Verneilh and others report, though they are now all but invisible. Verneilh interprets this device as being an abbreviation in the medieval manner of "Pour

Faus Serment" (For False Oath), a crime punished on the bishop's ladder, which was set up on the parvis (square) of Notre-Dame occasionally for that purpose.[22] The revenge that four students are taking on the wretch would further illustrate this point. It was the custom in the Middle Ages for interested persons to be allowed to express their resentment against a convicted criminal in this brutal way. But they were told to confine their missiles to mud and garbage and to avoid "stones or other bruising objects."[23]

Two officers of Notre-Dame's police force are standing by and one of them, evidently thinking that the situation is getting out of hand, seizes the hilt of his sword. But his companion restrains him. Various authors have told of the enjoyment people of the Middle Ages took in witnessing scenes of torture.[24] Such an audience is represented by the people watching from the upper windows of one of the houses, which old prints show once crowded the parvis. In another interior one sees a young man scuffling with a young woman, which seems to offer a pithy reminder that the bout with vice is never ended and that some students are still prone to engage in the condemned practices. This could explain the oath-taking scene in the following quatrefoil, the last of the quartet.

Here three students are seen with an ecclesiastic who administers the vow to them. The Bible is open and three hands are laid upon it. The taking of oaths was very prevalent in medieval academic practice. Students had to swear to obey any new regulation and every examination started with the candidate's pledge not to bribe the examiner.[25] The bishop's throne in the background identifies the setting as that of the cathedral sanctuary, into which the young couple on the right* seem to have come to publish their banns, an act that was declared obligatory by the Lateran Council of 1215.[26] If this interpretation is correct, the young couple's presence would be meant to serve as a didactic contrast, i.e., symbolizing sexual regularity.

The right-hand series of quatrefoils, in contrast to the first set, seem to treat of what we might qualify as approved activities of the students, all carried out under the bishop's benign supervision [Pl. 4]. We begin again at the lower left. During this period, it should be explained, many ecclesiastics were deeply involved in a broad movement to reclaim church rights that had been lost for hundreds of years. This had occurred during the great adversity of the deep Middle Ages, when in return for protection against the marauders who ravaged Western Europe from the ninth to the eleventh centuries the churchmen were forced to sacrifice many of their privileges to the barons, including even church tithes. Like any other feudal tax these had become proprietary and could be bought and sold, deeded, divided, or otherwise disposed of by their lay owners.

The drive for the restitution of tithes often met with strong resistance on the part of lay seigniors. The quest continued far into the thirteenth century and

---

*The young man's hood would not necessarily mean that he was a cleric.

4. *Notre-Dame de Paris*. The Martyrs' Portal (13th century). Series representing the
"Life of the Students." The four reliefs at the right. Lower left, collection of tithes;
lower right, the artisan in his booth; upper left, group-studying scene; upper right,
attending a lecture.

when preparing to leave for the last Crusade in which he was to die, St. Louis
tried to give the drive a strong impetus by decreeing that in his territories
thereafter tithes could be restored to the Church "without requiring our consent or that of our successors."[27] This was in the year 1269, when work on
the eight reliefs was proceeding. It would not be surprising therefore if this
important concern of the Church should find an echo in them.

In this campaign large numbers of collectors would have been required by the bishop and chapter of Notre-Dame to cover their vast landed possessions spread widely over the Île de France, and it is altogether probable that scholars were brought into this work. The first scene appears to describe an excursion of this kind, three clerics having come to a peasant household to make a collection. Everything about the action indicates that they are cordially received. At the right, the young peasant, whose wife hides behind him in a demure gesture prescribed by the mores of the time, reaches into his purse. His old mother at his side is too feeble to rise in deference to the important visitors. But her still hale husband fusses about them ceremoniously and delivers to one of them the "kiss of peace," a customary accolade in such circumstances.

The following scene, at the lower right, is more easily identified. Here, it seems clear, is an artisan at work in his booth, which could be located either on the parvis of Notre-Dame or in the cloister, in both of which workshops of this kind existed during the thirteenth century. Here in fact a royal decree permitted the churchmen to place a goldsmith and other skilled workmen, who would be independent of the powerful guilds that controlled the city's trades.[28] But these artisans had to conform to other accepted regulations, like that of working "on the street, their window or door ajar."[29] Churchmen of the Middle Ages were far from considering such activities as beneath notice! Thus, in the popular thirteenth-century *Dictionarius*, a student's manual prepared by a local cleric, Jean de Garlande, among all the other useful information of a purely scholarly nature which it contains is also included a modern-type directory of the various shops and other tourist attractions of the capital.[30]

At the artisan's side is a tout, loudly vaunting his skill. It is not exactly clear from the worn sculpture what type of work the former is engaged in. It is certainly on some small object, which from the *Dictionarius'* descriptions might be a buckle, a brooch, or a pin. Even more likely, it could be a ring, if the couple at the far left of the scene are the same young persons who appear in the fourth relief of the first set, where we have identified them as publishing their banns inside the cathedral sanctuary. The present couple are dressed exactly the same as the other and the young man has one arm about his fiancée. All the other hands are unfortunately missing but there is an inescapable suggestiveness to the byplay that is taking place here: The young man seems to be extending to his lady the money for a purchase.

The relief in the upper-left quatrefoil plainly represents a group-study scene, common in the Middle Ages. If the lettering originally inscribed on the wall-scroll were legible we would probably be able to read on it the printed version of one of those oaths that students were required to take during the campaigns of reform that were urged upon them periodically. Or it might have been a reference to the decree of excommunication issued, in 1269, by Bishop Étienne Tempier, against those "clerics, scholars, and their servants, who go armed about the city, day or night, kidnap women, violate young girls, break down the doors of houses, and commit homicide, robbery, and all sorts of other crimes."[31]

Or the scroll might simply have reproduced Robert de Sorbon's six recommendations on "How to Study," extracted from his sermons to the students. St. Louis' chaplain and confessor was full of wise counsel on this subject, sometimes sounding like a modern dean at chapel advising his young charges on how to extract one true thought from each day's reading and to write it down, "for the words which are not confided to writing take flight like dust before the wind." And above all other methods to be recommended, he added, was discussion with one's fellow-students and especially "disputation." For the latter was "even more advantageous than reading, since it clarifies all doubts, all obscurities that reading may have left."[32] These prescriptions all appear to be faithfully reproduced in this scene, which contains some of the most fascinating sculpture of the series.

The final quatrefoil shows students attending a lecture, a duty that needed emphasizing since the delinquency on this score was widespread and minimum requirements had to be set. The master is identified by his cape and biretta and by his elevated position.

Preserving his right of justice over a thousand students might not have exactly filled the episcopal strongboxes but it was indispensable if the bishop was to maintain his claims over the city's other clerics who were far more numerous, to say nothing of the thousands of laymen in various sections of Paris over whom he held seigniorial jurisdiction. That there was constant danger of invasion of these rights by the king's officers is illustrated by the repeated violence that was used against students and other clerics by the royal police, right under the king's beard as it were and in contravention of his solemn pledges of protection. There is no doubt that the monarchs often blinked at the excesses of their officers, recognizing their ultimate usefulness to the royal cause. As one authority has explained it: "It cannot be doubted that the repeated encroachments of the royal agents on ecclesiastic possessions and privileges contributed to a large degree to the development of the central authority."[33]

Nevertheless, the kings did make some effort to curb these infringements. Provosts of Paris, before assuming office, were required to appear in the church of Saint-Julien-le-Pauvre, right across the Seine from Notre-Dame, and take an oath before the masters and students that they would respect their rights. This mandate was still operative at the beginning of the fourteenth century, when the students' privilege was ordered read publicly every two years to the provost and his men, after which he was to say to them—"in French," it was specified— "I want you to know that I have sworn to observe this privilege."[34]

Yet violations of the academic immunities continued. In one reported instance that took place in 1303 or 1304, the University once more shut down in protest, this time because of the hanging of a student. The strike compelled the king to punish his provost, who was required to cut the student's body down and kiss it. Then the entire clergy of Paris marched on the house of the offending magistrate and threw stones at it while solemnly exorcizing the Devil.

Other similar happenings were considered important enough to be memorialized by epitaphs or even art works. In one case a police officer who had "forcefully taken two scholars out of the church of the Carmes" was made to offer "honorable amends," while wearing only a shirt, carrying a tall candle, and kneeling before the clergy, all of which was represented in a painting that a seventeenth-century writer could still see hanging, "in the nave of the said church to the left of the great portal."[35]

Unfortunately, that picture has disappeared. But another very similar incident left an artistic monument in its wake which has been preserved. Involved on that occasion was the convent of the Grands-Augustins, from which three armed constables dragged Nicolas Aymery, a member of the order. The monks must have put up a resistance and one of them was killed. The religious community was outraged and as Aymery was a master in theology of the University, that body entered into the vehement demand for redress. Punishment was draconic, the three constables being stripped of all possessions and permanently exiled from the kingdom. But first they were required to give "honorable amends" in three public places—"in shirttail and with uncovered head and bare legs and feet, and each holding a burning four-pound torch and begging pardon and mercy of all."[36]

Before the constables' goods were turned over to the king two deductions were made. One was for 1,000 livres, which, after payment for prayers and masses, were divided among the University rector, the prior of the order, and his monks. The other was to pay for the making of a stone cross which was to be erected on the spot together with a sculptured representation of the "honorable amends" scene. This relief was given a prominent place on the outside wall of the convent church, from which it was removed during the Revolution of 1789 by Alexandre Lenoir, the amazing volunteer guardian of monuments who by ruse, cajolery, and personal purchase and at times at the risk of his life saved many of France's most precious art treasures from destruction or sale out of the country.[37]

Still to be found [Pl. 5] in a court of the Petits-Augustins (at present, the École des Beaux-Arts), where Lenoir stored his priceless harvest, this remarkable relief shows the three culprits on their knees before a group of churchmen. To the fore is the prior, molded somewhat larger than the others, in keeping with his dignity. He holds a scroll in his hand, probably a reference to the by then legendary Philippe-Auguste charter of 1222. On the other side, in addition to the prisoners and their armed guards, a group of townsmen is represented. The inscription which runs around the four sides of the relief is in both French

and Latin, one verse in the latter language implying that a statue of the mur-
dered monk could also be seen here.

Still another conflict between ecclesiastic and royal justice, which likewise
resulted in a victory for the Church, won commemorative tablets at both the
cathedrals of Sens and Paris. In the former, seat of the archbishop, the inscription was placed beneath a statue of the king, "armed and on horseback." This
was Philippe de Valois, recently acceded to the throne (1328), who had earned
this splendid tribute for having refused to deprive the archbishop of his secular
justice. In doing so, he had ruled against the plea of his own advocate, whose
ignominy (in the Church's eyes) was thereafter broadcast by the malicious association of his name with an ugly grimacing little devil on the roodscreen at
Notre-Dame, which was always shown to visitors and against whose nose
choirboys were encouraged to extinguish their candles.[38]

But such victories could not arrest the relentless process which has been
described as "that daily war which only the complete triumph of the monarchic
power was destined to terminate."[39] Indeed this steady growth of the central
(royal) power, so essential to the developing economic forces, is one of the
most salient facts in the history of medieval French society. It began at the
time that Western Europe emerged from its cocoon-like state in the eleventh
century and intensified through the twelfth and thirteenth. The royal power,
itself a feudal sovereignty, grew at the expense of all others as a line of shrewd
Capetian kings divided their opponents. Among the latter, as we have seen, the
ecclesiastics were by no means spared.

Nor were the churchmen's quarrels solely with the royal power. Innumerable
were their collisions with lay seigniors and as frequent, often bitter to the point
of violence, with other ecclesiastics: abbot against abbot, bishop against abbot,
bishop against churches of his own diocese. A famous case involving Paris' renowned Bishop Maurice de Sully and the monks of Saint-Germain-des-Prés,
with whom he was in constant turmoil, occurred when the pope came to dedi-
cate a new church at that abbey. Maurice tried to enter the convent in the
procession of prelates that accompanied the pope. But the monks would not
permit the cortege to proceed while the bishop was part of it. After a hurried
conference between pope and bishop, Maurice agreed to retire. He later took
the matter up at a church council, arguing that as a Christian he had a right to
visit the abbey. But his protest was laid aside.

The conflict of the bishop with the University would inevitably have been
seen by the former in feudal terms. The masters and students were "his men"
and were seeking to slip out of his jurisdiction by way of their unholy "*Universitas.*" The bishop was often at odds likewise with his own chapter at Notre-
Dame on a variety of jurisdictional questions, as, for example, over their rival
claims on the cathedral's offertory boxes. In this latter case an accord was
eventually reached partitioning the church's earnings, the bishop retaining

rights over the sanctuary and part of the choir while the canons got the nave and the aisles.[40]

Reported instances of such conflicts often impress us as being incredibly petty today and yet they might in the end have called for papal action! Others are ludicrous or just simply funny though they certainly did not strike the principals that way. One dispute between the bishop and Notre-Dame chapter, which occurred in 1273, lacks a few pertinent details that might have added zest to a suggestive tale. It began when two of the bishop's constables broke into a residence bordering the cloister and caught a man bathing "in the company of the mistress of the house."

The officers demanded payment of a fine and as the sinners, under the circumstances, were hardly in a position to argue, they turned over a vase to them. The canons were infuriated, not by the transgression of the couple, however, but because they claimed jurisdiction over one of them! They won their point. The vase was restored and in addition the bishop had to turn over a pair of fur-lined gloves as a penalty, a conventional adjustment in such cases. Whether the recipient was the person whose ease had been disturbed and what his connection with the cathedral chapter was were not mentioned in the account, however.[41]

The eight reliefs at the base of Notre-Dame's south transept portal were carved at a time when the political world was unlike anything we know today,

5. Paris, *Former Convent of the Grands-Augustins*. "Honorable Amends" relief (15th century). Three of the king's constables (kneeling at right) make amends to leaders of the Augustinian order, one of whose monks they had killed. Now at the École des Beaux-Arts.

when every geographic area down to city or town was fractioned into a myriad of sovereignties, each imposing the confusing variety of obligations—taxes, services, tithes, etc.—characteristic of the feudal order. An idea of this political patchwork quilt can be ascertained from the circumstance that Paris had at least two dozen seigniors with autonomous courts of justice. The great majority were churchmen, the bishop leading in the extent of his jurisdiction which covered 105 scattered streets, followed by various abbots, priors and other church dignitaries, and the king.[42]

Jurisdiction over a street could be split several ways and might be sliced down to a single house or even part of one, or the justice inside and outside of some houses might be divided. All of this loses its apparent insanity when one understands that medieval justice was regarded as a kind of private property, "an important source of revenue."[43] And by all accounts it was enormously remunerative. Sentences were far harsher than modern ones and fines extraordinarily high. Jews particularly were heavily penalized and seigniors vied for justice over them.[44] Complete confiscation of property often figured as a punishment and the assessors were thorough, leaving a gentleman, for example, nothing but his palfreys and two saddles, his packhorse and his squire's jade, also his bed, his ceremonial robe, a buckle, and one ring. His wife fared somewhat worse, saving merely her bed, one dress, several chemisettes, a belt, a purse, a buckle, and a ring.[45]

How such fines could mount up is shown by figures of the annual earnings of the bishop's temporal justice. This court, which handled only cases of the prelate's thousands of lay subjects, was located in a separate building called the For-l'Évêque, situated on the right bank of the Seine on the Quai de la Mégisserie. Thus it was sharply distinguished from the bishop's Officialité, the court covering the clerical population (students included) which was housed in the episcopal palace, facing the cathedral portal we have been discussing. The latter complex also included the bishop's jail and an area where judicial duels were fought.

We have no accounts for the bishop's income from the Officialité, but there exist "lettres patentes" from 1374, giving earnings of his judicial officers at the For-l'Évêque, from which we can obtain a comparative idea. The chief magistrate here drew a total of about 30,000 livres* while his chief assistants received "more than 6,000 livres each." Income from the prison and from various fees which were farmed out was thousands of livres more. The profits accruing to the bishop from these sources can only be guessed at. When, in 1674, Louis XIV assumed all temporal justice under the crown, he indemnified the then archbishop of Paris for his jurisdiction by an annuity of 10,000 livres, raised in 1681 to 16,000, plus other allowances.[46]

*These sums must be multiplied many times to bring them in line with modern equivalents.

Under this arrangement the For-l'Évêque became a royal prison. It had been on this site since the thirteenth century. Writers of the seventeenth and eighteenth centuries have described as still visible over its portals two old reliefs. One presented a bishop and a king, most likely Guillaume de Seignelay and Philippe-Auguste, kneeling together before the Virgin, marking the accord of 1222. On this relief, Jean Lebeuf reported in 1744, were also "the arms of France in innumerable fleur-de-lis and traversed by a bishop's crosier." And on the other portal, a judge in a robe and hood was depicted, with his assessors and a clerk of the court, "dressed like a churchman."[47]

It would be interesting to know what might have happened to these extraordinary sculptures, so relevant to the matter that we have been studying. They must still have been in good preservation in 1652, since Paris' first archbishop, Jean-François de Gondi, had them kept in place at that time when a complete reconstruction of the For-l'Évêque was undertaken.[48] That they remained after the transformation of the building into a royal prison, in 1674, is also certain since Lebeuf mentioned seeing them long after that date. They were probably still there when, in 1780, the For-l'Évêque was ordered torn down by Louis XVI, for assertedly humanitarian reasons, the royal edict beginning: "Full of desire to solace the unhappy . . . we have been touched for a long time by the state of the prisons in the majority of the cities of our kingdom. . . ." The demolition did not take place until 1783, the "lands and materials" being sold to private buyers.[49]

Were the reliefs broken up at the time and tossed into the Seine or was the stone out of which they had been carved used, in reverse, on some other building? Whichever happened, their disappearance probably caused little regret. For, aside from the eighteenth-century viewpoint of Gothic art as downright barbaric, the subject could not have recommended itself to the monarchal notions of the time. A king of France humbly kneeling side by side with a mere bishop! Yet, for whatever hope there may still be that these interesting old sculptures will one day be found, the fact that the prison on which they were located was torn down a few years before the Revolution is a fortunate accident. If the For-l'Évêque had continued to stand until 1789 there is little doubt that it would have been wiped out without a vestige, as were so many other monuments to human misery.

In any event it is a pity that the sculpture is gone. But such losses (and there have been many of them, knowledge of which has come down to us) merely increase the more the value of what is left. Among these remnants the eight reliefs should hold a preeminent place. On a par artistically with any similar sculpture that has survived from the thirteenth century, they have the unique merit besides of presenting to us in exact and profuse detail vibrant happenings, as actual as photography, from that amazing period.

CHAPTER II
THE SOCIAL FACTOR

THE EXPERIENCE with the Notre-Dame reliefs opens the question as to how general the neglect of social motives may have been in the study of old art. We have been asked to assume, for example, that medieval churchmen unfalteringly avoided the temptation to use art in their own or in the Church's worldly interests and that laymen were likewise reluctant to intrude into this sacred area. But this attitude, many now agree, has been highly overplayed.

Nevertheless, it is certainly true that concrete historical events or their leading protagonists were not a major preoccupation of medieval church art. Even if we take into account the amount of this kind of work that was subsequently destroyed, it still would not add up to a massive portion of the total art product of the time. Yet there were other ways that historical currents could have impinged upon and variously influenced this art, causing changes in the handling of the leading Christian figures, for example, rises or falls in their popularity, evolutions in their legends. In all of these the possible mediation of nontheological factors has been but scantily explored.

This neglect is the more surprising when one considers the broader outlook that marked much earlier scholarship. With a few notable exceptions, on the other hand, contemporary art historians have failed to make a study of the social background a systematic matter, their occasional concern with the history of a period being often merely applied to the dating of some monument or the solution of some problem of filiation.

In the field of iconography the limited scope of many authors is particularly marked. Thus, for example, in tracing some change in the pattern of the Nativity, if the influence of an earlier art work is not demonstrable, it would be considered perfectly adequate to find a literary or liturgical or homiletic source. And it might not often strike the scholar as worthwhile to go beyond book or document to ask why the author or preacher might have felt urged to make his new formulation at the given time and place. The failure to do so may of course imply that the change had simply originated with the person making it.

At times, however, a writer has made a frank ideological profession of his interpretation. This is what occurred in the great debate that raged some years ago as to whether the Gothic architectural form was primarily of esthetic or technological inspiration. The latter viewpoint stemmed from Eugène Viollet-le-Duc, the renowned nineteenth-century architect and restorer. The old forms of cylindrical vaulting and the semicircular arch, he argued, had proved deficient for the wide, capacious city-cathedrals that began to be needed in the mid-twelfth century, the outward thrust of the heavy vaults often causing them to collapse soon after the scaffolding was removed. After a series of costly failures, architects mastered the use of the Gothic arch, which by elevating the vault shifted its major thrust from out to down. This push, Viollet-le-Duc suggested, was carried by the ribs—upon which the weight of the vault rested—toward the supporting columns. "It is by the skillful application of this principle that [architects] quickly came to apply the entire weight and thrust of enormous vaults onto extremely thin pillars," he explained.[1]

This attractive, but rather too neat, explanation imposed itself nevertheless on architects for many years, backed by its originator's overwhelming documentation. In the first quarter of the twentieth century, however, various objections began to be raised to it. The results of the bombing of Reims cathedral and other churches during World War I added to these doubts, when the ribs of some Gothic bays were found completely blown away while the vaults above them remained standing. In 1928 a Chief Engineer of the "Ponts et Chaussées," Victor Sabouret, made a thorough study of the subject, finding "quite frequently" organic fissures in the arch-ribs "not only in bombed churches but also in non-restored old vaults." This proved that the Gothic ribs gave no support to the vault, he concluded, and they had not been very helpful during its construction either.[2]

In 1934 these arguments were taken up and developed by Pol Abraham, who adopted the frank viewpoint that while Gothic architecture was esthetically magnificent it was technically thoroughly deficient. Most Gothic churches would have soon toppled if not for the timely addition of sustaining elements and especially of the flying buttress. Marcel Aubert replied by taking up the cudgels for Viollet-le-Duc's basic thesis. Where architects had previously feared to cover the large naves of churches with vaults, he pointed out, the Gothic arch had provided the solution. The earliest ogival arches were heavy and thick, the ribs large and strong, which proved that Gothic builders had indeed regarded them as powerful supports to the vault.

As for the effects of the bombings, Aubert felt that they had been exaggeratedly generalized. If some vaults had remained standing after the ribs had fallen this merely proved that they were extremely solid; others had given way.[3] These bombing effects, another author agreed, did not prove that the vaults would have survived "had they been deprived of their ribs after seven weeks instead of after seven centuries."[4]

It was in their secondary conclusions that Viollet-le-Duc's critics revealed their special "viewpoint." Sabouret held that since the Gothic rib served no practical purpose its role must have been conceived by the old architects themselves as purely decorative: employed for its "effect of ascension which was pursued with obstinacy" by the medieval builders.[5] And Pol Abraham went even further. He was frankly troubled by the influence that Viollet-le-Duc's "rationalist" theories had had on modern builders. According to this approach, he explained, beauty must be attained "solely by necessary construction elements and without recourse to artifice." Modern architects had allowed themselves to be saddled by this notion, he added, concluding that "on pain of death architecture must utilize the technics invented by the engineers and bow to the narrow economic and social necessities."

They should free themselves of this tyranny, Abraham urged, and concern themselves more appropriately with matters of style and with those "caprices of taste which have played and will always play in architecture a superior role to the technics which serve them."[6]

There are undoubtedly compelling reasons for architects to be concerned with materials and methods. Modern architects in any case seem to have resisted Pol Abraham's efforts to liberate them from these base necessities. Nevertheless, it would be folly to deny the enormous part that the esthetic element has played in Gothic architecture. Aside from all else, a potent stimulus to the full development of this form, with its light walls and open bays, was undoubtedly the perfection of the stained-glass technic, which was to make of the thirteenth-century cathedral a great blaze of glowing color.

A famous example in which mystical rather than technological motives were assumed to have influenced the form of many medieval churches was the long-favored theory regarding the "meaning" of the slight deflection of the choir from the line of the main axis, which can be observed in so many old churches, as for example in Notre-Dame de Paris. This deviation, it was held, was meant to symbolize the head of Jesus Christ dropping to his shoulder as he expired on the cross. Various symbolisms of a similar nature have been suggested. Émile Mâle, for instance, thought that one door at Notre-Dame's north side, because of its traditional name—the "Porte Rouge"—might have been meant to figure the wound pierced in Christ's right side by the lance.[7] However, as Robert de Lasteyrie has pointed out, this opening is in the church choir, which should symbolize the head of Christ, not his flank!

De Lasteyrie, in a masterful study, proved that axial deviations and particularly those of the choir, far from having a mystical origin, could usually be traced to very mundane causes. They were the consequence of the nature of the site, of obstacles due to preexisting structures, of belated changes or additions, or—and that most frequently—"the involuntary result of the conditions in which architects of the Middle Ages worked and of the imperfect methods they possessed to align the successive constructions of vast edifices whose various parts were never set down at the same time."

Medieval churches were almost always built section by section and often at considerable gaps of time between sections, de Lasteyrie explained. The completed part was each time shut off for the use of the cult by means of temporary partitions, which obstructed the view from the section that was being built. Lacking the modern instruments for taking readings under such complex conditions, the medieval architects got into trouble and "a tiny error often caused a marked divergence in alignment." Since the choir was usually done first, that was the reason for the frequency of the deflection at that point, he added, but he gave examples of divergences in other parts of numerous churches.[8]

There have been a variety of other factors that have influenced the form of medieval church architecture. In Southern France, for example, churches were often built with smooth, thick outside walls, heavy towers, machicolated galleries, and other military features of defense aimed at Saracen raiders, who completely controlled the Western Mediterranean far into the eleventh century. It has been suggested also that the monks of Cluny found tunnel vaulting advantageous for their churches because of the excellent acoustics it provided. This would be of primary importance to this order, whose members chanted their offices from one end of the day to the other.[9]

The cult of relics, on the other hand, was without question at the origin of those strange, bulbous excrescences that rim the eastern exteriors of many Romanesque churches. It might be difficult at times to account for them on esthetic grounds [Pl. 6]. But the great masses of visitors that were attracted into the churches by their miracle-working relics do in any case explain the apse, as they do also the development of crypts and ambulatories, multiple naves and narthexes. At first, relics were kept in a crypt, often right beneath the pavement, and there might be a little window through which the bones or other holy remnants could be seen. But people wanted to get closer to the revered objects. Accordingly, a stairway and a narrow passage would be built and as the number of visitors to the crypt increased, a room was added where the pilgrims could gather for contemplation and prayer.[10]

An accidental circumstance, at Saint-Martin de Tours, may have helped bring about a departure from the custom of displaying relics in the church crypt. This was the high level of the ground water of the Loire at that point, which necessitated raising the place of display aboveground. When this was done, the new construction was worked out in the form of an "annular aisle or corridor enclosing the sanctuary, giving access to the tomb of St. Martin" as well as "to a series of round chapels attached to the peripheral wall of the corridor," where other relics or images were displayed.[11] Whether or not the ambulatory, thus called forth by topographic chance at Tours, was the first of its kind is irrelevant to this discussion. What is interesting here is the fact that this form was eventually adopted universally as the increasing crowds of pilgrims caused grave traffic problems inside the relics-containing churches.

The way this took place is described with great verve by Abbot Suger of Saint-Denis, who explained that the rebuilding of his basilica was made necessary by such circumstances. As the hordes of pilgrims thronged into his church, he narrated, the people up front would hold onto their places, fighting off "those who strove to flock in to worship and kiss the holy relics . . . [so] that no one among the countless thousands . . . could move a foot." Women were crushed by men as in a winepress and "cried out horribly as though in labor." Sometimes they would faint and have to be carried above the heads of the crowd into the cloisters, "gasping almost with their last breath." And when the brethren displayed the remains of St. Dionysius (Denis) and his companions, the crowd's agitation became such that rioting often resulted and the monks would have to escape with the relics by leaping out through the windows.[12]

Into this chaos the system of divided nave and ambulatory—with one-way traffic leading the pilgrims from the front entrance to the apse, then around the sanctuary and back out again by the transept portal or through another door at the front—became a solution whose utility was swiftly appreciated [Pl. 7].

The belief in the efficacy of relics was so strong and widespread, it has been suggested that the Middle Ages might be properly called "the epoch of the cult of relics."[13] And out of this cult of miracle-working remnants evolved the whole complex of pilgrimages, some of which played an extraordinary commercial and political role, to say nothing of their artistic one. These pious journeys were often organized with astonishing acumen. After the fire of 1134 the cathedral of Chartres was rebuilt by the chapter with the deliberate aim of attracting pilgrims to the shrine containing the relic of the Virgin's Tunic. Appropriately a series of miracles began occurring around this relic and the stream of visitors began to flow.[14]

The development of the cult of relics was likewise largely responsible for the increase in the number of altars and chapels in the churches. In the early centuries every altar had had to have its holy remnant,[15] a synodal requirement that limited the number of altars, many churches having only one or two at most. The acquisition of large numbers of relics, especially during the Crusades, and other circumstances played havoc with this austerity. As altars and chapels multiplied, a writer has noted, "the change was reflected in the design of [the] churches. . . . The east end was not merely lengthened; it was expanded with

6. *Conques-en-Rouergue, Church of Sainte-Foy* (12th century). Exterior view of church apse.

7. *Saint-Denis, Abbey Church.* The ambulatory (12th and 13th century). The passage of pilgrims was directed around the holy relics, which were displayed in the sanctuary at the center.

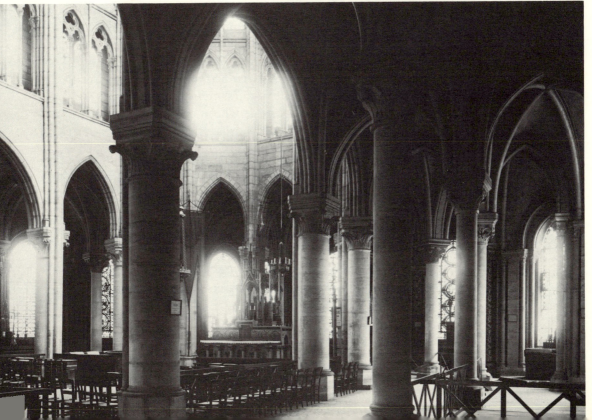

a cluster of chapels growing out of the ambulatory, round the shrine, and sometimes a second, eastern transept was added to contain more altars. . . ."[16]

The possession of famous, miracle-performing relics was paramount for churches wishing to attract the faithful. Competition developed sharply among them. In this manner the question of who had the true remains of Mary Magdalene became a burning issue between the monasteries of Vézelay and distant Saint-Maximin-en-Provence. Around 1100 Bishop Norgaud of Autun intervened, trying to keep pilgrims from making offerings at Vézelay. But Pope Pascal II quickly lifted his ban. Vézelay went on in its controversial career, which did not affect its phenomenal prosperity, nor the steady growth of the abbey church with its superb sculptured façade and pillar capitals. Doubts of the genuineness of its relics continued to cloud the abbey's fame, however, until Abbot Jean I, in 1265, offered to settle the matter on the evidence.

In the presence of St. Louis, the papal legate and other high church dignitaries, and "numerous barons," the saint's tomb was dug up, whereupon a letter from Charles the Bold dating from the ninth century was discovered in a vase, "authenticating" the remains! St. Louis was so impressed that he gave the abbey additional relics from among those he had brought from Constantinople, including two thorns from Christ's Crown, a fragment of the True Cross, and scraps of the Holy Shroud, the Purple Mantle, the Infant's Swaddling-Cloth, and of the Cloth with which Christ had wiped the Apostles' feet.[17]

The possession of certified relics was of such immense concern to the prosperity of religious bodies that it is not surprising to see miracles performed by them repeatedly appearing in the art of the churches involved. An example among many is the one at Saint-Benoît-sur-Loire, showing the monks transporting the saint's remains to this church. The sick rise from their beds as they pass [Pl. 8]. This was a way not only of presenting to the faithful ocular proof of the efficacy of their relics but also of authenticating them in good, solid stone. It has been said that in ambiguous cases, where the presence of a particular saint in the art of a church cannot otherwise be explained, one can usually assume possession in the past of some relic of the saint in question.[18]

The pilgrimage to Santiago da Compostela, whose enormous influence on medieval architecture and sculpture has been exhaustively studied by many scholars, unquestionably had its origin in political and economic, as well as religious, motives. The discovery* of St. James' tomb, around 830, at Compostela by Bishop Théodemir of Iria Flavia was not favored by the times. It was not until 250 years later that the political situation was ripe for the full exploitation of this incident. The papacy saw in Spain a possible source of strength in its struggle with the German emperors and, in 1077, Pope Gregory VII laid claim to it as a fief of the Church. The crusade for the reconquest of

---

*The pretty French synonym for "discovery" when applied to relics—"invention"—would appear in this case to be more appropriately understood in its more usual sense.

the peninsula won the support of all important elements of the population of Southwest France, who perceived the economic as well as political advantages of the campaign.[19] And as the knights moved across the Pyrenees they were closely followed by merchants, churchmen, and masters of "piedras tallar" and of "jometria" (masons and builders).[20]

The Compostela pilgrimage, which developed into Christendom's leading circuit in the twelfth century, was energetically fostered by the Cluny order, which encouraged the building of roads, bridges, and hospices and saw to it that the perilous route was properly policed. It established dozens of its subsidiary abbeys along the four major passages into Spain, a number of which had their own relics that merited stopovers for pilgrims. To keep the latter from going astray toward other goals, Cluny crushed rivals or bought off possessors of competitive relics. When, for example, the powerful chapter of Saint-Sernin at Toulouse set up the counterclaim of possessing the bodies of six Apostles, including the greater part of that of St. James himself, the bishop of Toulouse, who was loyal to Cluny, summarily expelled them. The pope ordered their reinstatement a year later, but the canons had evidently learned their lesson by then and thereafter Saint-Sernin became a leading stopping-off place on the Compostela pilgrimage road.[21]

8. *Saint-Benoît-sur-Loire, Abbey Church*. North portal (13th century).
The sick rise from their beds at the passing of St. Benedict's remains.

What poetry could do to help imprint the glories of this journey on the popular imagination was accomplished by such epics as the *Chronique de Turpin* and the *Chanson de Roland*, the former anachronistically describing Charlemagne himself as an early Compostela pilgrim.[22] The pilgrimage even had its own guidebook (which the latest scholarship seems to attribute to the Knights Templars rather than to Cluny[23]), and an excellent one it was, telling the wayfarer how much money he needed for the journey, what rivers he had to cross, the climate and other circumstances he would encounter. The author described the Gascons as loudmouthed and primitive, eating off the floor, servants sleeping with their master and mistress. The Navarrais were equally benighted: In warming themselves at the fire both men and women showed what should be hidden and the men "fornicated shamelessly with beasts." However, they were "regular in the payment of their tithes," he added, to their credit.

The writer cursed boatmen and others who cheated pilgrims as well as rival institutions that presumed to possess relics that pilgrimage churches claimed. He vaunted the efficacy of the latter, saying about those at Saint-Gilles: "Oh, how beautiful and profitable it is to visit his tomb. The very day that one has prayed to him with all one's heart, one's prayer will be granted without any doubt." Also he described glowingly the art possessions of various pilgrimage churches, much of them long since disappeared. Often, he was frank to the point of indiscretion, as when he told of how Compostela's great corps of seventy-two canons divided the church's enormous earnings with the archbishop. Only one week of the year did the offerings go for the benefit of poor pilgrims. This should be increased, he suggested, adding that the city's lepers already got whatever came in at the altar on Sunday mornings up until 9 o'clock.[24]

Artistically, as has been pointed out, the pilgrimage route was very much a two-way passage, with influences flowing in both directions.[25] As early as the mid-tenth century, a bishop of Le Puy led a conducted tour of 200 monks to Compostela and the marked influence of Moorish architecture at Le Puy proves that the returning pilgrims had brought back other things besides cockleshells and tales of miracles.[26] All along the routes leading across France the gifts of pilgrims helped Cluny build and decorate some of the country's most splendid churches. And sculpturally, the determination to give stature to St. James is everywhere evident. Undoubtedly the saint's apotheosis which can be seen on the portals of so many pilgrimage churches helped popularize the trip and many began to wonder if St. James were not greater even than St. Peter as "the son of Zebedee elbow[ed] from the position of honor the prince of the apostles."[27]

St. James' transformation into a warrior-horseman and "killer of Moors" in twelfth-century Spanish sculpture was due to a natural association with the major problem of the crusaders to that country.[28] Other saints were "elevated" during this period from the pedestrian to the cavalier status. Pilgrimage sculpture was also concerned with miracles in connection with the passage, like that of the boy who was hanged when falsely accused of theft. His parents sadly continued their journey to St. James' tomb. On returning they found their son still alive on the gibbet, having been held up by the feet by "ung preudome" (a righteous and wise man), presumably the appreciative saint. They ran to the judge who would not believe their story: It was as likely as if the cock and hen roasting on the fire there would come out and sing. Which they promptly did, in honor of which miracle sculptured effigies of the fowls were put up in the village church: "and I have seen them in truth and they are both white," a pilgrim wrote.[29] The whole story, with variations, of the miraculous delivery of the young boy is told in a stained-glass window still to be seen at Tours cathedral.

Other rewards, including the most precious of all, eternal bliss, were held out attractively to the pilgrim, as illustrated in the lintel across the great tympanum at Autun, where a figure bearing the familiar staff of St. James and the traveler's wallet decorated by the Compostela scallop shell leads the procession of the Elect. Other pilgrimage art stressed the importance of granting food and shelter to pious wayfarers, like the charming capital of San Gil at Luna (Zaragoza), which shows six of them lying together, alternating head and feet, each in a sort of individual sleeping-bag, his head covered by a hood.[30] Two other capitals at the portal of the still-standing hospice near Notre-Dame du Puy show the pilgrim receiving bread and being bedded down solicitously.[31]

Too much has already been written about the influence played by feudal relations and the medieval notions of royalty upon the character and posture of Christ, Mary, and the Apostles on church tympana to require anything more than a mention here. An American scholar has commented in this manner about the Moissac tympanum, for example: "The hierarchical relations of Roman Christianity, the temporal claims of the Church, are presented here in terms of the most advanced conceptions of centralized feudal power possible at the moment."[32] While Émile Mâle held that the directly historical references in church art were limited to the baptism of Clovis, the exploits of Charlemagne, and the first Crusades, he made an exception of the cathedral of Reims, where France's early kings are displayed in great stained-glass figures. But this was the consecration church of French royalty, he explained, and each sovereign is accompanied by his bishop so as to remind Christians "that a king anointed with holy oil is more than a man."[33] However, Reims is not the only church with this type of royal apotheosis.

The sacred character of the French royalty is just as highly developed at Paris' Sainte-Chapelle, built by St. Louis to house the Crown of Thorns. He had paid a king's ransom for this relic at that great mart of blessed bones and vestments, Constantinople, where another just like it was up for sale a few years later. The king had the chapel decorated by a profusion of stained-glass scenes from the Old and New Testaments, in which the ever-recurring motif of coronation was meant to be more than a mere reference to the shrine's chief possession. Many of the subjects are unique in medieval art, drawn from Kings and Numbers (one of the Bible's most arid sectors and the art going with it is often just as boring), from Esther and Judges. In one scene Gideon, contrary to Scripture, is shown wearing the crown which actually he refused.*

The inordinate and at times anomalous repetition of these royal themes "probably reveals one of the essential meanings of the edifice," says one commentator, all of which was meant to lead up to the final window glorifying "the relics of the Cross, the Crown of Thorns, and the founder of the edifice, Louis IX. We must not forget the sacred and sacerdotal character of the French royalty in the Middle Ages," he goes on. "The political ideology of St. Louis was nourished by all the Christian and sacred 'themes' justifying royalty, and it is normal that they are expressed at Sainte-Chapelle, which was created by him, inspired by him, and which assumes all its meaning only in relationship to his personality."[34] And St. Louis, devoutest of the devout, permitted his own effigy to be put into the Sainte-Chapelle lancets, as he did moreover others of himself and of his wife on a portal of Notre-Dame. It was, as a matter of fact, a practice that sovereigns and nobles frequently followed, at Strasbourg, Chartres, and elsewhere.

They did not even disdain to use hallowed church space for what would appear to us today as highly improper purposes. Thus Louis VII, who in his never-ending efforts to expand the royal authority had led a series of expeditions into Burgundy, was able, in 1166, to bring an especially troublesome baron, the Comte Girard de Mâcon, to heel. This success, which he accomplished ostensibly in behalf of his ally, the bishop of Mâcon, whom the comte had repeatedly harried with his raids, Louis solemnized by paying for the erection of a church at Avenas, located within the bishop's diocese and on the border of the comte's domain. Inside this church and over its altar, he had carved a large relief in which he is depicted as its founder, piously kneeling and presenting a model of it to St. Vincent, while at the same time, in the symbolic language of feudalism, leaving no doubt about his readiness to return to administer punishment to his enemies [Pl. 9].[35]

The Catholic prelates themselves were scarcely more reticent about appearing in church art or of building up the authority of the hierarchy by adept associations with illustrious predecessors. This was especially true of the papal dignity, which was sedulously developed as an accessory of the character of

---

*Judges 8:22–23: "Then the men of Israel said unto Gideon, Rule thou over us, both thou, and thy son, and thy son's son also: for thou hast delivered us from the hand of Midian. / And Gideon said unto them, I will not rule over you, neither shall my son rule over you: the Lord shall rule over you."

St. Peter. Indeed, the latter has been shown to have been completely metamorphosed from his evangelical role by a repetition of second thoughts, whose inspiration is often only too apparent.

It was, significantly, at Rome that he was first placed, in art, at the top of the hierarchy, distinguished from the other Apostles by his tonsure. Later the chasuble was put on his shoulders and he was shown saying mass. It was Pope Leo III who had Peter presented with the highest symbol of ecclesiastic dignity: the pallium. He was the first pope thereafter. This occurred in the famous mosaic of the Triclinium arch across from the papal Lateran Palace, where Peter is shown presenting the papal stole to Leo and the royal banner to Charlemagne, both of whom are kneeling before him. A Latin inscription reads: "St. Peter, you give life to Pope Leo and victory to King Charles." Later an even more daring innovation was introduced showing Peter wearing the pope's tiara. In the eleventh century he was figured as consecrating his successor, St. Clement, in another mosaic at Rome, and soon after began to turn over the keys (symbolic of the power to absolve sin) to succeeding popes. At the origin of these changes, whose purpose was obvious, there was "almost always a pope."[36]

In an ingenious study, Meyer Schapiro has shown how the legend of Theophilus was adapted to the tensions of feudal society in twelfth-century sculpture. Analyzing the story from the famous relief at Souillac, he points out that in this region of Southwest France ecclesiastics were constantly in conflict with lay nobles who laid claim to church holdings. Thus the vidame Theophilus, who sells his soul for worldly advancement, can actually be regarded as the victim of an iniquitous contract into which he is maneuvered by his seignior-devil. The ceremony follows the pattern of the time, feudal homage being figured by the Devil's taking Theophilus' hands into his own [Pl. 10, see also Ch. VI and VII and Pl. 108]. From this awful pledge only a divine intervention can free the vidame. This is accomplished by the Virgin, the queen of heaven, whose enormously elevated position in French art at the time, the author suggests, "was undoubtedly conditioned by the important administrative and even judicial role of the queen in the French monarchy."[37]

In some of the lesser subjects illustrating various feudal relationships medieval sculpture has at times been strikingly topical. At Mervilliers there is, for example, a remarkable relief representing the donation of some property to the church of Saint-Georges. The donor, a fully armored knight accompanied by his squire and horse, kneels as he presents the deeds to a seated dignitary, who has been identified as the dean of the chapter of Sainte-Croix-d'Orléans, to which the village church (now gone) was attached. The local priest, in the process of celebrating mass, turns to bless the event while the hand of God points toward the altar as though to say, in the words of a church commentator: "Always remember that your pledge has been taken before God and if you prove false to it you will be accursed as a perjurer!"[38]

9. *Church of Avenas* (12th century). Relief of Louis VII offering the church to St. Vincent. The act of donorship is recorded in the sculpture and in the inscription below.   10. *Souillac, Abbey Church* (12th century). Theophilus pledges allegiance to the Devil, who grasps his hands in the symbolic act of feudal vassalage.

This type of warning was by no means superfluous though it would have been more proper to make it to the descendants of the donor. For the church chronicles are full of violent challenges of pious bequests raised by heirs, sometimes many generations removed from the original benefactors. Churchmen would, wherever possible, get seigniors to confirm grants made by their ancestors.*[39] Even more effective, it seems certain, would be to record the deed in stone. The Mervilliers relief underlines this point variously. Far at the right a tiny scribe chronicles the event on a scroll which, leaving his desk, climbs up and around the tympanum. The Latin inscription not only certifies the gift of the donor, "Rembaud, chevalier," but also confirms it in the name of "Herbert Guillaume," son, brother, or nephew, his heir [Pl. 11].

Perhaps even more astonishing are the two reliefs, at Saint-Georges-de-

*Donor documents were read before a witnessing public, at times in the church, at times outdoors.

Boscherville and Souvigny, presenting money-coining scenes. In the latter place, two monks are shown putting the imprint on coins under the supervision of the prior while another monk weighs the pieces in a scale before putting them into a bag [Pl. 12]. This singular scene is probably meant to emphasize the priory's right to coin money, which might have been under challenge at the time.[40] At Vézelay there is a relief which seems to refer to the abbot's right of justice, which was contested all through the years that the abbey church was going up,[41] as we shall see in Chapter IV. One scene shows two men at odds; a second, the abbot rendering his verdict; a third, witnesses seemingly marveling at his fairness and sagacity.

At Saint-Benoît-sur-Loire, a relief presenting a judicial duel, which the abbot's champion will surely win, probably relates to a contention over land, judging from the sheaves of grain in one of the scenes [Pl. 13]. There are, amazingly, two other capitals dealing with donor subjects in this church. In the one, several members of the family of Hugues de Sainte-Marie have their gift consecrated by Christ. In the other, a donor of land to St. Benedict has been tied and tortured by the apostate, Zalla. But the saint reforms the heretic and incidentally wins the land back from him!

The desire to exorcise a feared enemy could explain the use of Saracen slaves, set back to back and chained, as caryatids in the Basses-Pyrenées church

11. *Former Church of Mervilliers* (12th century). Tympanum relief representing the donation of some property by a seignior to the church. A mold at Chartres Museum.

at Oloron-Sainte-Marie. On the other hand, the sculpture at San Domingo da Silos, in which the patron saint is shown capturing runaway Moorish slaves and putting them back to work on the abbey's lands, was probably based on fact. San Domingo was one of the great administrative geniuses that the Church produced during this period of economic revival that followed the stagnation of the deep Middle Ages, beautifully mingling in his person the complex motives of the Spanish Crusade.[42] And the realities of eleventh-century travel seem to be reflected in the Flight into Egypt carving on the porch at Saint-Benoît-sur-Loire, where the sculptor would not allow the Holy Family out on their perilous journey without the accompaniment of an armed guard [Pl. 14].[43] This may be the converted robber of an apocryphal legend, but the story reflects the realities of travel in the Middle Ages, nevertheless.[44]

A celebrated art work whose political motivation is, of course, unquestioned is the Bayeux Tapestry. But this, it is always emphasized, is a secular work; hence its worldly content is scarcely surprising. Usually ignored, however, is the fact that though the Tapestry was primarily an a posteriori justification for William the Conqueror's invasion of England, it was by equal intention a church piece, having probably been fabricated for the cathedral of Bayeux, where it was hung from the earliest epoch.[45]

Some scholars have suggested that the Bayeux Tapestry is an Anglo-Saxon work, purportedly prepared for William's triumphant return home. It is established that he made many lavish gifts to various churches on that occasion. It was long the custom with Teutonic tribes to commemorate their exploits with "elaborate paintings, sculptures or embroideries" and this tradition was continued after they crossed over into England. There was, for example, one embroidered tapestry done by Aethelflaed at the end of the tenth century and presented to the church at Ely, celebrating her husband's heroic deeds. But she was only one of a "multitude of English needlewomen whose work was famous throughout Europe from the tenth to the fourteenth century," an author has noted, concluding that "the historical hanging at Bayeux is unique only in surviving."[46]

Was the Tapestry's endurance over the centuries due to its having belonged to a church? This would not have helped it much during the Revolution or the religious wars, to be sure, but it would have been of considerable importance most of the rest of the time.* The Tapestry was more than a mere possession of the church at Bayeux. It was prominently displayed there periodically in commemorative celebrations: during the "Octaves des Reliques," at the feting of the consecration of the cathedral in July, and on St. John's day. Nor was it

---

*This is a consideration that is sometimes lost sight of but it must undoubtedly have played an important part in producing the enormous overweight of surviving church art as compared to the secular.

12 . *Souvigny, Church of Saint-Pierre* (12th century). Capital relief of monks in a money-coining scene.

Saint-Benoît-sur-Loire, Abbey Church: 13. Capital relief of a judicial duel (12th century). 14. Porch capital relief (11th century). The Holy Family on the Flight into Egypt, accompanied by an armed guard.

shown for esthetic appreciation on these occasions, but rather for the ethical-political message that it enshrined and for which it found its appropriate place inside a cathedral.

For the story of the Bayeux Tapestry is not only an account of a battle and a victory. It is a tale of high morality, of the breaking of a solemn oath and the punishment of this crime. Wace in describing Harold's vow to William says "his hand trembled, his flesh quivered."[47] And Harold's brother, Gyrth, according to all chronicles, tried to keep the king out of the fighting at Hastings because he had admittedly done this dreadful thing. It was for this reason, too, that William demanded Rome's endorsement of his punitive expedition, sending Prior Lanfranc of the Abbaye de Bec to Italy to register his claim. The pope not only agreed to condemn Harold as unworthy of the throne because of his broken pledge but granted its investiture to the Norman claimant, sending him with his blessing a banner bearing a cross, which is shown in the Tapestry accompanying William in council and in battle.[48]

Other scenes from the Tapestry make this sacred aspect of the expedition supremely clear. It also accounts for the primary role played throughout by Bishop Odo de Conteville of Bayeux, William's uterine brother. When news of Harold's accession to the English throne is brought by a messenger, it is he who counsels war. And at the time of the invasion he passes over the Channel with the troops and is shown blessing the first meal eaten on English soil. More important, he even takes part in the battle of Hastings, armored and on horseback though without a sword, at one point rallying William's troops with a bludgeon when they are in retreat [Pl. 15]. It has even been suggested that the Tapestry was made on Odo's orders.[49]

Medieval art, religious or other, has been enormously helpful in revealing how people of the Middle Ages lived, worked, dressed, furnished their homes. The Bayeux Tapestry itself is wonderfully instructive in this regard, containing highly descriptive scenes of shipbuilding and navigation, of the various arts of war, and of the preparation and serving of food. Its artists did not miss even such a detail as the difference in the way the English and the French wore their hair, the former long, the latter short, or how they trimmed their horses' manes!

It was on the basis of this type of information, furnished by artists throughout the ages, that a nonprofessional French scholar, Commandant Richard Lefebvre des Noëttes, was able to make some highly suggestive discoveries, earlier in this century. A retired cavalryman, he began his new career by trying to date the Bayeux Tapestry, which he found had been done "at a moment when the cavalry was abandoning materiel and methods of combat that had become antiquated and adopting new ones."[50] The key innovation was the stirrup, which, Lefebvre des Noëttes explained, is entirely absent from ancient art and first appeared around 850, becoming generalized only in tenth- and eleventh-century work. Gradually this invention, together with the saddlebow and snaffle, completely transformed the posture of fighting horsemen.

15. *The Bayeux Tapestry* (late 11th century). Bishop Odo, at left, drives a retreating warrior back into the fighting at the Battle of Hastings. Now at the Musée de la Reine Mathilde.

Up to this point art works had shown them carrying their lances extended before them as they went into attack. They would arrive before the enemy in tumultuous gallop, stop short, dart their lances, and then retire momentarily, returning finally sword in hand. All this changed radically when cavalrymen realized the full utility of the new equipment. Then, "solidly installed upon their stirrups, with body bent forward, lance held firmly under arm, they hurled themselves upon their adversaries, seeking (not avoiding) a collision."[51]

Lynn White has warned that in the early Middle Ages artists "were little concerned with depicting the observable objects of the world about them. . . . As a result, iconography lagged behind actuality, and innovations were seldom reflected in objects of art until their novelty had worn off and they were taken for granted."[52] This would seem to invalidate the use of art works for delicate points of dating, but it would not for historical observations of broader scope. This Lefebvre des Noëttes demonstrated as he went on to other problems, still drawing upon his specialized training, which he applied to old works of art. Though likewise concerned with the equipment of horses, his next observations were made on the animals when used as beasts of burden rather than in combat. And once more the commandant found important innovations dating from the Middle Ages—especially a new kind of harness—playing a key role.

The basis of the old traction method, he explained, was the use of a leather band about the throat. The collar passed right over the trachea and was joined to the yoke above the withers, having no contact with the shoulders, where the animal's real strength lay. To avoid choking itself, it had to draw its head back, the worst possible position for traction. Added to this handicap was the absence of nailed iron shoes, without which heavy loads could not be drawn without damage to the animal's feet. Disadvantageous also was the prevailing practice of ranging the animals side by side instead of tandem. How much could a team of two horses draw equipped in this manner? The commandant was not content with guessing but built the old equipment and conducted a series of experiments, finding that such a team could pull all of 500 kilograms. This was about one fourth or less of the draft power of a modernly geared pair of animals.[53]

The invention of the rigid horse collar, "resting on the bony base of the shoulder blades and thus mustering the full force of the animal," together with the nailed iron horseshoe and the method of placing the animals in file, which made possible the use of an almost unlimited number—all these innovations dating from the Middle Ages revolutionized traction and had profound effects on other phases of medieval life, Lefebvre de Noëttes argued. This change in draft power he was able to demonstrate in many art works, the wagons depicted being sturdier, their loads heavier. One of his illustrations was from the famous Herrade de Landsberg illuminated manuscript (twelfth century), where two horses could be seen drawing a massive chariot in which were standing no fewer than sixteen men.[54]

More interesting for our purposes were the probable effects of the new traction methods on medieval building. In the Middle Ages, carting stone from the
quarry was a most tedious and expensive process, huge teams being required to
haul relatively small loads over the primitive roads. Medieval chronicles tell
glowingly of how the pious—even kings and nobles, women as well as men—
would pitch in and help the animals. But the significant thing about these stories
was that such nonprofessional help was very occasional and at best more in-
spirational than serviceable. (This question is more fully discussed in Chapter
IX.) For man's role as a beast of burden had become dated! Formerly, however,
the deficient traction force at hand had caused this responsibility to devolve
upon the only effective medium available: human muscular power. This was,
Commandant Lefebvre des Noëttes contended, a basic reason for the continued
use of slave labor in the past, as was illustrated in building scenes in art works
of all the previous historic periods.

Even the most advanced of the ancients, however radiant their literary and
artistic accomplishments, had been unable to free themselves of this monstrous
degradation. It was a "suggestive coincidence," the commandant observed,
that it should have died out in the West during the very period—the tenth to
the thirteenth century—when the revolutionary improvements in the equipment
of draft animals had come into effect there. Historians had sought to explain
the disappearance of slavery by the influence of Christian moral force. But the
Apostles and the early Fathers had all sanctioned slavery as divinely ordained,
the commandant noted, and he might have added that medieval prelates had
continued to do the same.

Moral factors, he concluded, "are not alone in governing human destinies.
There are, besides, imperious material conditions. One could not possibly
understand the social progress of the Middle Ages, one of the most profound
that humanity has known, if one fails to consider that invention of genius which
under the first Capetians revolutionized the means of transport, endowed
industry with new and almost limitless possibilities and made of man a con-
ductor of forces."[55] Thereafter it became easy, even advantageous, to substitute
the animal for the slave.

"Is it not admirable," Lefebvre des Noëttes asked, "that in the eleventh and
twelfth century, in absolute contrast to the previous rule, the 'white mantle'*
of abbeys, chateaux, and cathedrals with which Western Europe adorned itself
should have been the accomplishment of free workingmen?"[56]

---

*Reference to the famous quotation of the monk, Raoul Glaber, regarding the great surge in
building that took place, in pious thanksgiving, after the world was spared its widely predicted
dissolution in the "Year Thousand."

CHAPTER III
EVE AND MARY:
CONFLICTING IMAGES
OF MEDIEVAL WOMAN

Built during the papal occupancy, on the crest of the "new town" across the Rhone from Avignon, the Chartreuse-du-Val-de-Bénédiction has long been abandoned by the monks. There is neither furniture nor any other amenity of earlier habitation in the spacious, barren convent, nothing but the pale remnants of Italian frescoes which the homesick popes had painted in various places of their temporary abode.

One's eye is the more struck accordingly by the sculptured relief above the door inside one of the cells that line the old cloister. Suddenly, as one looks at it, the empty, echoing monastery seems to be peopled once again. There are certain art works that have this faculty of recall; yet what this one summons up is less the physical life than the very special order of ideas that once prevailed here.

The subject of the relief is wild and obscene, presenting a recumbent woman in a scabrous posture with a goat. "The old hag is letting the goat do to her," the concierge commented disgustedly [Pl. 16].

His attitude toward the woman, one realized, was perhaps not much different from that of the early occupants of the cell, that vanished community for whom this revolting bit of sculpture had been carved.

Not aimed at the public but at single pairs of cloistered eyes, what could its message be other than a warning against woman's bestiality, meant to rally the monks' resistance at faltering moments? For the lives of the most saintly ascetics—St. Anthony's, for example—show that Satan reserved his most redoubtable trials for the cloistered brethren. And in the monks' catalogue of transformations the Devil might often assume a woman's guise.

By the fourteenth century, when the Chartreuse was built, the general view of woman had considerably softened so that this kind of treatment of her in art strikes one as rather anachronistic for its time. But the battles of the convent

41

were abiding ones and the monastic attitude toward woman changed more slowly than did its secular counterpart. This viewpoint regarded woman as the Daughter of Eve and by that descent still primarily responsible for man's fall. As St. Bernard expressed it in sermons addressed to his "sons" at Clairvaux, Eve was "the original cause of all evil, whose disgrace has come down to all other women."[1]

This view of woman inevitably influenced the manner of her presentation in church art of that time and continued now and then to break through into works of later periods. She might be shown as repellently ugly or hatefully seductive. The latter delineation is strikingly illustrated in a capital relief at Autun representing the mortal Vice of Unchastity. A young man stands rapt before the naked body of his temptress, whose flaming hair associates her with the Devil. The latter is also present, his fingers coiled into the hapless youth's hair [Pl. 17].

At Vézelay, on the other hand, it is the woman herself who is bewitched, supposedly by the "profane music" of a jongleur, under whose influence she permits herself to be caressed by a grimacing demon. But from the time of Eve woman was known to have this denatured fondness for foul things, taking the serpent into her arms on occasion and stroking it adoringly [Pl. 18]. In the case of Potiphar's wife, she is frankly a member of the Devil's team, listening confidently to his evil counsel while extending to him the eager intimacy of a co-conspirator [Pl. 19].

Surely it is not without meaning that the sculptured presentation of the Vice of Unchastity which one finds on so many church façades of the twelfth century should invariably be a woman, suffering eternally in Hell. She is usually shown in a revolting posture, her naked body entwined by serpents which feed on her breasts and sexual organs. Sometimes, too, she is accompanied by the Devil, who assumes an intimate relationship to her [Pl. 20].

The typical "male" Vice, on the other hand, is either Pride or Avarice, the former denoting the chief failing of the feudal nobles, the latter that of the middle class. There was a shift of emphasis from one mortal Vice to the other in the twelfth century, which one author has traced to the Church's increased concern with the rising clamor of the burghers for communal rights. But the major female Vice as depicted in church art remained unaltered. Whatever her class, woman's characteristic corruption was still Unchastity.[2]

In any event, it is the cloister's accent on the baleful influence of woman on man that gives much twelfth-century sculpture a misogynous imprint. At its cruelest perhaps the viewpoint is expressed in the Expulsion from Paradise reliefs of Notre-Dame-du-Port, at Clermont-Ferrand [Pl. 21]. Adam hurls wailing Eve to the ground, kicks her, and drags her by the hair in a series of realistic gestures that were inspired, it has been suggested, by the liturgical drama, *Le Jeu d'Adam et Ève*, which was acted during the Middle Ages both

16 (above). *Villeneuve-les-Avignon, Chartreuse-du-Val-de-Bénédiction* (14th century). Relief of the Vice of Unchastity.
17 (center). *Autun Cathedral* (12th century). Capital relief of the Vice of Unchastity.   18 (above, right). *Reims Cathedral* (13th century). Eve showing her fondness for the serpent.
19 (below). *Chartres Cathedral*. North porch (13th century). Potiphar's wife listening to the Devil's advice.

inside and outside of many churches. The high climax of the play, whose verisimilitude was heightened by costumes and stage scenery, was reached when Adam, robbed of eternal bliss, cried out his fury and dismay:

> Oh, evil woman, full of treason. . . .
> Forever contrary to reason,
> Bringing no man good in any season:
> Our children's children to the end of time
> Will feel the cruel whiplash of your crime![3]

It was hardly the kind of teaching calculated to spread affection for the wives and mothers in the audience. But it did suit the Church's purpose of combating in behalf of its clergy woman's terrible attractiveness. How dangerous this was considered to be is shown by the action of one church council forbidding priests to visit their mothers and sisters.[4] And the monk, Bernard de Besse, warned his confreres against even touching their baby sister's hands.[5] The rules of the Cistercian order held that the prohibition against contact with woman must not be breached even for the purpose of granting charity and that if a member of the feared sex penetrated by accident into the convent church, services must be suspended, the abbot deposed, and the monks put on bread and water.

20. *Bordeaux, Church of Sainte-Croix* (12th century). A woman, illustrating the Vice of Unchastity, shown with her lover, the Devil.   21. *Clermont-Ferrand, Notre-Dame-du-Port* (12th century). Adam kicks Eve and pulls her hair, as the Archangel drives the couple from Paradise.

These harsh regulations have been related to Gregory VII's struggle for Church reform.[6] As is known, moral regeneration of the religious community was only one phase of this campaign, which involved ultimately the political power of the Church, its independence of lay sovereigns, and the centralization of control at Rome. An indispensable part of this program was considered to be the prohibition of legal marriage or concubinage, both of which were widely practiced not only by the secular but by the regular (monastic) clergy as well.

The drive to tear the priests and monks from the arms of women continued to color the ecclesiastic attitude toward the female sex long after other circumstances had brought about important improvements in woman's social position. Into the late thirteenth and even the fourteenth century priests sermonized about the malice of women toward men. The wisest of males were helpless before their wiles. Reflections of this viewpoint are not lacking in art. Thus Aristotle and Virgil—those summits of genius among the ancients—are seen portrayed in ignominious Boccaccio-like situations illustrating woman's perfidy. Aristotle is shown on all fours with the Indian courtesan Campaspe on his back, whose favors he seeks. And Virgil is left dangling in midair in a basket by a lady who had granted him an assignation, to be laughed at by the entire populace of Rome the following morning.[7]

It would be impossible to discount the great contributions of the Church over the centuries to the dignity of marriage and to woman's position within it. As one author, otherwise critical of the Church, has put it, "from its origins Christianity has exalted marriage, proclaimed the equality of husband and wife, and in particular divided impartially between the two the rights conferred by society and nature on the children." But this writer goes on to document the Church's ambivalence on the question of woman's emancipation, pointing out that it rejected most other privileges for her, including the right of communal property.[8] Church apologists have admitted this disparaging attitude. One of them, while seeking to emphasize its role in improving woman's lot, nevertheless agrees that it considered her to be morally inferior, which was the formal basis, for example, for her exclusion from the priesthood.[9]

The Villeneuve-les-Avignon relief raises another disturbing question. How could one square this monkish execration of women with the universal apotheosis of Christ's mother, who already in the twelfth century had assumed a preponderant position in so much of church art? Even the most passionate of reformers, the Cistercians, who played a key role in the Church's moral-purification movement as well as in support of the papacy's political ambitions, had a most particular devotion for the Virgin. They dedicated all their churches to her and the mother-abbey at Cîteaux adopted as its device an image of Mary, under whose mantle the abbots of the order were shown kneeling while above the church portal verses in her honor were engraved. St. Bernard, whom Dante called "the knight of the Virgin," devoted a whole series of his homilies to the mother of Christ, that "strong woman" upon whom "Our salvation, the recovery of our innocence and the victory over our enemy [Satan] depends. . . ."[10]

However, a closer examination will show that there is actually no contradiction between the monks' adoration of Mary and their very low view of ordinary woman. The relationship between the two stressed contrasts rather than similarities. In the glorification of the Virgin, it was the Woman-Without-Sin, the non-woman Woman, the anti-Eve that was revered. This distinction is often explicit in the art of the time, as at the church of Saint-Martin-d'Ainay, at Lyon, where sculptured versions of the Original Sin and—plainly antithetical—the Virgin of the Annunciation are placed side by side. That type of confrontation seemed, to subtle medieval minds, to be marvelously validated by the inversion of letters in the words "EVA" and "AVE." The exegetical spotlighting of this anagram was put into a Latin poem by Peter Damian, the great eleventh-century reformer:

> That angel who greets you with "Ave"
> Reverses sinful Eva's name.
> Lead us back, O holy Virgin,
> Whence the falling sinner came.

And the twelfth-century poet Wace, in his *La vie de la vierge Marie*, vowed that the anagram was meant

> To allow us all to recall
> From what high point Eve made us fall.[11]

In the doctrinal opposition of Mary and Eve, common woman was uncompromisingly associated with the latter. Even with Mary Magdalene and Mary the Egyptian, those sinners to whom she could feel most naturally drawn, the ordinary woman could hardly forget that their sainthood was sanctioned by a decision that she herself was not prepared to take: the abandonment of their sex. Her identification with their earlier transgressions could scarcely bring her solace for her continuing sins, as numerous representations in art were always prompt to remind her. A famous example, which unfortunately a prudish seventeenth-century priest suppressed, was a stained-glass medallion from a Parisian church showing Mary the Egyptian poised suggestively on the bridge deck of the ship taking her to Jaffa from Alexandria, with her skirts raised up to her knees, prepared, as an inscription explained, to pay for her passage in trade. There was masculine malice in this portrayal but it was entirely consistent with the Church's view of woman: once fallen and forever after prone.

The glorification of Mary in the West had been a recent development. Unlike the Eastern Church, where her festival days had been celebrated from earliest times, they passed almost without notice in France. It was only toward the end of the tenth century that the cult of the Virgin as the "Mother of Mercy" was initiated by the order of Cluny, interpreted iconographically by Mary's taking her protegés under her ample cloak. This was, it has been suggested, possibly in response to the terror of the world's end that spread abroad with the approach of the Year Thousand.[12]

It was not until the twelfth century that the Church's cult of Mary came to full flower, when also the "amour courtois," that strange deviant among love poetries, began to be sung in all the feudal courts of Southern France. It used to be thought that the cult of the Virgin had inspired the origin of this courtly love poetry. But modern scholarship has rejected the hypothesis, arguing that the two are profoundly contradictory in essence, the frankly hedonistic nature of the one and the sex-denying emphasis of the other being only one phase of their antagonism.

However, though the erotic content of the courtly love poetry could not have failed to make it abhorrent to such men as St. Bernard and Hugues de Saint-Victor, it is curious nevertheless how their own literary style was influenced by it. In the former's sermons in praise of Mary he gives vent to a type of sexual symbolism that would give Freudian amateurs a field day. She was "the bush, the arc, the star, the flowering stalk, the fleece, the nuptial chamber, the door, the garden, the dawn, Jacob's ladder."[13] The celebrated Catholic encyclopedist, Honorius d'Autun (who wrote from 1090 to 1120), composed a hymn in which Jesus praises the beauty of Mary. "He extols her freshness," an author paraphrases him, "her loose hair, her lovely throat, her brow which he likens to a tower, and her sparkling teeth. He gives each feature a moral sense and the poem, a mixture of voluptuous images and noble thoughts, shines with a kind of abstract passion."[14]

The Church's Mariolatry reached an intense stage in the thirteenth century, its widespread acceptance being fostered by prayers, hymns, liturgical drama, legends, and especially art. The lovely *Ave Maria* dates from this impulse as does the beautiful name of "Notre Dame," a pure hand-over from the language of chivalry. The rhymed version of the *Miracles of Notre Dame*, by Gautier de Coincy, canon of Soissons, helped spread the idea of Mary's accessibility. Even the worst sinners could now touch her heart. She was known, for example, to have protected an adultress against the clamorous accusations of the woman whose husband she had seduced simply because the siren had honored daily in her prayers the Annunciation, considered to have been the Virgin's most pleasurable moment.[15]

Iconographically, Mary's image responded richly to these various influences. Earlier she had been so little estimated that she once was actually left out of the Nativity.[16] But in the twelfth and especially the thirteenth century she came into her own. Émile Mâle described this evolution admirably.[17] At first, he pointed out, the Virgin was never seen apart from her son. Then in such scenes as the Annunciation and the Visitation she began to appear alone. But even when with Jesus the artists would put the dramatic spotlight on her. The wide popularization of such a subject as the Adoration of the Magi, for example, was merely an excuse for presenting Mary. Shown in a kind of majesty and mounted on a throne, from this position she (along with her son) received the feudal reverence of kings. This royal treatment came naturally to medieval artists, Mâle noted. "The Virgin of the twelfth century and of the beginning of the thirteenth is a queen."[18]

It was only somewhat later that the Magi were withdrawn and the Virgin appeared alone on church tympana—still bearing the infant Jesus on her knees, to be sure—in the same superb posture as before. This "daring innovation" was used at Chartres (among other places), it has been suggested, in order to give an impulsion to the great pilgrimage in the Virgin's honor that was directed toward that church in the first half of the twelfth century.[19] Soon after there began to appear the great chain of miracles associated with Mary that one can see effigied in so many churches of France and elsewhere. Then representations of the Death, Resurrection, and Assumption of the Virgin were appended to her plastic repertory, each adding further to her glory. And finally that ultimate scene of her triumph was invented: the Coronation. First shown as an already accomplished fact, then carried out by an angel in the presence of her Son, it is by Christ's own hands in the end that the crown is put on Mary's head.

Much of this elevated the Virgin to a position that tended to put her out of reach of the ordinary woman. But this overawing side of Mary was only one facet of her complex personality. There was another phase that began to evolve in the thirteenth century, which had the effect of popularizing her image. Simple, literate minds found Scripture altogether too meager as to detail and out of their desire to see the great gaps in Mary's life filled in, there arose a whole series of popular apocrypha, which eventually passed over, in part at least, into church liturgy and art.

Starting before Mary's birth, the legends early amplified the story of her parents, Anne and Joachim, going on to the Virgin's early years, her marriage, her relationship with her son at the different epochs of his life, which the Bible had left so barren, and finally to Mary's life after the death of Christ. Even the already established elements of her story were in this manner completely transformed. In the early twelfth-century Nativity, for example, she is presented as overwhelmed by the event, hardly accepting her own role in it. She does not even dare look at the Infant, who is extended on a kind of altar, which is set above and at some distance from her [Pl. 22].

But this austerity changes gradually, taking on one after another those gracious little touches we now normally associate with the subject—and all of them apocryphal. Even the ox and the ass had to be produced out of whole

22. *Chartres Cathedral*. The Nativity stained-glass panel (12th century).
Note Christ's crib in the form of an altar. Note also the sleeping Joseph.

cloth, and the midwives. As the story goes, when the great moment drew near Joseph ran distraught out of the stable looking for assistance. But he could find no one and when he returned Jesus was already born and there were the midwives quietly preparing his bath. The tendency of all this (before the mawkish exaggerations of the fourteenth and especially of later centuries) was to humanize Mary's story, making her a real girl, a real woman, a real mother.

Accompanying this trend, as we shall see, was a deep-going change in the social position of medieval woman. In art, besides what has been called the "feminization of the Divinity,"[20] which referred specifically to Mary, went a softening of attitude in the representation of other women. This tendency can be more readily seen in works covering Old Testament stories than in those of the Christian legend, which remained under stricter doctrinal control. Though material about the Hebrew prophets and other predecessors was rarely used in church art except to prefigure important elements of the dogma involving Christ and Mary (Abraham's offered sacrifice of Isaac symbolizing the Crucifixion; Habakkuk's feeding of Daniel in the lions' den without breaking the king's seal designating Christ's passage into and out of his mother's womb without marring her virginity; etc.), nevertheless there was less rigidity in the handling of details and characters in these accounts than in subjects drawn from the New Testament.

Thirteenth-century art is particularly inventive in this regard. Thus the Noah story often furnishes striking family scenes like those on the sculptured frieze of Bourges cathedral's west façade [Pl. 23]. And at Amiens an incomparable series of small quatrefoils covering the entire base of the church front has most gracious material of this type, such as the story of the Queen of Sheba or of Hosea's harlot. The latter represents a medieval version of a theme which in modern times has continued to be highly popular: the rehabilitation of a fallen woman by an honest man. In medieval art it had the added effect of alleviating the tragic heritage of Eve, whose descendant puts on a bourgeois hat to symbolize her reform [Pl. 24].

As for Esther and Judith, both frequently found in thirteenth-century art, they were equally memorable for their patriotic and heroic roles. Psychologically they often represented a great advance in the handling of women, as illustrated by the beautiful carvings on the north porch at Chartres, where Esther is shown pleading for her people at the feet of Ahasuerus [Pl. 25] and Judith is seen piously pouring ashes on her head in preparation for her mission [Pl. 26]. Such scenes are rarer in the twelfth century but they do exist, as in a capital relief at Vézelay, where Judith is shown returning from her perilous self-imposed task. She stands, magnificently conscious of her accomplishment, brandishing Holofernes' head before the astonished eyes of the men cowering on the city's walls [Pl. 27].

23. *Bourges Cathedral*. West façade frieze (13th century). Noah's family going to the Ark.   24. *Amiens Cathedral*. Hosea and the Harlot quatrefoil (13th century). Above, he pays fifteen pieces of silver, plus one and one-half homers of barley, for her; below, he marries her.

Chartres Cathedral. North porch (13th century):   25. Queen Esther at the feet of Ahasuerus.   26. Judith, in prayer, covers her head with ashes before going out to kill Holofernes.

27. *Vézelay, Church of La Madeleine* (12th century). Capital relief of Judith returning triumphantly from her mission, bearing the head of Holofernes.   28. *Chartres Cathedral*. West façade frieze (12th century). The Massacre of the Innocents.

29. *Bourges Cathedral*. The Prodigal Son stained-glass window (13th century). Returning home after his misadventures, he is greeted affectionately by his father while his mother presents him with a handsome robe.

Other important sources of stirring scenes involving women have been the *Golden Legend* and certain narrative sections of the Evangels, especially those occurring in the absence of Christ or Mary. The Massacre of the Innocents, for example, often furnishes affecting illustrations of motherly love, as in the tiny frieze that threads across the façade of Chartres cathedral, where the whole story of Christ is told in frequently exquisite images [Pl. 28]. By extension, delineations of fatherly affection also begin to appear, seen in many representations of the return of the Prodigal Son [Pl. 29] or in the marvelously touching scene of the Creation of Adam, on Chartres' north porch, where the love of God wells out of his gaze upon the still inert form of his firstborn, whose nodding head he embraces on his lap [Pl. 30].

As the attitude toward woman improved, it was inevitable that the relationship between the sexes, as exemplified in art, should undergo a like alteration. Nowhere is this more movingly portrayed than in Judgment Day scenes, inescapably charged with the thought of eternal separations. But the artists at Saint-Trophime at Arles, at Notre-Dame de Paris, and at Amiens cathedral strike a reassuring note. Forgetful that associations by the flesh would cease after the Rising, they depict husband and wife as lovingly taking each other's hands [Pl. 31]. The principle of human solidarity is extended at times to include the whole family of man, who are shown eagerly helping each other out of the grave.

In this manner likewise the thirteenth-century narrative of the Original Sin and its punishment was transformed, taking on a totally different character from the early misogynous one. The Devil retires into the background and Eve is no longer portrayed as the chief instigator of disobedience but shares her guilt with Adam in an act of complete moral as well as artistic balance [Pl. 32]. At times, regard for the sentiments of the unfortunate first couple overflows into an attempt to shield them from harrowing despair after the Expulsion. In the south rose at Lyon cathedral this is accomplished by accompanying the latter scene by a sort of flash-forward of Christ's Descent into Limbo, out of whose jaws he reclaims the repentant sinners, thus serving to reassure them (as well as their descendants) that they will not be abandoned for eternity.

Nor is the entry of Adam and Eve into mortality any longer treated in the thirteenth century as the ultimate calamity. The first couple fall to their labors with zest in the Genesis window at Tours, and when Eve pauses to have her baby, she proudly lifts it up to its father, who offers fervent prayers to God. But the ultimate in reverses is undoubtedly that amazing scene at Strasbourg, in which an elegant young seignior offers the fruit of temptation to the Unwise Virgin. It is no longer Eve who is associated with the Devil but rather the male partner, the back of whose cloak reveals a family of crawling things. And whereas Adam was formerly the pathetic dupe, it is now the giddy girl whose

30. *Chartres Cathedral*. North porch (13th century). The Creation of Adam.   31. *Amiens Cathedral*. Porte du Sauveur (13th century). Detail of the Judgment Day: The Rising Dead. Upper right, a man helps his wife out of the tomb.   32. *Reims Cathedral* (13th century). The Original Sin: Adam and Eve shown sharing the guilt equally.

credulity is imposed upon—and she promptly begins to unclasp her robe [Pl. 33].

Sexual love as such is no longer automatically covered by taboo or pictured in almost animalic terms, as in the famous vignette on the border of the Bayeux Tapestry. It can now be the subject of extraordinary finesse and even sympathy. A charming example is the young couple sculptured on the pendant of a stone console at Lyon. Each caresses his partner with one soft hand while holding his favorite pet in the other. It would be hard to find a good theological reason for including this scene on a church façade. The portrayal of Castor and Pollux had a firmer iconographic tradition but its manner of presentation sometimes went beyond prescription, showing the twins warmly embracing. This gracious treatment of men reveals the same humanizing trend that we find softening the artistic effigy of women. Indeed, the process developed to the point where a type of pure "genre" scene began to insert itself here and there amid the austerities of church art [Pl. 34].

And startling is the representation of Herod's love for Salome in the famous Saint-Étienne relief, whose pathos inspired a whole library of literary comment. The tetrarch chucks his stepdaughter under the chin, a favorite gesture in the Middle Ages, but his sad, sad face displays a striking maturity in the description of this anomalous passion, whose purely human side effaces for the moment its calamitous consequences for St. John [Pl. 35].

It is difficult to think that such complex changes in the artistic interpretation of women could have failed to have their social counterpart. As a matter of fact, woman's legal position was undergoing a great transformation during this period, the fundamental element being her acquisition of the right of inheritance.

Under the feudal fief the possession of land by a vassal was at first inseparable from the obligation of military service. But around the tenth century a change began to establish itself, an inheriting son being required by civil law to indemnify his sister with a dowry at her marriage. But even if the young woman failed to wed she could, by the thirteenth century, acquire possession of up to one third of her parent's landed property.[21] Marriage itself was considered a strictly feudal service and choosing a mate without the seignior's consent was severely punishable. But eventually a rich heir could buy off this servitude and a woman, too, could pay to marry the man of her choice.

With the woman's acquisition of the right of inheritance went all the feudal privileges pertaining to it. Since land superseded the person under feudal law, as one author has pointed out, "the woman possessing fiefs had . . . all the rights of sovereignty, that of raising troops, coining money, conducting civil and criminal justice." To be sure, these prerogatives were not won without opposition, on the part of both the lay seigniors and the Church. The latter seemed to be particularly horrified by the trend and a synod at Nantes early denounced

33. *Strasbourg Cathedral.*
West façade, south portal
(13th century).
The Tempter and the
Foolish Virgin.

as a "barbaric" innovation the practice of allowing women to discuss public
affairs with men: Let them return to their own quarters and gabble among
themselves![22]

It was woman's assumption of the judge's mantle that particularly exercised
the conservatives. Canonic law even prohibited them from serving as witnesses
in court, their testimony being considered unworthy of trust.[23] But by the thirteenth century matters had developed to the point where Pope Innocent III
was forced to concede that Queen Aliénor, though a woman, had full rights of
justice as a feudal suzerain. The pope's decision came on an appeal by the order
of Hospitalers, in a case in which the queen had claimed jurisdiction over the
Knights, which they challenged.[24]

It is significant that in the middle class of the cities woman's social position was early characterized by almost complete equality with that of man. The burgher, who in the twelfth and even in the thirteenth century continued to carry various disabilities of his former serfdom, had even to fight for the right of endowing his children or any other heirs. His daughters were co-beneficiaries of the positive outcome of this struggle, and the equal division of his possessions between male and female descendants was a right that was written into most communal charters. As for the woman merchant, all legislation of the Middle Ages concurred in granting her full civil status, "even if married."[25] And the artisan's wife paid her own poll tax.

In some trades women had their own guilds ("corporations") and in thirteenth-century Paris they worked in the following categories: as embroiderers, seamstresses, spinners, wool combers, weavers, headdress makers ("coiffières"), hatters, dairywomen, retail food merchants, and female doctors.[26] Several of these occupations are beautifully illustrated in the sculptured series representing the "Active Life," on Chartres' north porch [see Pl. 69]. Silkmaking was almost exclusively a woman's trade and one of the great poetic bequests

34. *Vézelay, Church of La Madeleine* (12th century). A mother combing her child's hair.

35. *Toulouse, Former Cloister of the Monastery of Saint-Étienne* (12th century). Capital relief of Herod and Salome. Now at the Musée des Augustins.

of the Middle Ages is Chrétien de Troyes' complaint of the women silk spinners:

> Forever weaving silken goods,
> But we ourselves so poorly dressed,
> Forever clothed in nakedness,
> Forever lacking drink and food. . . .[27]

While it was through the elimination of the military service requirement that woman finally obtained the right of inheritance and hence moved closer to equality with men, it was by no means unusual for them to fight during the Middle Ages, whether in tournaments or in wars. "Many women appeared in armor in the ranks of the Crusaders," one author reports.[28] Another has pointed out that the mortality of men in the Crusades was so high that women had to be used in the armies, where they were assigned special tasks such as filling moats during sieges and pulling artillery into position.[29] Their role in defending their homes has been consecrated in the romantic image of their standing guard at the barbicans, preparing to pour hot oil on the heads of the city's attackers.

The picture is hardly fictional, judging from chronicles of the great defensive battles fought by the people of Southwest France during the religious wars of the thirteenth century. Organized ostensibly to root out heresy but strongly animated also by a goal of political domination and absorption, the invasion by the Northern forces roused a great tide of patriotic resistance. Women often played heroic roles in accounts of this popular upsurge, as in the epic poem describing the death of the leader of the "crusaders," Simon de Montfort, outside the walls of Toulouse.

A projectile-thrower devised by a carpenter and mounted on the city ramparts was operated "by young girls and married women," the poet assures us. It hurled the stone that smashed Simon's head open, spilling eyes, brains, upper teeth, forehead, and jaw. The delighted populace lighted candles in all the city's churches, crying: "Joy! For God is merciful," while trumpets and drums, cymbals and bugles sounded throughout the grateful city.[30] The incident might well have been commemorated in one of those artistic monuments that were put up by the freedom-loving communities of Central Italy. But the course of the "crusade" soon after shifted again and the final subjection of the South would have made any such memorials historically anomalous. On the other hand, there is a relief in the church of Saint-Nazaire at Carcassonne which is supposed to be the story seen from the eventually winning side [see Ch. VI and Pl. 94]. The fact that this church also has a tombal effigy of Simon tends to authenticate this assumption.[31]

There is evidence suggesting that the great Crusades played a significant part in the evolution of woman's improved social position. They occurred during that critical period when her legal right to inheritance was being slowly won, not without strong opposition, as we have seen. But as the male seigniors were now called out to the holy wars, remaining away for years on end, the capacity of women—their wives—to conduct the affairs of the seigniories in their place was often given a kind of sharp laboratory test. Many thousands of these husbands never came home at all and although twelfth-century "chansons de geste" show Charlemagne, as prescribed by custom, marrying off the widows of his slain barons en masse on the return home, a time must have come when there were no longer enough men to go around. And some women may have simply decided to remain unwed, intoxicated by the heady wine of their new-found freedom and importance.

That they could be competent administrators and at times tough ones is a well-documented fact. One of these "strong women," the Comtesse Catherine de Chartres, ran her husband's affairs while he was off to the Crusades. When he was killed, she retained the fief in her own hands as dowager. She had her court of justice, her marshal of the palace, and her provost and like any aggressive feudal lord conducted sharp jurisdictional battles with the cathedral canons. On one occasion she encouraged or even helped organize a mob which invaded and sacked the church and other chapter buildings, the conflict ultimately requiring the intervention of Philippe-Auguste.[32]

It is generally held today, despite the sharp contradictions between them, that courtly love poetry strongly influenced the cult of Mary, at least in the latter's code and trappings. That this should have been possible implies a sharing by the two, in part anyway, of important background influences. That the changed social position of women should be more clearly mirrored in the love poetry than in the cult of the Virgin (and, derivatively, in religious art) is understandable. The former was declamatorily predicated on the superiority of women while the Church was, if anything, misogynous.

The panegyrics of the court poets addressed to their paragons, usually married women, were formerly read at face value, from which was derived a strange notion of the feudal marital relationship. Certainly the nobles' morals were no better than might be expected. They are said to have populated the manors with their bastards. But that these egoistic and bellicose men should allow their wives a similar freedom strains credibility.[33]

Modern scholars have been able to find "internal evidence" in the courtly poetry pointing to an entirely different interpretation. The strong parallel between the postures assumed by the poet with regard to his lady and the feudal relationship has been singled out as particularly meaningful. He conducted himself toward her entirely in the manner of a vassal to his suzerain. "To be in love . . . was like a knight taking an oath," declared the famed troubadour, Bernard de Ventadour: "With patience and discretion, I am your vassal and your servant."[34] One author, when discussing the allegedly biographical content of the troubadour's poetry, goes so far as to insist that "one could not find a single example of the dreams and beliefs of the courtly love being carried into practice."[35]

It could hardly be otherwise in the socially rigid Middle Ages. The poet most frequently belonged to a lower social class than the lady to whom he sang. As the authoritative writer on this subject, Eduard Wechssler, exhaustively demonstrated, it was indeed through his poetry that the troubadour hoped to get advancement at the seigniorial court, over whose spiritual life (and often its physical one as well) his lady presided. Since it was known to all concerned that the favors he demanded were purely conventional, her good name remained unblemished. She could enjoy the luxury of being passionately and publicly craved—and often in excellent verse—without paying the usual price, unless, of course, inclination and opportunity combined toward that end.

The poet, on the other hand, had the strongest non-amatory motives for his songs. Often starting as a lowly jongleur, who had to travel from court to court to earn a precarious living, one can see him suddenly presented with the opportunity of stabilizing his position. He could ask for nothing better than to be "taken up" into his lady's household, which to him meant the nearest thing to security and social position attainable at the time. And the kiss he asked for was nothing else, Wechssler argued, than the token by which the pledge of vassalage was customarily sealed. (The vassal first kissed the lord's shoe, then was raised by him and given the accolade.)[36]

Nevertheless, as such things happen in the creative life of man, the poems that were meant as "bread and butter" pieces ended by acquiring an artistic independence and at times a depth and richness that have helped them retain their attractiveness over the centuries. Their remarkable originality consisted in the circumstance that for the first time in the West was sung the ennobling effect on man of his love for a superior woman. This emphasis contributed importantly to the spiritual position of the female sex and, in consequence, to the relationship between the sexes.

It is all the more surprising to find the greatest love epic of the time, the *Roman de la rose*, containing some of the most ferocious attacks on women in all literature. "There are fewer honest women than phoenixes," Jean de Meung sang, "fewer honest women than white crows." And his is that truly bestial couplet:

> Either by act or in your hearts,
> You all are, were, or will be tarts![37]

It would almost seem from this savage misogyny that the poet was lined up with the monks. But the affinity is illusory. Actually there were light-years of difference between the two attitudes toward woman. Jean de Meung's poetry could never have been the inspiration of the atrocious relief at Villeneuve-les-Avignon!

Jean de Meung's attacks on women have been interpreted as essentially an act of dissociation from the mawkishness and exaggerated self-abnegation of the courtly poetry in favor of a natural, candidly hedonistic relationship. That of Abélard and Héloïse, for example. Ah, there was a woman! "Never has her like been seen since," the poet sadly exulted. Freely and courageously she took the man she loved to her bed, mating him out of wedlock, by nature, as it were. It was only when they did marry, on Abélard's insistence, that tragedy ensued. For marriage was a hateful and treacherous state, the source of lies and villainy. The only true relationship between the sexes was honest sensuality, the poet insisted, ending his long epic with an amazingly graphic allegorical description of the sex act.

Héloïse herself was no shrinking violet when recalling their passionate affair to Abélard. She preferred, she admitted, the flat but "more expressive" word —"fornication"—to the ridiculous euphemism—"delights of love"—that was usually applied to the physical relationship. (It should be said, of course, that she could hardly have known that her burning letters to her lover would ever become public.) It is a significant fact, however, at a time when the positive feminine influence on man was beginning to be vaunted, as by Abélard himself who argued that women's prayers always had a special grace in Scripture, that it should have been this great and extraordinarily modern woman who acted the Devil's disciple. She forthrightly reasserted Eve's sinful role and countered her former lover's references by quoting from Gospel various instances where woman's influence had been pernicious. Even so, Héloïse declared, she had brought evil into Abélard's life, for which she would now atone by a lifetime of penance. But she would not lie either to God or herself by asserting that she was reformed. How could one talk of repentance when one's soul burned with the same passions as before?

"The delights of love which we enjoyed together were so sweet to me that their memory can neither displease me nor be effaced. Wherever I turn, they are present, reawakening the old desires. . . . Even at solemn mass . . . the licentious pictures of those passionate acts seize upon this miserable heart." She caught herself while asleep, she said, making motions that recalled their passion. The very places where they had embraced were indelibly imprinted on her mind. Do not ask for my prayers, she cried, for my chastity is nothing but hypocrisy. It is your prayers that I need since you have always been the first to me, coming even before God. To which Adam-Abélard replied, bitterly recriminating, blessing the mutilation that had put him beyond temptation's reach, finally succeeding in bringing his tormentor to reason.[38]

It has often been said that everything that medieval man has thought or felt or dreamed can be found in the art of the cathedrals. Unfortunately, this is a great exaggeration. Perhaps if the word "found" were changed to "alluded to," it would be closer to the truth for then manner would be left out of account.

And even so, there are whole areas and depths of the human soul revealed in the exchange of letters between Héloïse and Abélard with which nothing in the art of the time shows the slightest familiarity. The plastic presence, of course, has its own inimitable qualities, and with these we must be content.

It would be incongruous to think of church art as depicting the extraordinary relationship between these two amazing human beings. That Jean de Meung glorified them was largely due to the fact that they symbolized for him a defiance of church morality and of the false monastic advocacy of sexual abstinence, which he held to be a course of life that was against nature, hence repugnant. In this sense his ideas may be considered as a kind of reply to the Church's glorification of the Virgin and to the various corollaries of her cult. And even his ideas about women, violently abusive though they might be, tended to free them from inaccessible, saintly models and to substitute more natural prototypes.

But, strangely, this was also an accomplishment, though only obliquely to be sure, of the church art of the twelfth and thirteenth centuries. For this art, as we have seen, had its own notable share in the humanizing of woman's image. Through representations of Mary and the saints, the softening influence of art made itself more widely felt in the portrayal of all the Daughters of Eve and beyond them in the depiction of various human relationships. The altered attitude toward the female sex in church art may have been largely unintended. But it strikes us as inevitable today, ultimately responsive to important changes in woman's social situation.

CHAPTER IV
THE NEW CLASSES AS DONORS
AND AS SUBJECTS

Anyone who has studied the capital reliefs at Vézelay with any care will have been struck by the extraordinary degree of violence prevalent in them. Half the subjects are turbulent in action and the general impression of the entire collection is tumultuous, unbridled, almost hysterical. It would seem that the person responsible for the iconographic program (generally credited to Peter the Venerable, who headed the abbatial school at Vézelay for several years before moving on to greater fame at Cluny) had especially conned Scripture for scenes of violence, finding in even familiar stories some convulsive incident that no one else would have thought of using.

Thus, although infrequently found elsewhere, one sees at Vézelay how Cain is killed by his son Lamech and how Judas ends his own life at the end of a rope. Shorn Samson is shown struggling desperately with his yoke and Jacob strives two times with the angel. Moses kills the Egyptian who abuses the Jew. The angel slays Pharaoh's son. Moses has a club ready for the man sacrificing to the Golden Calf. Amnon is killed by Absalom and the latter in turn has his head chopped off by Joab, which is Holofernes' fate at Judith's hands [see Pl. 27], Goliath's at David's [Pl. 36], and almost that of Isaac at his father's. Normally artists were content to show Abraham simply in the act of raising his sword, which the angel seizes. But here its sharp edge is placed against the boy's throat, a contact that is highly favored at Vézelay.

True, whoever wanted to illustrate the Old Testament could hardly avoid scenes of homicide and bloodletting. The tale of Gentle Jesus provides nothing comparable. But Vézelay's artists found plenty of source material of their preferred kind in the legends of the saints, who, it will have been noticed, were most vulnerable to decapitation, usually resisting other forms of martyrdom. The chastisement of the Vices, a Christian and medieval innovation, furnished another field for exploitation of this kind at Vézelay: punishment of Avarice;

63

Calumny having his tongue ripped out; Anger plunging the sword into his own chest. And everywhere are demons, devils, and evil spirits, orchestrating the Walpurgis Night of torture and carnage [Pl. 37].

Writers have alluded to the pall of fear that hovered over medieval man, doubtless a reflection of the constant presence of danger, the nearness of death. For aside from the intermittent catastrophes of foreign invasions, epidemics, natural holocausts, and famines, there was the everyday reality of the feudal system itself, wefted of anarchy and rapine. All of this, added to the terrors of spiritual damnation, ended by giving life a sense of awful precariousness and doom. This incubus, from which man in later centuries was progressively delivered, by a quirk of history reappeared in all its terror in recent times, furnishing many contemporaries with an extraordinary insight into the medieval nightmare. By a cruel coincidence, one of the most eloquent writers on this subject happened to be the famous medievalist, Marc Bloch, who in the end became a victim himself of Nazi bestiality.

It was inevitable, as the co-authors of one work have pointed out, that medieval art should reflect this basic reality of that time and be "charged with the terrors lived by those who created it." The conflicts that are to be found in Romanesque church art, they added, go beyond a symbolic or religious intention and can be explained only by historic realities. "The impression of fright, even anguish, which the viewer can hardly escape, imposes itself upon him even before he has had the time to appreciate the beauty of the art."[1]

But in addition to this general background of violence that characterized life in the Middle Ages, there existed at Vézelay another source of tumult: the conflict between the abbey and its dependents of town and country that raged through half a century and which swept into its torrent popes and prelates, barons and kings. The Vézelay conflict was a part of the broad struggle for relief from the heavy load of imposts and for the abolition of mortmain and other remnants of serfdom which the rising middle class of many parts of France would try to cast off during the course of the twelfth century.

An interesting circumstance about this communal strife at Vézelay was that its first eruption, in 1106, occurred soon after construction work on the monastery's new basilica was begun and may have been directly related to that event. Pope Pascal II had authenticated the abbey's relics of St. Mary Magdalene in 1103 and the pilgrims who began thronging to Vézelay made the erection of a greater edifice indispensable. In order to help defray the enormous expense the abbot imposed new taxes on the citizens, who thought that their burdens were already heavy enough. As so often happened in the Middle Ages, the controversy reached a sudden and violent climax, the townsmen breaking into the monastery and killing the abbot.[2]

Peace was reestablished but work on the new church proceeded only fitfully since the atmosphere at Vézelay never lost its tension. In 1120, new distur-

Vézelay, Church of La Madeleine (12th century). Capital reliefs:
36. David and Goliath.   37. The Temptation of St. Anthony.

bances resulted in the burning down of many of the monastery buildings, including the old basilica with over 1,000 people in it. Work on the unfinished new
church, which was fortunately spared, was now pressed forward. In 1137,
townsmen joined with the peasants in renewed demands and a temporary
settlement was reached. But this gave no assurance of peace since the abbey's
immense prosperity invited covetousness. Controversies continued to rage, with
other ecclesiastic houses and especially with the Comtes de Nevers, who had
long claimed seigniorial rights over the abbey's dependents.

After his return from the Second Crusade, Comte Guillaume III quickly
forgot his vows and renewed his demands on the abbey, shrewdly involving
the help of the town's burghers in his behalf. Addressing them in the same
field where St. Bernard's eloquence had a few years earlier incited Louis VII
and countless barons to take the cross, he encouraged the townsmen to break
their feudal ties with the abbot, who was forced to flee Vézelay under the
protection of two cardinal-legates. On appeal of the pope the king intervened

and the townsmen found that the count's pledges of protection were worthless. The abbot proceeded with brutality against them. His mercenaries took over the town with the sword, confiscating the property of the communal leaders and forcing a number of them to take to the forests and a life of banditry.

The communal struggle at Vézelay was not exactly typical since the support of lay seigniors was certainly not an unfailing circumstance of such conflicts. The opposition of churchmen was more consistent since many towns of France were under the seigniory of ecclesiastics, who were hard put to it to handle the ebullient middle class. And in the end many prelates began to look upon the communes as devilish instruments directed specifically against the Church. Councils and synods repeatedly denounced them and preachers inveighed against those "modern Babylons" which "establish diabolic customs opposed to ecclesiastic organization and tending toward the almost complete overturning of the Church's jurisdiction."[3]

A "Marxist" writer has suggested that the demons on the capital reliefs at Vézelay were meant to terrorize the restive peasants of the abbot, who found the Devil "a most precious auxiliary" in helping to keep his charges under heel.[4] This viewpoint ignores the fact that the churchmen themselves were just as terrorized by devils as were their serfs. Their presence in the art of so many cloisters (as at Moissac, for example) where none but monks ever penetrated would indicate a different purpose. It has been pointed out that wherever one finds a church in which a large part of the imagery is concerned with devils and their antics, it is a certain sign that the sanctuary was originally monastic.[5] "Satan was the terror of the cloisters," an author has noted,[6] an observation which the novelist Huysmans described as still valid in modern times, in his firsthand account of a Trappist colony. His point of departure was the assumption that the concentrated virtue of the convent attracted the concourse of demons, eager to disrupt such holiness.

When, in art of the cloister, even the most accomplished saints like Benedict or Anthony were shown tormented by salacious dreams or devils, the obvious purpose was to reassure the inmates that they, too, could overcome their torturers with piety and virtue. Nevertheless, church artists may very well at times have been referring to a contemporary model for some evil spirit that they put into their work. In Chapter I, for example, there was an allusion to the carved demon on the roodscreen at Notre-Dame de Paris, which was associated with the king's advocate who had had the effrontery to try to strip the bishop of his secular justice.* The case was considered so important that other grimacing effigies were identified with this attorney in various churches of the archdiocese.[7]

If a similar personification of the abbey's secular enemies had been made at

*Actually the carving antedated the ascription but this does not alter the significance of the thought behind it.

Vézelay, the reference undoubtedly would have been pointed at the communal rabble or the Comte de Nevers' men, about whom a papal legate wrote, in 1119, that they "broke down the doors of the cloister, threw stones on the reliquaries; . . . they did not even respect the crucifix in which is preserved a piece of the True Cross; they beat the monks, drove them off with stones, and having captured one of them treated him in an infamous manner."[8] This description is not too much different from the one that Peter the Venerable gave of the devilish disturbers of the monastery's peace, telling how they held nocturnal assemblies, broke forcefully into the abbey, and attacked the monks with wheelwrights' adzes while planting firebrands across their paths.[9]

The substitution of Avarice for Pride as the leading "male" Vice in art of the twelfth century, it has been argued, reflected a change in the class relations of the Church.[10] Formerly it had most frequently been in conflict with the nobles and, accordingly, had preached humility and the perils of Pride to them. But as the clamorous burghers became more and more the chief opponents, Pride was replaced by Greed as man's basic error.

To castigate Avarice, and through it the middle class, church iconographers usually chose the parable of Lazarus and Dives. The latter symbolized one of the "nouveaux riches" of the time, who had acquired his fortune by trade or usury. Far from disdaining the wealth that was derived from these activities, however, the ecclesiastic seigniors took it with bad grace when the burghers demanded the right of passing their fortunes on to their children!* And if Bishop Maurice de Sully of Paris compared the merchant to the Devil it was because he wanted him to be more liberal in his donations to Notre-Dame's building fund.[11] So if the greedy burgher would not loosen up with his lucre, he could take it with him, down to Hell, as Dives does indeed in the great façade tableau at Moissac, where he is shown with his moneybag strung around his neck. On his deathbed, his ministering devils, waiting for the release of his soul, hold up the pouch reassuringly to him [Pl. 38].

Allusion has been made to the apparently contradictory circumstance that the sharp conflicts which often divided burghers and local churchmen did not prevent their joining together in erecting such admirable monuments as the cathedrals of Laon, Reims, and Beauvais, in all of which the communal spirit was very strong. This was possible, it is argued, because the middle classes saw in the cathedral "a kind of neutral zone, open to all, where you could fix a rendezvous, exchange ideas, and do business, all of which had nothing to do with religious service."[12] This is a great oversimplification of the matter, as we shall presently see. For one thing, it sometimes occurred that when the com-

---

*Even well into the thirteenth century there were still many subjects of churchmen who had not shaken the yoke of mortmain.

38. *Moissac, Church of Saint-Pierre.* West porch (12th century). Detail of the parable of Lazarus and Dives. Right, death of Dives; left, he is dragged down to Hell with his moneybag.

mune and the local churchmen were in violent opposition the burghers were banned altogether from the cathedral precincts!

It is significant that the kings (and, to a lesser extent, the lay nobles) were quicker than the ecclesiastics to perceive the advantages of a peaceful adjustment with the middle class. At times, it is true, the royal friendliness was little more than an excuse for extracting money from them, the methods used being often crude enough. A celebrated case was one that occurred, early in the twelfth century, during the great controversy between the townsmen of Laon and their ecclesiastical seignior, which Louis VI purported to arbitrate by putting the burghers' freedom on the block. The commune offered 400 livres and the bishop, a beneficiary of simony who had never even been ordained, outbid it by 300 livres. The king slipped out of town with his booty and the bishop tried to raise the 700 livres he had paid Louis by putting a new tax on the town. This was the spark that touched off a savage insurrection, in which the bishop, who is reported to have tried to hide in a barrel, lost his head.[13]

By the end of the twelfth century and the beginning of the thirteenth, however, the wealth of the burghers had become such that they were not likely to be outbid in this manner. Philippe-Auguste, Louis VI's grandson, became the staunch friend of the communes, which he saw as dependable allies in his struggles with the puissant barons and prelates. Before leaving for the Crusades in 1190 he instructed his bailiffs to set up committees of burghers, "wise, loyal, and of good report," to help them conduct their affairs.[14] When passing through Lyon, he encouraged the townsmen there to set up a commune, which they promptly did, organizing it on a quasi-military basis, each guild having its company, its captain, and its standard.[15] The help of the burghers to royalty was mainly financial at first, but at the great battle of Bouvines, which Philippe-Auguste fought against the Germans in 1214, mentioned among the troops assembled with the king were the "communes of Corbeil, Amiens, Beauvais, Compiègne, and Arras."[16]

Louis VIII and especially his queen, Blanche of Castile, both as regent and as dominant influence in the reign of her son, St. Louis, continued this royal friendliness toward the bourgeoisie. Joinville in his fascinating chronicle tells of a coterie of angry barons on one occasion barring the queen's and the young king's entry into Paris. But the tradesmen and artisans of the guilds demanded arms and delivered their rulers, who made a triumphant entrance into the capital along roads lined with cheering people. The incident evidently made a lasting impression on the young ruler, who remembered it forty years later when preparing his political testament for his dauphin. St. Louis urged his son to give particular attention to the "strength and wealth of the great cities" so that the barons of his and other lands would "fear to undertake any inimical acts against you."[17]

That the ecclesiastics were slower in adjusting to the new bourgeoisie may have delayed the full exploitation of the middle class as a major contributor to the construction and ornamentation of churches. Burgher donors in the first half of the twelfth (and even as early as the eleventh) century are not unknown, a famous example being furnished by a relief at Notre-Dame-du-Port, at Clermont-Ferrand, showing a person making a donation of a carved capital to the church. His features and dress would seem to identify him as a merchant and he is even named, in a book held open by an angel: "*Stefanus.*" But such cases are infrequent enough to attract attention when they do occur.

The background of the circumstances that led to a radical change in this situation during the thirteenth century remains obscure. However, the wealth of the burghers must have been strongly suggestive at the time. There is much circumstantial evidence indicating that the stained-glass window may have played a significant role in this development. Louis Grodecki, in a provocative analysis of the development of Gothic architecture,[18] has conjectured that this form evolved largely as an excited reaction to the introduction of stained-glass windows: "the desire to offer larger and larger surfaces for storied translucid decoration." The heavy Romanesque wall, its windows kept very small so as not to detract from its supporting strength, was replaced by the open bay with a wall so narrow as to be hardly more than a partition, this author notes. The purpose was not primarily to let more light in, since the more window space that was won the darker the glass used, so that in the end Gothic churches were hardly more luminous than Romanesque structures.

What was behind this seemingly irresistible impulse to enlarge the surface of colored glass? Was it indeed, as the writer suggests, a straining toward "the realization in matter of the formal and spiritual ideal of a dream of total light, of unlimited transparence?" He refers to the intense preoccupation of church thinkers of the twelfth and thirteenth centuries with the mystical properties of light. And it is well to recall that Abbot Suger, who is the first churchman credited with having used colored windows on a monumental scale, was deeply motivated in this precise sense. Holding with the doctrine of the abbey's patron saint (St. Denis) that all nature was a reflection of the original source of light, Suger believed that through contemplation of precious stones (and likewise stained-glass windows), which in a manner trapped this divine essence, man could be transported beyond his material nature toward "the purity of heaven."[19]

There would seem to be a logical consistency between this mystical intoxication with light and the desire for large areas of decorative glass in a church. But one wonders if either is a sufficient motivation for the amazingly swift proliferation of the radically new Gothic style of architecture or even of its stained-glass ornamentation. If nothing else, one must consider the financial means of the churchmen who were responsible for construction. For, as is known, the cost of the windows with their legendary accounts in jigsaw patterns was very high, "nearly equal to that of the structure."[20]

As we shall see later (Chapter IX), churchmen often overextended themselves in their building plans. If, in their frantic search for funds, the wealth of the bourgeoisie had at first remained largely untapped, it could not possibly continue so for long. To a great extent this wealth was liquid besides, an important circumstance when we remember that building workmen were mainly freemen by the twelfth century and had to be paid in cash. It was helpful, too, that the richer and older crafts often had organizational contact with the cathedral, had "their" chapel in it, and celebrated their saint's day there in considerable splendor.

Another circumstance that seems to have favored this entire development was the fact that so many of the great cathedrals had to be rebuilt in the thirteenth century following ruinous fires (Chartres, Reims, Amiens, etc.). The bishop of Amiens consulted the townsmen of mark before launching the rebuilding of his edifice. But the most striking case is that of Chartres, whose church was all but obliterated by the conflagration of 1194. The city was reportedly in a state of moral collapse after the tragedy when the papal legate, the Cardinal of Pisa, put vigor into the plan of an immediate rebuilding. Even the Virgin's Tunic, the church's most precious relic which each year brought thousands of pilgrims to celebrations of Mary's festival days, was miraculously discovered unblemished and the campaign was launched amid nearly ecstatic conditions.

Chartres' merchants and artisans had special reason to feel attached to the cathedral since the city's four important fairs were, as such things were arranged in the Middle Ages, set to coincide with the Virgin's festivals. And religious souvenirs—small leaden images of Our Lady of the Sacred Tunic or even real little chemisettes—"seem to have comprised the bulk of all goods sold." In fact, the relationship between merchants and the cathedral chapter was excellent, due in no small degree to the canons' practice of taking into their ranks as counselors ("avoués") the wealthiest of the bourgeois class. Since this withdrew the favored burghers from the jurisdiction of the count, the seignior of Chartres, the custom was repeatedly challenged by that noble, at times violently. As chance would have it, the matter was permanently settled by arbitration—in favor of the chapter and the burghers—just shortly before the fire.[21]

So favorable a burgher-cathedral association as subsisted at Chartres was by no means general, however. Indeed, the opposite sometimes occurred (particularly when a city was under an ecclesiastic rather than a secular seignior), often with deleterious effects on a church's building fortunes. Such a situation prevailed at Lyon over many decades, as a result of which the burghers were disinclined to make generous gifts to the archbishop's cathedral. They even had to construct a chapel of their own when they needed a place for their meetings, which in other cities were usually held in the cathedral.[22] It seems related to these circumstances that when windows were paid for at Lyon cathedral the benefactors mentioned are exclusively the churchmen themselves. Small wonder also that many of the lancets turned out to be of plain glass, much cheaper to produce than the colored, storied panels.[23]

An even more glaring example was that at Reims, where a fire in 1210 required the total reconstruction of the cathedral. All measures of the archbishop and chapter, aided by the pope, to raise funds proved inadequate and extraordinary pressure was put on the townsmen. "The burghers were in the habit of lending money to other cities and about this time a loan was negotiated with the commune of Auxerre. Henri de Braine demanded the tenth on the money to be exported, which the leaders . . . refused to pay. The archbishop then ordered the burghers not to leave their parishes, and the result was a riot." They stormed the prelate's palace (he himself was out of the city at the time), killing his marshal, and erected barricades with the help of cathedral "tombstones and even stones which had been prepared in the workshop for the . . . new edifice." Work on the cathedral halted for several years.[24]

Significantly, no windows at Reims—at least among those still existing today —were donated by the guilds. The considerable number of lancets remaining, either in their original thirteenth-century or restored form, were paid for entirely by feudal donors and especially by the archbishop and his bishop-suffragans. All these dignitaries are depicted, as though in "a solemn pontifical

session," in the upper choir lancets, the same area in which, it should be underscored, are to be found windows given by the richest guilds at Chartres and
other cathedrals. In two of the Reims lancets four of the ten bishops are doubled
up, a curious circumstance that has not been explained. Space was not lacking
since exactly two other window spaces were available in this area which had
to be filled with earlier panels in grisaille (gray monochrome) taken from the
old church. The implication seems inescapable that "funds ran out."[25] Certainly, little help could be expected from the infuriated burghers!

Ecclesiastic church-builders who had the relatively peaceful support of their
bourgeois subjects must have in the end appreciated this advantage. It is certain, on the other hand, that the burghers obtained what they felt was an ample
quid pro quo for their money. They could not have failed to appreciate the
opportunity it gave them for acquiring social status. It has been said that the
major political aim of the burghers was to assume a legitimate place in the
feudal structure—but not as lowly serfs! What they finally attained was a
kind of "collective fiefdom."[26] In this sense, for a guild to be allowed to set its
emblem at the bottom of the lancet it donated to the cathedral was—in the
thirteenth century—an enormously meaningful progression.

It is not accidental that donors of the stained-glass windows of the twelfth
century about which we are informed were almost exclusively feudal and
chiefly ecclesiastic. This is true of Abbot Suger's lancets, most of which are
now gone, and of the bits and pieces still remaining at various other churches.
We know also that Chartres cathedral had a whole set of old glass lancets.
These were largely lost in the 1194 fire, except for the three great western
windows and the so-called "Belle Verrière," now located on the south side of
the choir.

We have the accounts of a necrologist, however, from which we can make
out that there were fourteen other windows in the old church at Chartres. The
chronicler listed their donors, fortunately. Only one of them cannot be identified—all the others are clerics, most of them members of the chapter itself.
These circumstances seem to substantiate the fact that there was a sudden and
dramatic shift to the burghers among those appealed to for funds, during the
reconstruction of Chartres cathedral.

If the most opulent guilds such as the drapers and furriers (picturesquely
called the "bourgeoisie de la rivière" at Chartres [Pl. 39]) or the money-
changers (yes, the money-changers would also be represented in many thirteenth-century churches) could easily finance this scheme, the more modest
watercarriers [Pl. 40] or porters did not want to be left out either. One can
imagine that the canon in charge of the cathedral "fabrique" would not allow
the matter to rest there but would engage the various guilds in a lively competition. Something of the sort is implied by the fact that the richer societies

Chartres Cathedral (13th century):   39. Ambulatory stained-glass window. "Signature" of the Merchant Furriers, the donor guild.   40. South nave aisle stained-glass window. "Signature" of the Watercarriers, the donor guild.

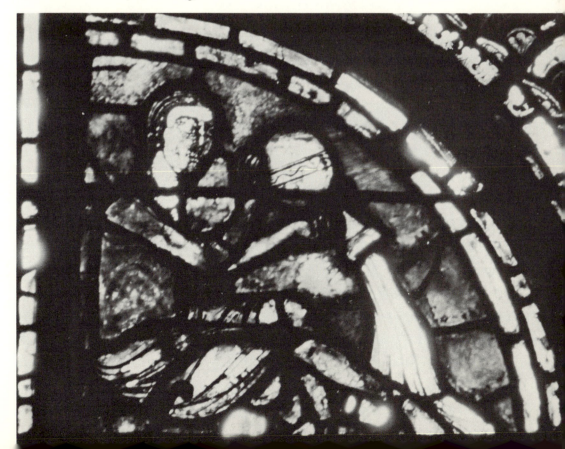

often made multiple-window endowments. At Chartres, for example, the drapers gave five windows, as did the bakers. The money-changers paid for four of them, including two magnificent lancets in the high choir.[27]

The mass patronage of church art by the burghers seems to have had the emulative effect frequently of loosening up the local seigniors as well. The donor barons could depend on a stellar advantage in the position of their windows: It would be taken for granted that they would get the choice of the upper registers of the church. Though the guilds at times were granted the higher lancets—as at Chartres or Le Mans—it was extremely rare for feudal donors to be placed in a lower position. Also they had the privilege of figuring personally in their lancet, armored and riding a charger, the background spangled with the family coat of arms.

We may assume that the guildsmen shared the general intoxication with this marvelous new medium. But the lancet held a particular attraction for them since with its numerous panels it was perfectly adapted to the narration of the legend of their patron saint. Inasmuch as certain popular saints were shared by several groups, it became necessary to distinguish the particular donors in some way. Thus was evolved that ingenious practice of identifying them by a work scene ("signature") in one or more of the bottom panels [Pl. 41, Pl. 42].[28]

The necessity of winning large numbers of secular benefactors early began to play havoc with the rigid control of the iconography by the clergy. With few exceptions the selection of subjects at Chartres was by the donors, according to one church authority. They would not have been too much interested in

Chartres Cathedral (13th century): 41 (opposite page). South nave aisle stained-glass window. "Signature" of the Shoemakers, the donor guild. 42 (above). Ambulatory stained-glass window. "Signature" of the Fishmongers, the donor guild. One merchant is extending a squid to his customer while his colleague counts the price on his fingers.

paying for a window if the subject was "imposed," he noted.[29] The donors of multiple windows especially troubled the harmony of the iconographic pattern, when, for example, they demanded a repetition of the same story in two or more windows of the church. Agreeing to this dictation by "outsiders" must have constituted a major concession by churchmen. It represents an early and exceedingly important development in the secularization of church art.

The merchants and artisans had to be content with a group display. But there can be little doubt that they considered the arrangement satisfactory since at Chartres no fewer than forty-two windows were given by the guilds and at Bourges, forty-seven. In working out the little scenes illustrating their trade the guildsmen must have frequently had a hand, as the selection of the most essential acts of their work and the inclusion of characteristic details that might have escaped the unalerted observer indicate.

43. *Chartres Cathedral.* Upper choir stained-glass window (13th century). "Signature" of the Butchers, the donor guild. The butcher has masked his victim's eyes, as his pet dog (lower right corner) watches the operation confidently.

When, for example, the butcher raises his bludgeon to stun a cow, its eyes are veiled by a cloth [Pl. 43]. In the shoeing operation at a smithy the horse has been placed into an ingenious iron frame meant to curb its frightened movements. And the scenes of the sculptors in their lancet are beautifully circumstantial. One of them stops to wash down the stone dust in his throat with some wine and in another scene the artist examines his work appraisingly [Pl. 44].

Both at Chartres and Le Mans there are windows whose "signatures" present what have generally been accepted as gaming scenes. These amazing representations in a church were evidently not considered out of order at the time since gambling was held to be a respectable upper-class activity. The windows were probably given by the makers of dice or of gaming boards, though it has been suggested, for the lancet at Le Mans, in any case, that it was donated by the players, who supposedly made up a pool of their winnings for the purpose.[30] It is even reported that the confraternity of Paris prostitutes offered a window to Maurice de Sully with an inscription denoting "their charity and their profession." But the bishop scornfully turned down this "scandalous offering."[31]

It seems entirely in order that in France the guilds having to do with the production and handling of wine should assume honored positions among the church lancets. Thus the coopers (who made casks for wine) gave the Noah window at Chartres, in reference no doubt to the fact that the Patriarch, grateful for the delivery of his wards from the flood, had planted the vine and then drunk of its first pressing—though a bit too liberally. It was hardly by inadvertence that the men who composed the window gave the Ark the unusual cylindrical form of a wine cask [Pl. 45]. Medieval artists were by no means lacking in this type of irreverent drollery.

The window of the local saint at Chartres, St. Lubin, was given by the tavernkeepers, most likely because that devout man had once been cellarer of his abbey. Indeed, he is thus presented in one medallion [Pl. 46]. The entire lancet, in fact, is dedicated to the marvelous crimson beverage, from the trucker who whips up his horse while on a delivery route [Pl. 47] to the presentation of a wine cup in a Eucharistic scene at mass or the portrayal of Christ at the top as "the wine that fertilizes virgins."[32] But that is only part of it. All about the lancet-rim are presented little vignettes of tavernkeepers, wineglass in hand—members of the donor guild—and one more considerable figure, evidently the guild's chief officer, who stands at the center-rim, his hand pointing inward in a presentation gesture [Pl. 48].

44. *Chartres Cathedral*. Ambulatory stained-glass window (13th century). "Signature" of the Sculptors, the donor guild. Left, a sculptor contemplates his work; right, a sculptor pauses to drink a goblet of wine.

Chartres Cathedral (13th century): 45. The Noah stained-glass window, donated by the Coopers' guild. The Ark is in the form of a wine cask. The St. Lubin stained-glass window, donated by the Tavernkeepers' guild: 46 (below). St. Lubin, as cellarer of his convent, drawing wine from a cask. 47 (opposite page). A trucker on a wine-delivery route.

Still another little scene shows a keeper with his wife; another a keeper hurrying to quench the thirst of a weary traveler; and in several he is followed by an individual who carries a kind of stick on his shoulder. Curious as it may seem, this person is none other than the early prototype of the modern bouncer! He is always represented as a youth, since this unenviable role was filled by the tavernkeeper's apprentice or "valet" (journeyman) [Pl. 49].

Fateful for the history of art patronage was the introduction of these little guild vignettes, which permitted the middle classes to break out en masse as it were in church art. Aside from the sculptured Labors of the Months on many church façades, which had an entirely different motivation, as we shall see in the following chapter, this is the first time in the West that the humble efforts of the productive elements of society were vaunted in art, on so large a scale and entirely by and for themselves. More than two hundred years would pass before the wealthy merchants of Florence and Venice would have themselves painted into the retinue of the Magi or their wives and daughters shown assist-

Chartres Cathedral. The St. Lubin stained-glass window (13th century): 48 (below). Left, a tavern-keeper offering a wine-filled goblet; right, the head of the guild pointing to the window in a presentation gesture. 49 (above). A tavernkeeper, followed by his bouncer, presenting a goblet of wine to a tired traveler.

50. *Chartres Cathedral.* The Aaron stained-glass window, upper choir (13th century), donated by *"Gaufridus,"* a rich hosier, shown in center, praying to Mary, who is in the next window. With him are his wife and two sons.

ing at the post-Nativity bustle in the Virgin's chamber. But the trend was started in these Gothic lancets.

Indeed, in the two windows at Chartres, presumably given by the hosiers, one can see an important transition already under way. Instead of a scene presenting the hosiers at work, we have what appears to be a family group: a man, his wife, and two sons. One of the youngsters is holding a white banner on which is painted a red sock. The other, an altar boy, has an incense-box in one hand and swings a censer in the other [Pl. 50]. The question rises as to what made the guild choose so curious a method of designating its sponsorship. The ambiguity is rendered more obscure by the fact that in one of these lancets the man's name, "*Gaufridus*" (Geoffroy), is prominently inscribed across it. Could this have been a leader of the guild, a particularly meritorious person whom the organization wished to honor in this manner?

It is hardly likely that that is the explanation of the origin of the lancet. It makes more sense to assume that the hosier "Gaufridus" was wealthy enough to endow the window himself. But even while doing this as a private individual he retained his identity as a hosier. It was the same sort of identification-by-profession that has created so many of our names. However, in the Chartres window there is the additional qualifying detail that constitutes a social fact of importance, the origin of a mark of bourgeois dignity. Allowed to rub elbows with barons and prelates, this "Gaufridus" could not match them with a family emblem. Accordingly, he used his guild's insignia![33] Thus we may be permitted to see in what might be called "The Sock Rampant" an early middle-class coat of arms.

One can imagine that the case of "Gaufridus" was not an isolated one, the more so since it was a manifestation of class cleavage expressing itself in art. For such wealthy middle-class individuals could no longer be grouped indiscriminately with simple artisans and tradesmen. These were members of the "merchant aristocracy," who in the thirteenth century, and sometimes earlier, began to differentiate themselves sharply from the humbler elements of the bourgeoisie, with whom moreover they not infrequently had harsh clashes of interest.[34] And so we find that at Tours cathedral the Tree of Jesse window was donated by a rich merchant, who is effigied in it together with his wife and whom a crediting inscription names as "*Matheus de . . . Dionisia uxor sua* [Pl. 51, Pl. 52]."[35] Similarly at Rouen a lancet dedicated to Mary portrays the city's leading burgher and his spouse, whom the Virgin honors with a charming circumlocution: "Ge sui ce por Ace le Tort" ("I am here because of Ace le Tort").[36]

But the lesser members of the middle class continued also to find an echo in church art, though still covered by group anonymity. One phase, that of the work scenes, attained a kind of ultimate expression during the fourteenth century in Semur-en-Auxois, where whole windows (drapers; butchers) were

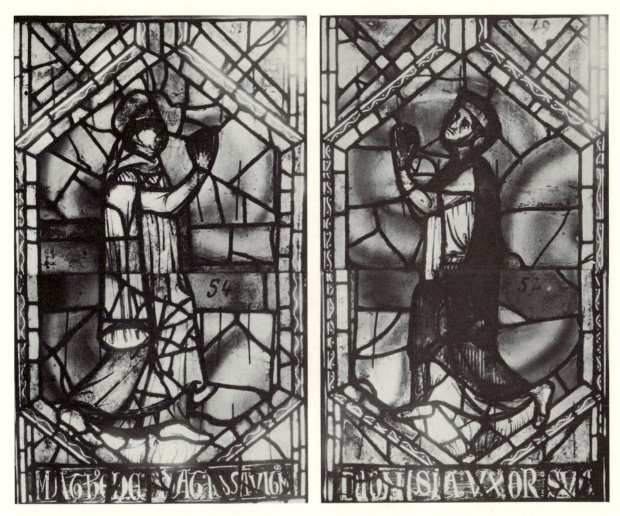

Tours Cathedral. The Tree of Jesse stained-glass window (13th century):   51. Portrait of a wealthy furrier-draper, *"Matheus,"* donor of the window.   52. Portrait of *"Dionisia,"* wife of *"Matheus."*

devoted to the various operations of a trade [Pl. 53]. An entirely different kind of development, seen at Strasbourg cathedral, was even richer in artistic consequence, the middle class serving in lancets of the south nave-aisle as models of the entire biblical cast in an amazing early anticipation of a village Passion Play.

The burgher-like geniality of the characters in these windows contrasts strikingly with the feudal rigidity of the kings on the opposite side of the nave, though the latter date from only a few decades earlier. The innumerable little people ("le menu peuple") of the south aisle are in a perpetual animation of busy-ness. The windows are a veritable festival of ardent "Gemütlichkeit,"

53. *Semur-en-Auxois, Church of Notre-Dame*. The Drapers' lancet (14th century).
The entire window is given over to scenes of the donor guild's trade.

upon all of which the Prophets look down benignly, leaning on their elbows and
commenting on the happenings like a chorus of Alsatian village sages [Pl. 54,
Pl. 55].

It would be difficult to account for so radical a difference in technic on the
two sides of the Strasbourg nave except on the basis of sponsorship. Therefore,
it should not surprise us that, late in the thirteenth century, a concatenation of
circumstances had turned the completion of Strasbourg cathedral over to the
city magistracy. The townsmen had been earlier involved in a bitter conflict
with the bishop, their seignior, which culminated in the pitched battle of Haus-
bergen, in 1262, when the churchman's cavalry was routed with the aid of the
guild militia. An oligarchy ruled the city for several decades thereafter but the
guilds, profiting from discords among the richest burgher families, seized power
in 1332. This was almost exactly the time when the south-aisle lancets were
begun.[37] And so we may be permitted to assume that they were done for and
by aid of the triumphant guildsmen, who disdained to steal onto the scene by
the disguise of their trade or service. Proudly and consciously taking all the

honors upon themselves, they gave Christ, Mary, and the Apostles their own flesh and animation.

Serving even more directly to corroborate the imprint of Strasbourg's new rulers on the cathedral's art was another lancet produced at this same time, but which unfortunately has disappeared. It was nothing less than a full-dress procession of the "Stadtrat." Everyone of importance was represented, it has been reported: the mayor, the magistrates, the guildsmen with their insignia, and even the nobles (who had been wisely conceded a minority of places on the town council), mounted and brilliantly accoutered. The guildsmen too were armed, though more modestly. And extended across a kind of chariot was spread out the great banner of the sovereign municipality.[38]

It is entirely likely that other examples of this kind had existed in other churches (it is certain that they were to be found in secular buildings) but about which even documentary traces have been lost. A fourteenth-century chronicler, Jean de Saint-Victor, described a colorful festival in Paris, in 1313, the high point of which was a parade by the combined guilds of the city, "all with their own banners, some with paintings of Hell on them, others with Paradise, and still others presented to the eyes of the public all the characters of the *Roman de Renard*, shown practicing the various professions." Another early writer reported that the guildsmen also acted out scenes from the New Testament and the fabliaux during this procession.[39]

Because of the peculiarities of the stained-glass windows, which permitted the quiet introduction of crediting medallions, this art remained the preferred medium of middle-class donors. There are, however, a considerable number of work scenes, other than Labors of the Months, to be seen in church sculpture of the twelfth and thirteenth centuries. Usually they refer to some prominent local industry, an example being the remarkable reliefs at Amiens representing merchants of the dye made from a plant grown in the vicinity, called "waide" (woad) [Pl. 56]. This pigment, which was in modern times replaced by indigo, continued to be used all the way into the twentieth century, in particular for the uniforms of English bobbies.

Another instance, from the twelfth century, of the same kind is a beautiful series at the church of Oloron-Sainte-Marie, in the Basses-Pyrenées, showing workers cutting and weighing salmon [Pl. 57]. Oloron is situated at the confluence of two mountain torrents and today, eight hundred years after this sculpture was made, the salmon fisheries are still important here, furnishing one fourth of France's supply. Now, to be sure, when the fish return from the ocean to spawn, there are man-made ladders to help them up the river rapids.

Of seemingly inescapable topical reference are the thirteenth-century reliefs around the pedestal of a statue of Christ at Reims [Pl. 58, Pl. 59]. Local tradition maintains that this sculpture was executed at the expense of a clothier as punishment for the crime of giving false measure. Since it was the function of the guild of each trade to police the honesty of its members, chief actors in the reliefs are presumed to be fellow guildsmen. The scenes are strikingly from the life of the times and have a religious reference merely in the sense that dishonesty was a violation of Christian morality.

In the first relief, we are shown a colorful group of men and women, dressed in the style of the thirteenth century, women in long robes, men in tunics, all standing before the counter of the merchant who displays his wares to them. A clerk is shown carefully scrutinizing items in his account book. The crime

54. *Strasbourg Cathedral*. South aisle stained-glass window (14th century). Story of the Passion: Christ Crowned with Thorns. Above, Old Testament Prophets commenting on the events.

can be assumed to have taken place at this time for in the next scene two men have the guilty merchant in hand as though to conduct him before the court of his peers. Imprisonment was rare in such cases. Usually the guilty person could expunge his crime with a fine. In the final scene the draper is shown kneeling before a statue of the Virgin, to whom he is apparently swearing a renewed pledge of honesty. The fact that churchmen are absent from all these scenes whereas the draper's fellow tradesmen are often animated participants illustrates the large measure of self-rule attained by the burghers of Reims and many other towns of Northern France by the second half of the thirteenth century.

55. *Strasbourg Cathedral*. South aisle stained-glass window (14th century). The Judgment Day: a group of the Chosen.

56. *Amiens Cathedral*. South wall, outside the chapel of Saint-Nicolas (13th century). Two merchants (members of the donor guild) beside a bag of woad, a plant used for dyeing cloth.

57. *Oloron-Sainte-Marie, Church of Sainte-Marie* (12th century). Relief showing workers in salmon fishery engaged in various activities.

Reims Cathedral. Pedestal relief representing an ex voto offering required of a draper as punishment of an act of dishonesty (13th century): 58. Center and left, the draper's shop with clients, the draper, employees. Presumably, the dishonest act takes place here. At right, the dishonest draper being led away by a fellow guild member. 59. The dishonest draper, surrounded by fellow guild members, pledges his amendment as he kneels before the Virgin's statue.

Among the many post-Passion incidents in Strasbourg's south aisle, that of the Doubting Thomas could not possibly have been omitted. A builder and architect, where could this Apostle have learned his imperious need for verification by direct visual and manual means except in his work? Thomas had made his name fashioning palaces for Indian princes. His thirteenth-century counterparts in the West built not only cathedrals and chateaux but also fine meeting places for the wealthy guilds. A possible example was the magnificent so-called "House of Musicians," whose members might have posed for the remarkable group of performers that decorated its façade, though it has also been suggested that this was simply a banker's house [Pl. 60].[40] Another early guildhall, likewise at Reims, which came down into modern times, was given a tympanum bearing not an effigy of the Virgin or a patron saint, but a trinity symbolizing Learning, Strength, and Love!

Much could be written about the burghers' selection of this dedicatory trio. Certainly in the field of education their interests and needs had by this time made themselves felt. Indeed, as early as the twelfth century, in the burgeoning towns of France, lay schools began to spring up, which taught reading and writing in the vernacular, arithmetic and other subjects indispensable to the merchants and artisans. To these men and to their helping wives (schools for bourgeois daughters were already available in the thirteenth century), a bit of Thomas' inquiring skepticism was more than just a characteristic turn of mind, it was a business necessity. Arnold Hauser has gone so far as to infer that the sharpened psychological insight displayed by thirteenth- and fourteenth-century art was rooted in the need of the tradesmen to become close observers of people's motives.[41]

In its early history the middle class has often been associated with the development of a materialistic philosophy. It seems almost inevitable, of course, with the life and work of this group turning it toward the active world, that its ideological outlook should reflect this basic preoccupation. But it is highly doubtful that the merchants and small manufacturers of the twelfth and thirteenth centuries were already so determinant an element in society as to give it their spiritual imprint. As a matter of fact, other contemporary classes reflected variously the same materialistic tendency, which appears to have been a strong, general current in the intellectual life of the time. Not only the burghers were engaged in trade and industry, after all.

While Pierre Abélard was not the earliest of "modern" forerunners, his enormous faith in the power of reason to correct error and attain knowledge seems always to define a point of departure. Adelard of Bath, who early observed that light traveled faster than sound as well as other natural phenomena, laid down the creed of philosophical materialism in a witty phrase: "I am not the sort of fellow who can be fed with the picture of a beefsteak!"[42] Robert Grosseteste made a remarkable effort to explain the physical properties of light in mathematical terms, in his treatise, *De Luce*.[43] And Roger Bacon, his student, was one of the great early contributors to investigatory science, flaying the slavish dependence on authority and holding that mathematical deduction and experimental induction were the foundations of learning.[44]

And all of these men were churchmen! It was savants of the Church also who forged the theoretical instrument that was to unify this entire trend, who "severed natural science from theology and paved the way for nominalism, the basic philosophy of modern times."[45] That John Duns Scotus and William of Occam, to whom this accomplishment is credited, were Franciscan monks seems no accident. The saint of Assisi, son of a prosperous merchant, was a sort of Christian pantheist who preached to the birds and signed a peace pact with the wolf of Gubbio. He originated the Christmas crèche with its crib and stall, ox and ass, because he wanted to see Christ's mysteries *"corporeis oculis."*[46]

This viewpoint, of course, signified basically an abandonment of the high Middle Ages' fashion of looking at the visible world as merely a superficial reflection of a deeper reality. As one author has explained this symbolic mode of seeing: "All that is red became to them a reminder of the blood of Christ; all that is wooden, a memento of his cross. . . . Fishermen lowering their nets reminded them of their redemption, and hunting scenes were allegories of the Christian's struggles with the forces of sin. The crab, walking sideways, was a symbol of the fraudulent; . . . the pelican, which was believed to nourish its young with its own blood, was the analogue of Christ, who feeds mankind with his blood."[47]

With such a viewpoint, this writer concluded, there was no use in hiding behind a clump of reeds to observe the habits of pelicans. Once the cosmological significance of these birds was grasped, the rest scarcely mattered. But a great change began to assert itself in the twelfth and especially the thirteenth century, characterized by a throbbing interest in the real world. Members of all classes responded to this fresh and novel outlook. Among them the artists were surely a privileged group, trained by their work to observe more sharply than most others.

In the field of decoration, where they were given pretty much a free hand, the trend toward naturalism established itself fairly early. Though cities were growing rapidly, urban man still was very close to the land and artists often displayed an acuteness of observation with regard to its flora and fauna such as they were not to attain with the human figure until much later. Denise Jalabert, in a celebrated study, showed how medieval floral art evolved toward realism by a seemingly irresistible progression.

In early Romanesque art, she pointed out, one could not even be sure that the sculptor was thinking of leaves altogether when doing his ornamental capitals. But between 1140 and 1170 his reference to actual vegetation became quite definite, though no species was as yet recognizable. About 1205, at Chartres,

60. *Reims, The "House of Musicians"* (13th century). Statue of a bagpipe player.

61. *Villard de Honnecourt's Sketchbook* (13th century). The Lion.

carved grape leaves appeared and a few years later, flowers and leaves of the eglantine. By 1230 many species were clearly discernible, details being so exact that the scholar concluded that artists must have worked from nature. And in the second half of the thirteenth century they even began to notice the delicate undulant movements of plants.[48]

This development has been explained on esthetic principles as well as by the almost mystical suggestion—put forward by Viollet-le-Duc—that the development of floral art followed the laws of nature, starting with a preference for buds (Spring), moving on to blossoms and leaves (Summer), and finally—in high Gothic work—to whole branches heavy with fruit (Autumn). Was it a mere coincidence, then, that medieval botany attained a remarkable sophistication around this time? The earliest herbals were concerned either with the supposed moral symbolism of different plants or their traditional medicinal uses. But a book, *Circa Instans*, appearing around 1160, revealed a marked interest in plants for their own sake. And the herbal of Rufinus, dated about 1290, was "descriptive botany in the modern sense."[49]

Similarly, early animal representation in art followed closely the old bestiaries, which were full of theological didacticism and fantasy. Progress in the science of zoology—and, derivatively, artistic realism— was stimulated by the arrival in the West, during the thirteenth century, of many animals from the Orient: elephants, camels, leopards, monkeys, giraffes. Frequent reference has been made to the "proud note" that thirteenth-century architect Villard de Honnecourt put down beside his drawing of a lion in his famous sketchbook: "Know well that this lion was sketched from life."[50] The drawing is hardly realistic [Pl. 61] and it might even be questioned whether Villard actually saw a lion. However, it is likely that he did but was so overwhelmed by the experience that he merely jotted down the conventional image that was already in his mind's eye. That he could observe nature closely is amply demonstrated by his many other drawings of more familiar animals.

The developing interest in zoology in the Middle Ages is symbolized by the astonishing researches of Emperor Frederick II of Germany, one of the greatest of early Western experimental scientists. He wrote a treatise on falconry that was full of acute personal observations regarding the habits of winged creatures, many of which he arranged to be delivered from distant lands for study. He had ostrich eggs transported from Egypt to test the report that they could be hatched by the sun and exploded the fable that barnacle geese were hatched from barnacles by having some of these shellfish brought down from the North, concluding that the fable had risen from ignorance of the actual nesting places of the geese. He tested whether vultures found their food by sight or smell by sealing off their eyes and carried on many other experiments, sometimes on living humans.[51]

That artists were slower in developing their powers of psychological observation stemmed to some extent from the persistence of dogmatic taboos in the portrayal of religious figures. Expressionistic variety was more readily developed in the presentation of devils, monsters, and evil spirits. The reason is obvious. The more striking their delineation the greater the terror or revulsion they would call forth. But the quest for variety here, while often producing caricatures of the most naïve kind, did come up now and then with some marvelously effective delineations. That artists enjoyed this freedom of presentation is attested by the frequently zestful character of such work.

In the slow emergence of fidelity in portraiture an important role was probably played by those small, unobtrusive self-portraits by which many artists laid claim to their work. These early "signatures" were usually very elementary and it might seem exaggerated to attach too much importance to such a piece as the architect's carving at Laon, for example, in which the sole distinguishing feature is the cut of his hair and beard.[52] And yet one cannot minimize such elements. Hardly more subtle than a popular nickname as yet—like

"Red" or "Curly"—their importance lay in their revelation of a new turn of mind—or eye—in medieval artists, showing that they had begun to look for differentiating traits in individuals. The rest would not be long in coming! Besides, in the self-portraits the search for distinguishing features was dictated by a solid urge: the demonstrable proof of authorship. In a new work, based on examples from Central Europe, a scholar has gathered an immense collection of such self-portraits, which show a steady "naturalistic" development.[53]

Similarly, in preparing funerary effigies artists seemed strongly impelled to give faithful representations, as if careful identification rather than flattery was the major motive. Not many thirteenth-century individuals went as far as one Parisian lady who "from humility" had herself painted naked on her tombstone: "Thus I was born, thus I am prepared to rise."[54] But others did not mind being shown squint-eyed, flat-nosed, or with other unflattering features as they prepared to face their Maker, confident that he had a different set of values from those prevailing on earth.[55] It was possibly from an impulse of the same order that the burial piece of Isabelle d'Aragon was produced, in 1270. The wife of Philippe III was killed in a fall on the return of the royal family from the disastrous last Crusade and her husband evidently decided on the spot that a monument be erected to his young wife. A mold was taken of the dead woman's face, then the flesh was boiled off her bones, as was customary, and the latter carried home for burial at Saint-Denis.

But, most astonishingly, the artist at Cosenza, in Southern Italy, who took the death mask of St. Louis' daughter-in-law and then proceeded to do her mortuary statue, did not seek to prettify any of her features but copied faithfully the molded face, with its pathetically twisted mouth, swollen jaw, and imprint of the deep-jagged wound [Pl. 63]. The plaster cast must then have been done away with for when, fifteen years later, another portrait of Isabelle was made, this one for the tomb at Saint-Denis, it was purified of the previous touching distortions and looks like any other conventional sculpture of the type.[56]

What made it possible for artists to begin to perceive the varying individuality of their subjects? It certainly was not the result of such accidents, which could only have brought into focus a tendency that must have been growing more and more overt. Yet even this trend followed a zigzag path. As we saw in the case of Villard de Honnecourt's lion, an artist might think he was copying nature when actually he was still far off the mark. Late thirteenth-century portrayals of burghers, on the other hand, at times present what appear to be extraordinary likenesses, as in the great dye-merchants' ("waidiers") relief at Amiens [see Pl. 56]. One seems to be witnessing a scene of bargaining before the sacks of woad and the expressions and gestures of the two men, one tall and slim, the other short and heavyset, are strikingly "true to life."

Idealization in the handling of royalty was habitual but not inevitable. The

62. *Naumburg Cathedral, Germany* (13th century). Ekkehard and Uta, donors.

portraits of St. Louis and his queen at Notre-Dame are highly stylized. But other work of the same kind and period is less so, the most extraordinary example in this category being those unforgettable portraits of Ekkehard and Uta, at Naumburg cathedral [Pl. 62]. Though these statues are located in Germany, it would be hazardous to identify the nationality of their artist. There was in general much international traffic among artists of the time, and in the case of the Master of Naumburg, his first works have been traced to Amiens.[57]

Even in representations of Christ, Mary, and the Apostles, in which idealization continued longest to be practiced, increased technical competence joined with more acute observation and what we might term the "spirit of the time" to bring about an inevitable individuation. In fact, one finds strongly marked personalities among some of the finer twelfth-century carvings, such as the

63. *Paris, Musée des Monuments Français*. Funerary statue (mold) of Isabelle d'Aragon (13th century). The original was done at Cosenza, Italy, and is in the cathedral there.

64. *Moissac, Church of Saint-Pierre*. Portal pillar of south façade (12th century). Jeremiah.

65. *Chartres Cathedral*. North porch (13th century). St. John the Baptist.

66. *Notre-Dame de Paris* (13th century). Adam. Now in Cluny Museum.

67. *Chartres Cathedral*. West façade, south portal (12th century). Aristotle.

trumeau figures of Moissac and Souillac and the great façade statues of Saint-Denis and Chartres [Pl. 64].

William Koehler has associated this development with strong influences deriving from Byzantine art, which in turn had inherited a rich legacy from classical antiquity. Two revolutionary ideas—that of the articulated body and that of the animated figure—had been brought in from the Near East, he argued, cresting at Chartres in the mid-twelfth century as "the cornerstones of a new style, the Gothic." Coinciding with these major changes in the plastic arts was a great resurgence of interest in psychological problems among Christian writers, the author added.[58] In monumental art the trend developed to the point where in the north porch at Chartres cathedral the head of John the Baptist becomes so subtle, so refined, as almost to argue modeling from life [Pl. 65].

Certainly, that seems to be the source of the anatomical fidelity of the naked Adam that once stood on Notre-Dame's façade and is now at the Cluny museum [Pl. 66].

The trend to naturalism in portraiture appears relentless. Artists looked more and more outward and carved and painted more and more faithfully what they saw. This was not a chance development or the result of special esthetic laws but a response to powerful influences in the life of the time. Its beating pulse drew all along with it: the spurt of industry and commerce prompting new methods and inventions; increased use of metals stimulating interest in metallurgy; refinement of clothes rendering work with dyes and other chemicals essential; the imperious demand for food for a swiftly growing population stimulating the agricultural arts, new cultivation methods and crops, plant experimentation, and development of animal husbandry.

Artists of the twelfth and especially the thirteenth century had come out of the cloister, André Michel has pointed out. "The atelier in which they worked was no longer a closed chapel, a seminary, or a high chamber." They worked from nature, "mother of heresies," producing iconographic innovations against which Church reactionaries stormed.[59] And were they not right? For "implicit in such novelties were those forces of scientific objectivity and religious subjectivism which were eventually to destroy the unity and authority of the Latin Church."[60]

Another author saw these disturbing forces as already declaring themselves in the eleventh century, "an era of veritable evangelization," when the multitudes that the Church had brought too swiftly to Christianity* rose to affirm their will "to understand, to act, to create an entirely new ideal completely opposite to the monastic one." And it would no longer be possible to say about the art of the Middle Ages, he added, that "all was in God" for on church façades "facing God, man asserts himself. . . ."[61]

Is this not the profound, the historic significance of the presence on Chartres' breathtaking western portal of those astonishing figures of Pythagoras and Euclid and Aristotle, all busily engaged in furthering man's knowledge of the world about him [Pl. 67]? That they should be created in a bustling medieval town, where the relations between the ecclesiastics and the middle class were extraordinarily cordial, was symptomatic. For both groups had the strongest interest in fostering the new economic developments from which their mutual prosperity stemmed. This sculpture and especially the merchants' and artisans' lancets of the cathedral choir and nave are astir with a like excitement, reflect the same vital interest in all that is awake and throbbing, that creed of the active life with which the thriving, striving middle class was destined to mark all of future society.

*It has been shown that as late as the eleventh century close to half of Europe's population was still non-Christian.

CHAPTER V
THE POPULAR IMPACT

Surprising to those unacquainted with the subtle motivations of medieval iconographers are those ubiquitous Labors of the Months, which are usually found in a carved series over the church portal or along the lower registers of the façade piers. They show the peasant pruning, sowing, reaping, threshing, and in other typical acts of the cyclical seasons. The theological inspiration for these presentations can be foreshortened into the phrase: "redemption through work."[1] It was a characteristic finding of the high Middle Ages, which by a logical progression led to a *respect for work*, never before so urgently proclaimed.

This concept attained the rather incongruous, if touching, expression of the effigies of sixteen oxen being placed at the crest of Laon cathedral. It was the usual size of a team employed in building operations though the sculptured troop was, according to local tradition, inspired by one particular animal which, at a critical moment of the church's construction, miraculously appeared to help drag stone from the quarry to the building site [Pl. 68].[2]

Other illustrations of the principle of "respect for work" in French medieval art are extremely varied. Among them can be counted the capital reliefs which were installed within the church sanctuary itself at Cluny abbey, showing monks involved in miniature painting and other crafts actually practiced by them at that convent. A secular reference, on the other hand, was made by the series on Chartres' north porch depicting "The Active Life," which serve as pendants to the six figures on the other side of the arch representing "The Contemplative Life." The two groups were clearly meant to illustrate the double route to salvation recognized by the Church. However, this theological concept furnished the point of departure for works of purest topical realism, revealing all phases of the preparation of wool [Pl. 69].

More unusual but still illustrating the idea of "respect for work" is the sprawled figure of a man that is to be seen at the base of a pillar at Saint-

68. *Laon Cathedral* (13th century). Sculptured oxen on tower. 69. *Chartres Cathedral* (13th century). Woman combing wool. 70. *Saint-Gilles, Abbey Church* (12th century). Man at base of a pillar. 71. *Amiens Cathedral*. West façade (13th century). The Vice of Ingratitude.

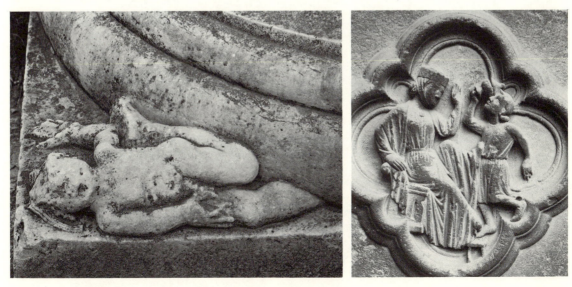

Gilles and which has been interpreted as a commemoration piece to a worker killed on the job [Pl. 70].[3] Consideration for the worker also emerges from the imagery for the Vice of Ingratitude, sometimes shown as a woman of the upper class rejecting a platter which a kneeling servant offers her, accompanying her refusal with a kick in the belly [Pl. 71].

In the widely used rural work scenes the artists' appreciation for the various occupations of the farm reveals how close the Middle Ages was to the land. Indeed, their sympathy for the drudgery of farm work makes them at times forgetful of the true character of Cain, who was a farmer, after all! He is so presented in a family work scene, together with Adam and Abel in Chartres' north porch [Pl. 72]. Elsewhere, too, he is handled sympathetically, as long as he is engaged in the arduous tasks of a farmer. Thus, in a stained-glass window at Tours, he is shown working in the hot sun while Abel, in contrast, is lazily seated as his flock does his work for him. The artists of the grain-bearing cen-

72. *Chartres Cathedral*. North porch (13th century). The First Family. Left, Adam and Abel, the latter portrayed as a shepherd; right, Cain (mutilated), digging the soil.

73. *Saint-Denis, Abbey Church* (12th century). The Labors of the Months: November.

74. *Strasbourg Cathedral* (13th century). The Labors of the Months: August.

tral plains of France may well have questioned at times the fairness of God's preference. Was it Cain's fault that the Lord loved the odor of burning animal fat? A different test should have been proposed! It is a safe bet in any case that if the Bible had been written in thirteenth-century France the roles of Cain and Abel would have been reversed.

Though the idea of redemption, which has been proposed as the explanation of the Labors of the Months, was strictly canonical, there was little restrictive iconography imposed in its application, as would have been the case in the handling of a purely religious subject. From this derived the early tendency of such scenes to vary with external conditions and to conform closely to actual life, much of it still the same today, as Joan Evans points out in a charming passage: "It is only when one travels in France at leisure that one discovers how much of the Middle Ages still exists for anyone who has time to look at it. I have seen cider-carts like those of the Bayeux Tapestry in the streets of that city; I have watched barley threshed with flails at Brioude and waited while oxen, hung in slings, were shod at Mesvres. Ploughing and sowing, reaping and binding, pruning and vintage, all the medieval labors of the months have passed before my eyes. . ."[4] [Pl. 73, Pl. 74].

Among the variations in the Labors which freedom from dogmatic restriction allowed to develop were particularities of country, climate, and tradition.* Thus

---

*It is not only in the Labors that such differences may occur. At Notre-Dame-du-Port, in Clermont-Ferrand, Eve is shown presenting Adam a bunch of grapes!

75. *Parma Cathedral Baptistry, Italy* (13th century). The Labors of the Months: September.

76. *Vézelay, Church of La Madeleine* (12th century). Honey-gathering scene.

77. *Amiens Cathedral* (13th century). The Labors of the Months: May.

there can often be seen differences between Italian and French cycles, as in the famous Labors at the Parma cathedral baptistry. Though reputedly the work of a French-influenced artist, Benedetto Antelami, several of the activities portrayed could hardly be matched in France. Thus September is pictured by two horses that are shown threshing grain by treading, a method still used in parts of Sicily [Pl. 75]. November is illustrated by a man digging up beets, a crop prominent in that area to this day. A third scene, sausage-making, presents a product for which this city is famous throughout the world.

A French scholar has shown that one series of capital reliefs at Vézelay displays "three important operations in the gathering of honey, which individuals, using known objects, accomplish with logical gestures that are in keeping with the habitual practices of ancient and even modern apiculturists. . . ." The writer stresses the extraordinary exactness of detail used by the artist in his presentation, alluding in particular to the way the peasants drive the bees from the full cone to an empty one by using smoke and the beating of sticks. One man activates the fire with a bellows and the cheeks of two others are bloated, their mouths evidently being filled with water, which they will blow at the bees if they get angry. A fourth peasant armed with a knife is carving the honey from the wax cells of a previously prepared comb [Pl. 76].[5]

James C. Webster, in a comprehensive study on the subject, has illustrated how differences in climate have caused shifts in the arrangement of the Labors.

Reaping, he points out, "will generally occur in June in Italian cycles, in July in French, and in August in German and English cycles."[6] Proverbs tend to show the same variations, he says, quoting the English saying, "March grass never did good," which in Norway runs "April's growth is rarely good."[7] Another author has referred to other differences of this kind. Thus in Italy the peasant is already shown trimming the vine in February, a month when his French equivalent is still warming himself at the fire.[8] English artists were so meticulous about climatic differences, Webster notes, that when they copied the cycles from French models after the Conquest, while still naming the months in the original language, they nevertheless displaced several of the work scenes, in keeping with actual practice on English farms.[9]

There are other exclusively national usages in these scenes. Thus weeding (June) is an English innovation. In Swiss glass, Winter is the Snow-Bringer, causing white flakes to fall by striking clouds with a staff. Peculiarly Italian are a hornblower (March), shown as a man with blown hair, a symbol of the wind, and a thorn-extractor. Also typically Italian is the flower-bearer (April). But a similar allegorical expression of joy at the return of the year's most fragrant time can be found in French cycles also (for May, however), as in the truly poetic quatrefoil at Amiens, where an elderly peasant sits amid lush foliage and warbling birds, dreaming on nature [Pl. 77]. But the month of May in the Gallic series is—exceptionally—most often granted to the seignior, who is shown riding or leading a horse, his favorite falcon clutching his extended finger.

The allegorical scenes occurring in the medieval cycles reveal the persistence of certain pantheistic motives of antique chronographs. Moreover, the mystical attitude toward the natural rhythms as reflected in the seasons is often rendered explicit in the medieval Labors through association with the signs of the zodiac [Pl. 78]. But the medieval art departed from its ancient models in one extremely significant way: by emphasizing real work scenes in contrast to the purely passive references in the antique works to the beauties of nature and the changing seasons.[10]

This accent on active work seems too marked, too insistent, not to have had a topical reference. Pointing to the same conclusion is the fact that the work cycles had almost disappeared, even from manuscript art, during the deep Middle Ages. Then they cropped up suddenly again in the eleventh century and exploded onto all the façades of France in the twelfth.[11] It can hardly be a total coincidence that this period parallels the inception of the Church's great "colonization" program, which was carried out mainly by its monastic orders.

These groups had acquired enormous grants of land, first as expiatory offerings prior to the anticipated world's end in the Year Thousand, then as votive gifts in gratitude that the dreaded Judgment Day had been put off. Added to the large holdings already in possession of religious organizations, which the increasingly successful campaign to establish obligatory celibacy for the clergy tended to perpetuate, church-owned property came in the end to monopolize a large proportion of the total acreage of France and other Western countries.

Meanwhile, as the great invasions from North and South ended during the eleventh century and as trade was resumed, cities grew and the prosperous times that resulted brought a rapid increase in the population. (Paris, for example, housed 100,000 people by the end of the twelfth century and more than twice that many by the end of the thirteenth.) More and more food was needed and as much of the new church lands were still uncleared the pressure to put them to work was doubtless very great.

The church groups set to this task with extraordinary zeal, putting to good use the experience already gained in the older monasteries. They cleared the forests, drained swamps, put up dikes against floods, irrigated, and fertilized. For this work the demand for hands exceeded anything that the monks themselves could supply. Accordingly, the system of taking on large numbers of "frères convers" (lay brothers) was instituted. The Abbaye-des-Dunes, for example, had thirty-six such "convers" listed among its personnel in 1150. A hundred years later this number had leaped to 1,248.[12] In addition to the "convers," church lands were also worked by serfs, who made up the great mass of feudalism's labor power, as well as by a lesser number of slaves.

Many writers have sought to endow the medieval Church with an anachronistic attitude toward slavery and serfdom. There was doubtless a certain amount of sincere sympathy felt by the clerics, especially the monks, for the peasants, whose labors they sometimes shared. There were even some powerful Christian voices calling for the liberation of all serfs and slaves. Nevertheless, slavery continued to be fairly widespread in Europe all the way into the fifteenth century. Slaves were owned, bought, and sold by many church dignitaries and the fact that they might be Christians or had consented to be baptized "did not bring about their liberation."[13] Slavery was eventually abolished everywhere in Europe. But this did not occur in response to a tide of moral indignation but rather because serfdom had proved to be a more productive system, answerable to changed technics and circumstances.

The great work of colonization undertaken by church groups is illustrated by a stained-glass lancet in Amiens cathedral dedicated to St. Leonard. One day, the *Golden Legend* narrates, when King Clovis was hunting in the Limousin, his wife, who had accompanied him to watch the sport, was seized by labor pains. The saint heard her cries and running to her aid delivered her safely with his prayers. Clovis offered him the entire forest as a reward but the holy man accepted only that part of it which he could circuit in one night mounted on his ass.[14] The Amiens glass shows the saint supervising the work of clearing the land donated by the grateful king.

78. *Amiens Cathedral* (13th century). Below, the Months of December, January, February, and March; above, their corresponding zodiacal signs.

The inclusion of this extraordinary scene among the more customary ones of miracles accomplished and church-building seems to underline a contemporary preoccupation of the local clerics. It could also have referred to the fact that by the mid-thirteenth century gifts of landed property by the nobles to the Church had sadly fallen off. In any event land and its cultivation and other related problems remained a major concern of churchmen. Most pressing among these problems surely were their relations with their own serfs, who in the dynamic circumstances of the times were spurred to action which occasionally took on a revolutionary scope. It was of his own serfs (and he had many) that Bishop Maurice de Sully of Paris was probably thinking when he sermonized at Notre-Dame: "Good people, pay your landed seignior what is his due. You should believe and understand that you owe him quitrents, poll taxes, percentages, services, transports, etc. Pay them all to him, at the place and time desired, and pay them in full."[15]

It is one of the interesting paradoxes of history that the peasants should have been taught their first lessons in associated action by their own ecclesiastic seigniors. The latter, unable to cope with the depredations of the nobles, organized their serfs to help control the feudal anarchy from which both commoners and the land-owning churchmen suffered. In the absence of a strong central authority, chronic local violence was the condition of life under feudalism. As a troubadour expressed it early in the twelfth century: "For the gentleman honor means stealing and pillage."[16] One noble who gave some land to an abbey pledged, in the grant charter, to "free it . . . of all those things which by violence the knights are accustomed to extort from the poor."[17]

Church property and even churches and abbeys were by no means immune to this brigandage, which became the more acute as the colonization program got under way. The Church sought to impose peace on the barons by moral persuasion. Councils and synods, starting at the end of the tenth century, decreed "That no Christian should kill another Christian."[18] But with little success. Around the year 990 Bishop Guy of Le Puy called a great outdoor meeting of all his diocese and tried to get the lay nobles formally to agree "to observe the peace, not to plunder the property of the church or the poor, and to restore what they had already taken. . . . "[19] The barons refused to take this oath but the resolute bishop, who had secretly armed some of his people, now brought them into play, forcing the nobles to sign a "Truce of God." Thus was initiated one of the most significant movements of the Middle Ages.

But the great task of pacifying the countryside was never completely fulfilled and late in the thirteenth century the prophet in the tympanum arch on Amiens' south portal still had work to do turning the weapons of war into tools of peace (Micah 4:1–3). The iconographers of this work were not making propaganda for just peace in general. They may even have had their own restless serfs in mind, fearing that they too might—like their brothers in many other places, armed with scythes and clubs, their "cavalry" mounted on asses—turn on their masters. Accused of attempting "the ruin of the institutions that rule us by the will of God and the ministry of the powers on this earth," the peasants were repeatedly crushed by the armed concert of bishops and barons. But still they kept rising.[20]

This is hardly the kind of story that would have found its way into the church art of the time. In fact, most struggles of the vassals of ecclesiastic seigniors are seldom even mentioned in the otherwise quite circumstantial chronicles that have at times come down about the institutions in question and historians have been able to piece their data together only from documents of other nearby communities. One of the most famous accounts of a peasant uprising is contained in Robert Wace's *Roman du Rou*. Written long after the events described, Wace's deeply moving narrative seems clearly to have had a contemporary model.

The peasants, stirred up by some unnamed agents, began holding meetings, "by twenties, thirties, and hundreds," to discuss their grievances. "Last year was bad and this year is worse," they complained as they listed the almost endless number of taxes and services required of them. "Everybody wants his share." No agreement of seignior or constable was a guarantee against additional extortions. Let us put an end to this, they cried, in lines that vibrate with the timeless throb of human dignity:

> We are men the same as they are:
> Our members are as straight as theirs are,
> Our bodies stand as high from ground,
> The pain we suffer's as profound.
> Our only need is courage now,
> To pledge ourselves by solemn vow,
> Our goods and persons to defend,
> And stay together to this end. . . .

If the nobles wanted to fight, they added, there would be thirty or forty peasants to every one of them, armed with clubs and pikes and hatchets and—for those who had nothing else to wield—with stones. All over the countryside the most glib and clever among them went, winning allies. Exposed by spies, however, the leaders were taken by their seigniors, who imposed a whole category of medieval tortures on them: tearing out teeth and eyes, cutting off hands, impaling some, boiling others in molten lead. The poet concluded with laconic satisfaction:

> And there the Commune did remain,
> No other villeins tried the same.[21]

But he boasted too soon.

Despite the reluctance that ecclesiastics may have had to use church art in a contemporary reference, it appears that this general rule fell down before the sharp problems they faced in keeping their serfs in check. The sudden swift rise in popularity of the sculptured Labors seems to reflect this urgency. One can see the local priest making the rounds of his church's art with his parishioners, as was indeed the established practice, urging home the subject of "redemption through work." It would be a sure solace to the peasants, weighted down by their worldly burdens, to see their familiar labors thus exalted upon the house of God.

Even more direct and effective would be the message of the parable of Lazarus and Dives, which likewise appeared on the fronts of many medieval churches. If the Unjust Rich Man, who swilled wine on earth but was denied a drop of water in Hell, represented the greedy usurer, who could his opposite

79. *Moissac, Church of Saint-Pierre.* West porch (12th century). Detail of the parable of Lazarus and Dives. Right, the rich man dines while the poor man is dying at his door; left, Lazarus in Abraham's bosom.

number (shown taken up into Abraham's Bosom) have imaged but the poor peasant (indeed, Lazarus was usually dressed as one), whose hard lot on earth assured him a brilliant heavenly reward [Pl. 79]? And could the priest have failed to refer to St. Jerome's words when describing the sufferings of the Damned, come Judgment Day: "And you, peasant, you, poor one, you will exult and laugh!"[22] Added to the satisfaction of this rosy promise to their kind was the symbolic revenge they could enjoy over Dives, the usurer, with whom they could identify the local moneylender, to whom many of them were in debt.

On first view one is inclined to consider the tradesmen's and artisans' stained-glass panels and the peasants' Labors of the Months as related manifestations. Both are concerned with men at work, after all. But there are fundamental differences in the background and presumed role of the two expressions. The tradesmen and artisans paid for the privilege of being displayed (it was in effect a kind of business advertisement) whereas the peasants were not then, and would indeed never be, in the financial position to commission art. The often touching and sympathetic descriptions of their toil were put on the churches and paid for by the clergy.

The middle class, on the other hand, were to go on paying for church art to the point, in the fourteenth and especially the fifteenth century, where they often became its leading patrons. But this would not be without a fundamental change in the social position of this class, entailing a deep-going dissociation among its members and the absorption of the wealthiest among them into a new nobility. In the process the commune, the instrument of bourgeois liberation, would be destroyed in behalf of the royal power, whose welling strength rendered it less and less tolerant of rivals. At the other extreme, the middle class would drop off the poorest artisans who would no longer be permitted to rise to the status of masters and were to constitute thereafter a permanent working class, forerunner of the modern proletariat.[23]

The workers were in no better position than the peasantry to commission art or to get their grievances or hopes expressed in church iconography. Unlike the peasants, however, upon whose labor a great part of the income of church bodies depended, the economic relationship of ecclesiastics to city workers was more occasional. Hence it is not surprising that their existence was less frequently referred to in church art. They would never attain to the splendor of the peasants' position in the Labors of the Months.

There is an extremely interesting contract, come down to us in the original manuscript, between the abbot of Saint-Aubin d'Angers and a serf named "Foulque," by virtue of which the latter was declared a freeman and a lay brother of the abbey and given an acre of vineyard and a house, in return for which he was to decorate the church with his art. He could even pass these great privileges on to his son, if the latter turned out to have his father's talents![24] The key word in the contract was "freeman" and since this was only the end of the eleventh century, "Foulque" probably went on from there to become rich and a leader of his class. The day laborers who waited outside Chartres cathedral with their tools on their backs for someone to hire them were also "free" but, at the end of the thirteenth century, this state was no longer necessarily an augury of prosperity.

Day laborers were not only free, they were also paid in money, another basic circumstance linking them with their modern brothers. Indeed, one can see among the baptistry sculpture at Parma a remarkable example in church art of hired laborers being paid in coin. Done or influenced by French-trained Benedetto Antelami, this series of carvings on the baptistry's west portal represents the "Ages of Man," a topic of medieval iconography that signified the transitoriness of this life below.

The artist had the ingenious idea of featuring the different Ages as so many individual workers, the evangelical reference being to the parable of the Laborers in the Vineyard (Matt. 20:1–16), each of the sculptured scenes representing workers hired at a different hour of the day. The carving at the top, which shows a paymaster with his purse handing over a piece of money to an old man leaning on his hoe, figures "*Senectus*," or Old Age. The men of the other Ages are also associated with the laboring class, carrying a spade, a knife, or other tools. The Second Age is represented by a youth, whose inscription reads: "HORA TERMINA PUERICIA."[25] It might have added: "And now begins your life of toil."

Whereas concrete representations of the lower classes in church art are admittedly quite limited, the question rises whether the common influence did not make itself felt in other ways. Reflections from "popular" literature are like-

wise very rare, however. The most noteworthy product of this type, the fabliaux, toward whose hundreds of thousands of verses many poets contributed,
won but a few minor allusions in church art. One favorite shows a monk trying
to teach a wolf to read. "Say 'A'!" he tells him, showing him the ABC. "Ag-
neau" (lamb), the wolf growls. The moral was: "Thus the tongue betrays the
secrets of the heart." A few others are occasionally found but they add up to
little enough [Pl. 80].

The slighting of the fabliaux by church iconographers is understandable if for
no other reason than their frequent bristling anticlericalism. Though the lower
classes were also often ridiculed by this poetry, it nevertheless seems to have
remained very popular with them. They could hardly help enjoying the misadventures of the seigniors figured by the chief characters, whose true identity
was not masked by their animal exteriors. And it sometimes occurred in the
denouement of a fabliau that when a four-legged noble was thumped by humans,
they might even be referred to as "villeins." The commoners would be accustomed to drawing advantage from works that were not created for them. Even
the swarming art of the cathedrals, so often referred to as the "Bible of the
Poor," was far from expressing their basic concerns.

And yet the voiceless laboring classes did succeed to a considerable degree
in making an imprint on this art. How the influence of the masses bears upon
the cultural expression of a period is hardly understood even for more recent
times. The matter is infinitely more cloaked for the distant past, when the
people were illiterate and left no documentary or creative trace of their own,
however fragmentary. It is only by accident that anything relating to the subject
has come down to us. Nevertheless, we cannot escape assuming that the classes
making up nine tenths of the population must have impinged upon their contemporary culture, if not in the final products of what we know as art, then at
least in its elements, the primary materials out of which art evolves.

It is a fundamental law of human communication that the sentiments and
thoughts of those whom one aims to reach must be consulted, even if only to be
combated. The medieval Church had assumed the responsibility of molding
man's spirit. In view of the pervading anarchy of the times and the great social
mobility that began with the eleventh century, the task was prodigious, if not
ultimately impossible. Even writers who assume a placid accomplishment of
this gigantic undertaking by the clerics accept a certain amount of resilience, if
not to say resistance, on the part of their wards.

When discussing the interpretation of the Prodigal Son parable in medieval
art (which some have attempted to give the theological meaning of a falling
away from and then a return to the true faith), Émile Mâle says: "It seems
that the theologians conceded to the masses this touching story," meaning as a
simple tale without doctrinal complications.[26] The word "conceded" is much
too condescending. The clerics were surely aware of the necessity to touch the

emotions of those they wished to reach. For the people would not pray at the altar that did not appeal to them. The designers of church iconography knew of their preference for certain saints, usually those who possessed attributes that had the common touch. Inevitably the clerics sought to satisfy these predilections.

Whatever their theological attributions, what the people appeared to see in these favorite blessed ones was always something "human" and easily understood. Thus it must have been greatly appealing to them that St. Christopher, whose wit was so slow that he could not learn the simplest prayer, was nevertheless able to find an important work to do. The fact that it was physical must have pleased the sturdy laborer, who could almost see himself bearing the Christ Child on his own broad shoulders. The commoner must also have felt close to St. Peter, most human of the Apostles. The ecclesiastics played up his hieratic role but the common man could weep with him when the cock crowed, and when Peter was dressed down by Christ for refusing to let him wash his feet, he too would want to cry out with all his simple heart: "Lord, not my feet only, but also my hands and my head." (John 13:9.)

The Virgin was enthroned and crowned but this majesty merely awed the commoners. It was a different Mary that drew them, the Mary of Theophilus, the Virgin who though pure herself was generous to sinners, who interceded in

80. *Saint-Benoît-sur-Loire, Abbey Church* (12th century). Two faces of a capital illustrating an animal fabliau: An ass tries to play a lyre while a man plays a viol.

behalf of even the most desperate causes. What seemed to appeal to them in Mary the Egyptian or in Magdalene, on the other hand, was the association of their own earlier sinfulness, which would help them to understand another's weakness.[27] And Magdalene's melodramatic style that was so unlike the restrained comportment of other saints—throwing her arms aloft, falling to her knees—appears to have agreed with the emotional patterns of the time, with people's sentiments mounting swiftly to extremes and exploding into extravagant outbursts and display.[28]

Some of the most popular stories, treated over and over in medieval art, were drawn from basic situations in human relationships whose appeal has not been lost to this day. The parable of the Prodigal Son (or the Forgiving Father) was one of these. It often assumed delightful touches drawn from the life of the time, as can be seen in many stained-glass lancets. The bedizened prostitutes beckon to the young man from their door, then bathe him, show him a mirror as he dresses, and thread flowers into his hair (a common usage in medieval bodily adornment) before sitting him down to a feast (see Pl. 3). But, alas, when they win all his money from him at dice, they strip the last bit of clothing from his back before putting him out. How close would the commoner feel to him when, naked and heartsick, he was set to serving pigs! But as certain as the poor man's salvation was the Prodigal Son's delivery: From this abject posture he would some day rise (see Pl. 29).

The legend of St. Eustace (or the Family Reunited) also owed its presence in the windows of so many churches to the popularity of its theme. The serf, who was not permitted to hunt in seigniorial forests (did not one peasant of the abbot of Vézelay have his eyes put out for committing this crime?), must have been touched to see the beautiful deer turn its reproachful eyes on its pursuer: It was enough to convert an unsaintly man. How sad too when the family turn back for a last look at their home; there must have been scenes like this every day in transitional France of the thirteenth century. As Eustace is driven from the boat one suddenly realizes with shock that saints never fight back, not in their own behalf. But his wife Theospita miraculously preserves her virtue, through all the years of separation and adversity. And though the reunited family end up in the martyr's pot, this was not exactly a tragedy in the medieval Christian view of things.

Sometimes a folk attitude ran counter to accepted dogma and still got itself expressed in art. This was the case with St. Joseph, for whom the commoner (and the artist reflecting his viewpoint) seems to have had slight respect. He was the virgin father, the impotent progenitor, a rather ridiculous old man whose role in the drama was difficult to understand. If iconographic tradition did not require his presence, he would undoubtedly have often been left out altogether and even so he usually appears in various ways diminished, undersized or stuck off in a corner or asleep when some important event is going on (see Pl. 22).

But, most serious of all, was a denigration to which the church scholars themselves consented. In Jesse's posterity, it was Joseph—not Mary—who was the final issue before Christ. Hence in those splendid illustrations of the Savior's family tree that summit with the Virgin and which can be seen in so many medieval churches, Joseph is robbed even of his genealogy!

In humor the folk touch is especially evident, as much in thirteenth-century French church art as in the Flemish peasant ribaldries of the seventeenth century. It is at its broadest in the supporting consoles of the large façade statues at Amiens. The drunkard lovingly embraces his pot; the gourmand sadly shows you his empty bowl; another, his face distorted with suffering, prepares to heave. Equally zestful are the figures representing a small boy or midget who serves as a sort of foil to a series of Virtues in a portal arch at Laon cathedral. As he is beaten by a switch, caught in the toils of a rope, shown in various postures of defeat, his expressive features and funny defensive gestures end by winning more sympathy than the sturdy females who can find no more useful occupation than to poke their javelin at the luckless little chap.

It is understandable that medieval artists should have been baffled by the abstract, metaphysical quality of the Virtues. Often they are nothing but a negation, a mere absence, like the series of "Shall-Nots" in the Ten Commandments. Hardly anything could have been more unrewarding than to have to translate such negative traits into art forms. Charity is the only Virtue that can call forth a positive act. In the Psychomachia sequences that appeared in so many medieval churches a curious solution was devised for this dilemma which shows every sign of a double inspiration.

The clerical mind seems to be reflected in the stalwart, masculinized female figures of the Virtues, one looking exactly the same as the others, differentiated merely by her clothing or props or by a symbol on a shield [Pl. 81]. The Vices, on the other hand, are full of popular verve and fantasy. Pride is a rider who is thrown from his wildly racing horse. Cowardice is a soldier who has dropped his sword in terror and runs away from a bounding rabbit. At Amiens and at Paris a bird looks on at this amazing performance in a kind of bemused surprise [Pl. 82]. Unchastity, though more often linked with Greed in a dramatic clerical attack focused on the wealthy middle class, is also at times included in these series, shown as a woman clutching a man in an adulterous embrace. And Discord is represented by a family squabble: man and wife have each other by the hair and drag each other about their hut, overturning objects or spilling the pot with the evening's supper on the floor [Pl. 83].

It can be safely assumed that the common people have played an important role in the engendering of the apocrypha. The pressure from them for more information about the scriptural figures they loved must always have been insistent, encouraging visionaries to "see" intermediate incidents that could fill out the terse outlines of so many evangelical stories. These new details probably

Notre-Dame de Paris. Façade base, central portal (13th century):
81. The Virtue of Courage.   82. The Vice of Cowardice.

invaded liturgical drama first by a kind of literary osmosis, then finally forced their acceptance for artistic treatment.

The elaboration of the story of the Adoration of the Magi by such accretions is typical and imbued with the folk spirit. Scripture is exceedingly brief on the subject. Only Matthew tells of the "wise men from the east" who came to worship the Infant Christ. Popular fantasy made kings of them, arriving on horse or (later) camel, accompanied by a retinue. Their number is not mentioned but the mystic "three" must have suggested itself as a matter of course. In this manner, too, their ages could be symmetrically distributed so as to take in the whole range of mankind: twenty, forty, sixty. The Bible does not name them but this deficiency was likewise supplied, by the pseudo-Bede: Melchior, Caspar, and Balthazar. This old writer also described Balthazar's color as being dark (*"fuscus"*), but it was not until the fifteenth century, when the great wave of oceanic exploration brought massive contact with African Negroes, that he appeared in art as a member of that race.[29]

Whatever other elements there are in church art of an upper-class emphasis,

83. *Amiens Cathedral*. Façade base (13th century). The Vice of Discord.

there is one theme whose applicability is universal. This is the Judgment Day, whose minatory message, spread across the great central portals of France's Gothic cathedrals, warned of the fate awaiting all men, high and low, fortunate and miserable alike. All the people of the time believed in its terrifying portent: the gaping Leviathan spouting flame and sulfur, its rabble of devils stridently contesting for the risen souls, promptly beginning their unspeakable tortures on those who fell into their hands.

No amount of wealth or power on earth could protect their possessor on that day. This was the central thought of the Christian faith, the vital fiber of its mass appeal: equality in death, equality before the Judge at the final reckoning. The clerics never wavered in their adherence to this doctrine and every tympanum had its crowned and mitered heads among the Rejected, women in the splendid costume of the bourgeoisie, and armed knights, whose violence against the weak and innocent would now be repaid a thousandfold. In this time of feudalism and rigid class division here was a striking symbol of democracy, a Democracy of the Damned as it were [Pl. 84].

84. *Reims Cathedral* (13th century). Detail of the Judgment Day.
The "Democracy of the Damned."

On the other side of the portal, among the ranks of the Chosen, the same inexorable impartiality prevailed, in what might with equal justice be called the Democracy of the Blessed. They were ordinary folk for the most part and one or two would be individuals bearing the mark of the upper classes. Usually, however, the lead would be given to a member of the lower orders: a peasant or a pilgrim or a poor monk.

The message of this great unfurled drama must have been potently effective. Whether chosen or rejected, it said, each individual's ultimate destiny was now beyond the partisan verdict of wordly judges. The laboring classes, though involved with all humanity in this fearful last test, could nevertheless see in it an aspect of their deepest longing, the final realization of that equality which Christ had promised in eternity but which seemed unattainable on earth.

CHAPTER VI
THE CHURCH FIGHTS HERESY:
WITH FLAME, WITH SWORD—
AND WITH ART

Few structures are more familiar to art lovers than Albi cathedral: its long elliptical form, its red-brick walls, high and smooth as those of a fortress. Yet even the best of photographs will hardly prepare one for the startling reality, particularly if one approaches the church from the southwest, crossing the small stream just below the Tarn and then going under the railroad bridge and up the escarpment.

Arriving at the western end of the church, one feels that one has somehow switched directions. Instead of the usual façade one finds an immense tower-keep that resembles an elevated apse. There is no sculpture or decoration of any kind, not even a door. Just vertical slickness. This continues virtually unchanged as one makes one's way around the enormous, thick-walled structure.

The church has but two doors in all, compared to the six or more that other cathedrals usually possess. That at the north once opened by means of a draw-bridge into the bishop's palace, which was as forbidding and shutoff as the cathedral itself. That at the south is reached by a long, high ramp and its flamboyant porch was clearly a much later afterthought. The church has no transept and the apse, which is turned toward the city, presents the beetling form of a second donjon. All windows are extraordinarily narrow and unrecessed, starting far off the ground [Pl. 85].

Inside, all artistic embellishment is of a much later date than the basic structure. The chapels are merely a tardy adaptation of the spaces between the powerful vertical buttresses which gird the church like the ribs of a carapace. The florid sanctuary and all the rest of the ornamentation strike one as something that has been borrowed for some celebration and would soon be removed, leaving the church in its primitive barren and hollow state. Had it been meant to be prayed in at all?

As one continues to contemplate this strangely anomalous structure, much becomes clearer about the extraordinary conditions under which it was fabricated, at the end of the great heretical movement which had raged in the South for two centuries and to which this city had given its name. A lurid light is focused on the amazing brain that had conceived it. Rewarded by a grateful Church with this episcopacy, Bernard de Castanet, the "most terrible of inquisitors,"[1] had set his heart on the cathedral as a personal memorial, devoting to it a considerable portion of the immense fortune that he confiscated from "heretics." Bishop Bernard made a fine art of extortion. When, for example, the cathedral's building funds ran out, in 1299, a new witch-hunt directed against twenty-five of the city's leading citizens brought an ample replenishment.[2]

All of this scarcely endeared the prelate to the people of his diocese, who greeted him with cries of "Death!" when he appeared in the city. Bernard finally had to be withdrawn from Albi, but he was compensated with the see of Le Puy and later raised to the cardinalship. But his stay at Albi had lasted long enough for him to put the mark of a bristling citadel on his cathedral. And there was reason enough. Though this was almost half a century after the fall of Montségur, "the heresy was disarmed but it was far from being destroyed."[3] The cathedral has been called a monument to "the inexpiable battle" of the Church against "a people in revolt."[4] Also it has been suggested that this "lair of the helmeted inquisitor" should have been named after St. George rather than the gentle Cecilia.[5] But the Cappadocian knight had gone about the country fighting Christ's enemies whereas the Savior's defenders at Albi preferred to shut themselves up in their high keep, spacious enough to hold a great troop, where they could watch from their battlemented gallery for the approach of some errant Christians who might have got the strange notion of wanting to pray in this Temple of Mars.

The justified fear that seems to have determined the form of Albi cathedral had rather general play in this area, where churches long after the suppression of the heresy continued to be built to fit the needs of defense.[6] Often their construction was imposed as penance. At Najac-en-Rouergue the inquisitors even fixed the dimensions of the church and specified that its vault must be stone-covered.[7] The long gap in building occasioned by the military campaigns occurred at the time of greatest change in style, and many churches, which had been begun in Romanesque form were completed in the Gothic.[8] The sobriety of Southern Gothic has been offered as a proof of spiritual exhaustion resulting from the Albigensian "crusade." It is certain in any case that the structural simplicity of these churches—usually featured by a single nave and a truncated apse and the absence of external decoration—was better adapted to military defense than the Northern exemplars, with their large, open bays and adorned exteriors.[9]

Still another phase of the duel with the heresy and its repercussions on architecture in Southern France seems to be exemplified by the famous "Jacobins" church of Toulouse. Begun in 1230, it initiated a long series of Dominican structures, whose form reflected the primary purpose they were meant to serve: preaching against the heresy. The salient feature in the Toulouse edifice was the row of high narrow central columns that served to open the great double nave to the throngs that gathered about the raised, centrally located, carefully focused pulpit. The altar was clearly secondary in this church-auditorium (in which the vernacular replaced the liturgical Latin, besides), where the ritual victory of Christ had to await the outcome of a more immediate threat [Pl. 86].

Heresy (or theological nonconformism) was a perennial in the history of the medieval Church. In the eleventh and the beginning of the twelfth century, when Europe was coming out of its defensive retreat and when social changes of broad scope got under way, the accompanying intellectual renovation gave rise to many unorthodox ideas. While most of these manifestations "never dreamed of assailing the essential truths of Christianity,"[10] some did advocate drastic revisions of basic dogma.

The two leading heresies of the eleventh century, aimed at the Eucharist and the Trinity, were successfully suppressed within the hierarchical apparatus. It

85. *Albi Cathedral* (13th–14th century). The cathedral-fortress.
At right can be seen a part of the bishop's palace.

was different in the twelfth and especially the thirteenth century, however, when heresies popped up in numerous places all at once. The general source of inspiration was the religiously fecund Near East, whence revived Manichean concepts penetrated into Italy and France by way of Dalmatia. In Italy the infection was widespread, affecting the entire region from the Alps down into Tuscany and beyond. At Rome itself the ranks of the heretics swelled and at Milan, Brescia, Florence, and other cities it was strong among all classes, even counting a good number of priests among its converts.

In France the greatest concentrations of the heresy were found in its economically and culturally most advanced regions: in Burgundy and Champagne; in the industrial North, where it so infiltrated the ranks of the weavers that the word *textor* became synonymous with heretic; and especially in the cultivated urban centers of Languedoc and Provence. Here the Cathars missionized openly, disputing with Church spokesmen at fairs and markets. Rome sent a series of legates into this area to combat the infection, among them the famed St. Bernard. But the people beat kettles to drown out his voice. The great mystic wrote despairingly of the low estate to which orthodoxy had fallen in this region: "The churches are without congregations, the faithful without priests . . . the sacraments are despised, the holidays no longer celebrated, men die in sin, the grace of baptism is denied to infants."[11]

The chief grievances of commoners against the Catholic clergy were their worldliness and their immorality. It was symptomatic that one of the leading heresies of France assumed the name of "The Poor Men of Lyon" and that its founder, Peter Waldo, a wealthy merchant, gave up his fortune and began preaching a return to the poverty and humbleness of the primitive Church. It was the same basic idea, though this one operated from within the Church, that launched the Franciscan movement, characterized by its founder's nickname, "Il Poverello," and by his legendary act of stripping himself naked when abandoning his rich mercantile family.*

As for the morals of the clergy they were so notoriously bad that the very name of priest was used proverbially in pejorative context, people saying: "I'd rather be a priest than do this or that."[12] They were said to hate the clergy "worse than Jews."[13] And when clerics went out into the world they hid their tonsure.[14] The lives of high ecclesiastics were no more exemplary. One authority maintained that a majority of the bishops in 1075 failed to live according to the canonic law and there was open mention of the "bastards of canons" at a Church council.[15] Pope Gregory VII died in exile, his great "reform" still largely a dead letter. The Cistercians carried his program into the twelfth

---

*Hardly accidental, it would seem, was the bourgeois penchant for heresy at a time when the burghers were often at odds with their church seigniors. Repeatedly excommunicated, they looked elsewhere for spiritual outlets in the end. And when the priest at Vézelay ran out on the embattled burghers, they buried their dead themselves.

86. *Toulouse, Jacobins Church* (13th century). View of the interior, built
to hold large audiences in the Dominicans' campaign against heresy.

century but even in the thirteenth there was still much that needed to be done in this regard.

At the beginning of the latter century the heresy in Southern France surged stronger than ever and the Church was in desperate straits. To suppress the heresy by force called for the collaboration of the lay sovereigns of this area. But the latter took advantage of the Church's weakened position to advance their own interests. The murder, at Saint-Gilles, in 1208, of the papal legate, Pierre de Castelnau, was shrewdly exploited by the Church to gain the armed intervention it needed. The military force was supplied chiefly by the Northern barons, with the discreet support of King Philippe-Auguste. The civil war, one of the most sanguinary in French history, lasted over twenty years. Dozens of towns were destroyed, tens of thousands of "heretics" massacred and other thousands burned at the stake.

While the religious phase of the "crusade" was, according to the lights of those conducting it, sincerely motivated, many of them undeniably harbored secular and pecuniary aims as well. Its history is one long balance sheet of confiscations, shared by religious and lay leaders alike and facilitated by Rome's preliminary mass lifting of the feudal vows that had been made to "apostate" seigniors, in the entire disputed territory. The cross-bearing knights had their eternal status cleared for any crimes they might commit by being given papal absolution in advance. Even the pope benefited from the expropriations, getting a settlement of three deniers "per hearth."[16] But the king was, of course, the greatest beneficiary since, by the treaty of 1229, the vast territories of the Comte de Toulouse went over to the crown and the royal power was well on the way to establishing its hegemony over all of France.

The chief instrument of this conquest, Comte Simon de Montfort, was fated to die before its consummation. Of Norman origin, he was a typical feudal personage, mixing worldly and spiritual aims in balanced parts. It has been suggested that the window he gave to Chartres cathedral, which was just then in the great fever of its first building campaign, was intended as an ex voto offering for the success of his "crusade."[17] Yet, despite a series of military victories, he never seemed able to consolidate his gains. Finally, in 1218, a kind of tiredness or fatalism took hold of him, if we credit that stirring poetic chronicle of the campaign, the *Chanson de la croisade albigeoise*.

Once more the people of Toulouse, nobles and merchants, tradesmen and artisans, had taken their city back from the hated Northern conquerors. Once more Simon prepared for an attack. Early that day, the troubadour narrates, he lingered at mass, which he heard every morning. When told of a sortie in strength by the beleaguered townsmen and that his presence was urgently needed, he replied: "Not until I've seen my Redeemer!" The mass continued its measured course. At last the priest raised the host and Simon recited the

Nunc Dimittis and left for his final battle, already fully armed and crying out over and over: "Jesus, give me victory or death."[18]

Though the narrative of Simon's last communion may be apocryphal, the circumstances of the story are of the highest interest for the iconography of heresy. That Simon could expect to "see" the host at mass was due to a new practice adopted by the Church in the observance of this Sacrament and which was a categorical response to one of the major challenges of the Cathars: the symbolism of the Eucharist. The "elevation of the host" in the missal ceremony was first introduced at Paris between 1196 and 1208. For this purpose, the altar on which the chalice was placed, a simple table previously, was transformed into a kind of raised tabernacle. Other church decisions confirmed this featuring of the Eucharist. The dogma of transubstantiation was enunciated in 1215, followed in the second half of the century by the establishment of the feast of *Corpus Christi* and the first processions in honor of the host.[19] All of these innovations figured prominently in church art and can be considered primary echoes of the fight against the heresy.

But they were by no means the only changes stemming from this impulsion. The iconographic response of the Church to the heterodoxies of the time was varied, subtle, and often extremely effective. Armed with hundreds of years of experience in expressing dogma in artistic terms, church iconographers sedulously searched out convincing demonstrations of the truth and efficacy of the Catholic tenets. This had already begun to happen in response to the eleventh-century heresies, as can be seen in the tympanum of the now destroyed church at Bourges, Saint-Ursin, where the Sacrament of the Communion is stressed in a subtle but inescapable manner. This occurs in the Labors of the Months cycle, for December, which presents the familiar scene of a man seated at a convivial board. However, the table has been changed to an altar and in place of the peasant who is usually set before it we find an exalted ecclesiastical figure, meant to represent Christ, in fact! The loaf he is prepared to cut has a cross on it and the fish on the table completes the reference to the miracle of the Loaves and Fishes, which at the time was understood to symbolize the Eucharist.

An entirely similar representation at Souvigny, about forty miles southeast of Bourges, indicates that the Saint-Ursin relief was not an accidental, isolated occurrence but an iconographic idea that had evidently been thought about. At Souvigny, moreover, the presence of six fishes and a raised chalice render the symbolism irrefutable [Pl. 87]. Christ's gesturing in both these works, it has been suggested, denotes a pointed reply to the attack on the Eucharist by the French heresiarch, Bérenger de Tours, who was obliged to declare at a Church synod at Rome, in 1059, in acknowledgment of his error, that in the Eucharist it was the body and blood of Christ that were "handled and broken by the priests' hands and chewed by the teeth of the faithful."[20]

The minds of church thinkers were so preoccupied with the arguments of heretics and the importance of replying to them that even esthetic theories were adapted to combat the Catharist challenge. One such theory was aimed at its dualistic opposition of Good and Evil as the twin creative divinities. All things are good because they come from God, a leading church writer countered. Even monsters may participate in beauty, he added, because they are a part of the whole and fit into the divine pattern.[21]

That these were not merely cloistered lucubrations is illustrated by the recorded reply of a peasant at an Inquisition. God could not possibly have created such harmful things as wolves which devoured sheep, he argued. This was the Devil's work.[22] The Church could not afford to ignore simple, commonsense views as persuasive as this and a beautiful artistic concept covering it is contained in the superb capital reliefs from the convent of La Daurade at Toulouse, presenting the story of Job.

Here all the afflictions that are brought on the Patriarch's head are the active work of devils. They pull his house down, kill his children, crash stones upon his flock. In the midst of all this adversity Job remains resolute, an example to suffering believers whose difficulties could not possibly be as great as his. When the Patriarch's patience is at last rewarded it is an angel that ministers

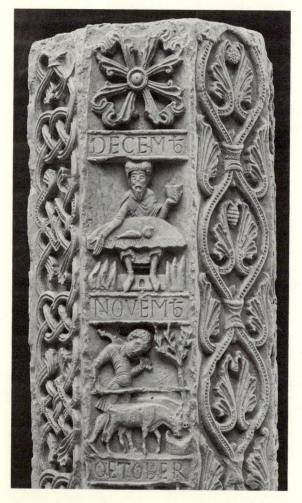

to him, treating his boils with the finest of medieval medicinal herbs and covering his naked body with shining raiment that dazzles the eyes of his family and friends. It all adds up to a brilliant and concise sermon on the Catholic concepts of sin and redemption, told in some of the most fascinating imagery of medieval art [Pl. 88]. At Chartres' north porch, on the other hand, the same idea is concentrated into one great carving that shows the Devil presiding over Job's sufferings [Pl. 89].

87. *Souvigny, Church of Saint-Pierre* (12th century). The Labors of the Months (mold): December. Actually a representation of Christ performing the miracle of the Loaves and Fishes. Now at Musée Lapidaire Farinier.

88. *Toulouse, Former Convent of La Daurade* (12th century). Capital relief: An angel treats Job's boils with medicinal herbs.

89. *Chartres Cathedral.* North porch (13th century). The sufferings of Job, presided over by the Devil.

The reply of orthodox art to heresy emphasized the most heavily challenged points of the Catholic doctrine. Thus as the heresy cast doubt on the divinity of Christ, scenes of the Savior in Transfiguration and in Majesty were multiplied to demonstrate his double nature as God and man. As for the Crucifixion, the heretics found the idea of Christ's suffering on the Cross repugnant. Even orthodox iconographers, as late as the twelfth century, avoided showing Christ in agony, presenting him habitually with his eyes open, his body calm, his manner relaxed. A jutting board was even placed beneath his feet so as to avoid the distressful notion that the full weight of his body might be tearing at the pierced holes in his hands and feet.

This reticence started to change in the second half of the twelfth century and especially in the thirteenth, when Christ began to be shown dying or already dead, his eyes closed, his head having dropped to his shoulder, the blood pouring from the wound caused by the lance in his side. Even the elimination of one of the nails that riveted Christ's body to the Cross was not without its dramatic purpose. This change was produced by twisting one of his feet upon the other, which had the effect of accentuating the sense of his suffering.

Whatever the humane view of such details their effect upon their audience can hardly be questioned. Was this naturalistic expressionism the result of a sudden emotionalization of medieval artists? It was, more likely, a determined assertion, in reply to the denials by heretics, that Christ *had* suffered on the Cross, had suffered infinitely, and by virtue of that suffering had brought man the possibility of infinite grace. We can assume that this emphasis on emotional imagery moved the faithful powerfully and on that account was found to be highly effective antiheretical propaganda. This in itself would have constituted a strong encouragement to its further exploitation. However, we must also recognize the fact that once begun, the tendency toward heightened emotionalization could have taken on a momentum of its own, leading eventually to those extreme representations of Christ's agony: his blood gushing from every wound, his body distorted, his forehead lacerated by the crown of thorns, his mouth ripped open to let out its supreme cry of anguish.

The Crucifixion over the right portal at Saint-Gilles, one of the first to be given so prominent a position, may have been related to events in this area, where Pierre de Bruys had been preaching his cross-burning heresy. Though Pierre was burned at the stake on the square outside the basilica, his disciples continued his heretical campaign. At the other end of the façade is another scene that would seem to reflect the contest that took place here for the souls of the faithful. Among those present at Christ's Entry into Jerusalem are two men at the extreme right, one of whom seeks gently to draw his companion toward the Savior—back into the Church, in other words. It is difficult to think that this unusual bit of quiet drama had any but a contemporary reference [Pl. 90].

Even more sharply assailed by the heretics than her son, the Virgin of the

90. *Saint-Gilles, Abbey Church* (12th century). Procession greeting Christ on his Entry into Jerusalem. Note the two men at the extreme right, the one urging the other to join the procession.

twelfth and thirteenth centuries may be considered to have won her exalted position in orthodox art, in part at least, as a reply to this denigration. It is extremely interesting that the East, where heretical doubts over the nature of Mary as the mother of God originated, also supplied one of the most effective iconographic responses to this skepticism: the legend of Theophilus. It should be recalled that the vidame's apostasy was Devil-inspired and that, according to Manichean belief, the Church was a creation of Satan. Theophilus, under the influence of this heretical doctrine, renounced Christ and the Virgin. (See Ch. II and Pl. 10.) But when he recanted, Mary promptly forgave him, winning him back to the Church and to a belief in its divine creation, thus flouting the arguments of the devil-heretics.[23]

As other reassertions of challenged Catholic dogmas, artistic representations of the Sacraments grew more and more common. Representations of the Confession, for example, began to appear, as in the scenes dedicated to Mary the Egyptian. This reformed prostitute, who lived a lonely penitential life in her desert hideout for almost half a century, had but a single request when she was discovered by the Abbot Zozime: to be confessed. The cleric was so moved by her radiant saintliness he kissed the ground where her feet stepped as she retired, after bidding him to return within a year with the Eucharist. This he did, carrying the chalice and the wafer all the way out into the wasteland. And when he came back once more the following year, the holy woman was dead and he had only to bury her [Pl. 91].

In this legend and in its artistic representation was enclosed the central doctrine of the Catholic faith, residing in the two basic Sacraments of Penitence and Communion. But it was especially on the symbolic sacrifice of the Eucharist that the church iconographers concentrated, using every opening that the liturgy offered. Scenes of the Last Supper, where Christ first enunciated this mystery, began appearing everywhere. The frequency of scenes of the Marriage at Cana, whose miracle of the water changed to wine was considered as symbolic of the Eucharist, can also be attributed to this impulsion.

At Charlieu a splendid sculptured setting of this miracle is set off by a lintel where the animals offered in the bloody sacrifices of the Old Testament are shown being led to slaughter: a calf, a ram, a goat. In another tympanum at the same church the Lamb of God is presented standing alone on the Christian altar, once again symbolizing the mystic sacrifice of the Eucharist. These subtle contrasts were all carefully explained by Peter the Venerable, famed head of Cluny abbey, in a treatise prepared to combat the heresy of Pierre de Bruys

91. *Former Abbey Church of Alspach* (12th century). Mary the Egyptian receiving Communion from the hands of Abbot Zozime. Now at the Colmar Musée d'Unterlinden.

and his followers. The ecclesiastic's arguments were descriptively conceived, almost as though the great debate were being conducted through artistic symbols, *these* artistic symbols in fact: "The ox, the calf, the ram, the goat soaked with their blood the altars of the Jews; only the Lamb of God, which cleanses the sins of the world, stands on the altar of the Christians." [24]

Scenes showing the presentation of the host to the faithful by clergymen of high and low degree were in all likelihood also meant to vindicate the challenged role of the priest. At Bourges, for example, in the façade Judgment Day sculpture, the point is graphically made in a kind of polemic of images. On one side is a Christian taking Communion from a priest at an altar: An angel is prepared to bear him straight up to Heaven. Opposite is a heretic who rejects the Eucharist: A devil already has hold of him. Inside the same church, a lovely lancet presents a similar confrontation, this one over the Sacrament of the Confession. The man rejecting it is rich, a usurer with his moneybag, who is shown receiving his merited punishment in the flames of Hell, which a devil agitates with a fork [Pl. 92].

In the St. Denis lancet, likewise at Bourges, the priesthood is elevated to its highest eminence when Christ is shown entering the jail to give the saint his wafer, which significantly has a cross on it. In his other hand the Savior holds a Communion chalice. The great amount of this kind of polemical art in Bourges would indicate a strong surge of heresy in this area. It was also widespread at the prominent fair town of Troyes, where a superb lancet at the cathedral presents an unusual setting of the Marriage at Cana. The miracle itself occurs on several levels, in such breadth and detail as to foreshadow Renaissance interpretations. There is repeated pouring of wine from pitcher to pitcher by the servants. These proceedings are agitatedly discussed by a group of men, among whom are several who seemingly contest the miracle. Wearing conical hats while their opponents are bareheaded, these quarrelers are doubtless meant to represent Jews, whom many ecclesiastics regarded as the original heretics, the heretics par excellence. (This disputation has been more fully discussed in an article published since the first printing of this book.[25])

In a famous sculptured scene at Reims (a prominent center of the heresy, where the Inquisition was also very active), the origin of the Eucharist is presumably carried far back into hallowed antiquity. According to one interpretation, the carving shows Melchizedek offering a wafer to Abraham before the latter goes off to battle [Pl. 93].[26] The iconographer who contrived this idea would have been no more disturbed by the anachronism than he was in presenting the ancient priest-king in the guise of a medieval bishop and the father of Jewry as a fully accoutered Christian knight. As such the latter could also be seen as one of the North's crusading barons, receiving the host before going out to destroy the enemies of the Church.

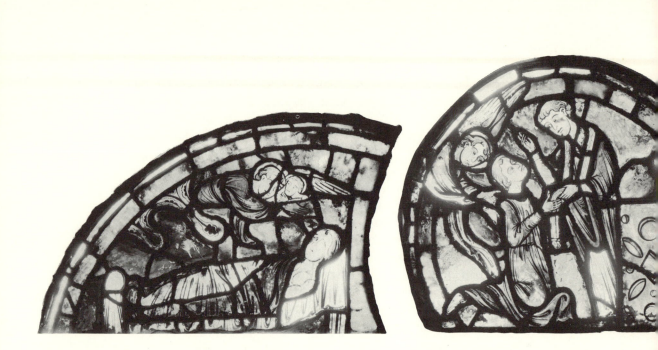

92. *Bourges Cathedral*. The Judgment Day stained-glass window (13th century). Center, man at left accepts Communion; man at right rejects it. Left, the communicant at death, his soul picked up by an angel. Right, the noncommunicant, broiling in Hell's fire.

Concrete references to the sanguinary heretical suppression in church art are, like other topical subjects, rare. Even if the orthodox iconographers were not constrained by delicacy, they would have been forced to consider the feelings of the conquered people whom they wished to win back to the fold. There are, nevertheless, a few echoes of those gory events and it is possible that there were others which it was thought proper to obliterate at some later date.

One of those still remaining is a relief at the church of Saint-Nazaire at Carcassonne, which has been interpreted as representing the battle by the walls of Toulouse where Simon de Montfort met his death [Pl. 94]. The clothes worn by the many participants in the scene mark it as definitely of the period in question. The setting is that of a city's ramparts near which is placed the kind of war "machine" which is described in the *Chanson de la croisade albigeoise* as having shot the stone that killed Simon. Another event told of in the *Chanson* seems also to be reproduced: the murder of one of Simon's men in full view of his army, for which the luckless man won martyrdom. Unfortunately, the section of the carving is gone where Simon himself would have been expected to figure. However, the fact that a tombal stone with Simon's coat of arms is still to be found in the same church (indeed, the warrior's remains lay here for five years) would seem to lend weight to the topical identification of the scene in the relief.[27]

132

Military resistance of the Cathars ended after the fall of Montségur, in 1244, which has inspired such a literary effusion in modern times. Recent findings indicate, however, that the Cathar heresy was far from being extirpated then or even beyond the thirteenth century. It used to be thought that the fleur-de-lis design that has been found on a number of Catharist funerary steles represented a final acceptance of orthodoxy, even if posthumously and by solicitous relations of the dead, who, it has been suggested, had prudently allowed the royal emblem to be chiseled on the stones.[28] But this viewpoint must now, it seems, be revised.

Very recent diggings in the hamlet of Saint-Marcel, near Cordes, one of the centers of the Cathar heresy in the Southwest, have yielded an amazing cache of copper book-cover ends spared from a fire. They were found to be decorated with fleur-de-lis, but each petal of the flowers ends in a raised ball, a well-known Catharist symbol. This would appear plainly to indicate that even if the political conquest was finally accepted by those responsible for this emblem, religious subjection definitely was not. Experts have identified the book-cover ends as belonging to the fifteenth century, which seems to indicate that the Cathar heresy, generally considered to have been obliterated by the fourteenth century, actually continued to have its secret devotees far beyond that period.[29]

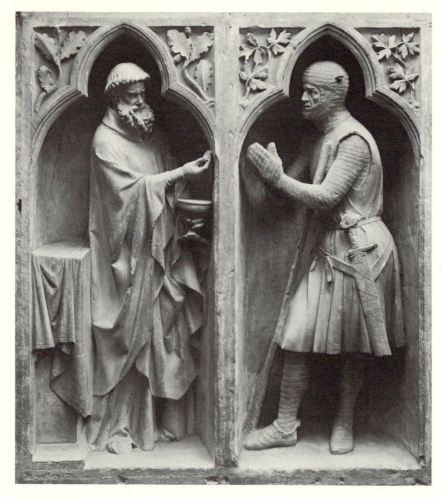

93. *Reims Cathedral* (13th century). Melchizedek offering Abraham the Communion wafer before he goes off to battle.

The Catharist attitude toward art seems to have oscillated between extreme iconoclasm as a revulsion from the dogmas illustrated in Catholic art to a busy fashioning of a series of new symbols, found in tombal decorations. These were mainly figures of doves, fishes, the Greek cross in a disk, a moon-crescent, solar triangles, and chalices representing the Holy Grail. There were also a few more complex subjects, containing even the human form, but many more of these have been found in Yugoslavia than in France.[30]

Often the heretics were exercised by an almost fanatical need to destroy Catholic symbols. The most famous example of this kind was the cross-burning heresy of Pierre de Bruys, which centered about the area of Saint-Gilles. This agitation, which included other challenges of orthodoxy, had a disastrous effect on the building fortunes of the renowned church, work having to be halted repeatedly for lengthy periods because of it. The stupendous façade sculpture was by some miracle completed but the church itself was brought up only to a point twelve meters from the ground when the religious conflicts ended work on it. When peace was reestablished there was neither money nor energy to finish the structure, which remained in an abortive state—services being conducted in the crypt—for five hundred years.

By an ironic duplication the truncated basilica was to suffer further damage in the religious wars of the sixteenth and seventeenth centuries, during which it was used as a fortress. When the Protestants abandoned it in 1622 they tried to blow it up but were forestalled by the timely arrival of royal troops. However, the tower was brought down, which undermined walls and pillars and gutted the vaulting. The façade sculpture was mutilated by musket volleys. The miracle is not so much that anything at all remains of this work but that despite so much willful amputation its grandiose creative pattern still shines so brilliantly and wholly out of it.

There may have been a good deal of Catharist iconoclasm about which we are in the dark since many churches were completely destroyed during the troubles. In one reference to the destruction of art by opponents of the Church the circumstances point to a political as well as a religious context. This was

94. *Carcassonne, Church of Saint-Nazaire.* Remnant of a relief presumably representing the Battle of Toulouse, 1218. Below, right, is one of the "engins de guerre" by which Simon de Montfort was supposed to have met his death.

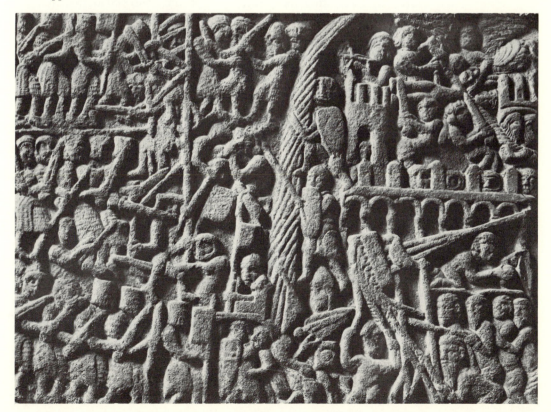

at Albi itself, where paintings of St. Dominic and St. Peter of Verona (an assassinated Italian inquisitor) were effaced from the city portal. In their places were
painted portraits of two royal commissioners sent down to curb excesses of the
inquisitors and whom the city canonized hopefully in this manner. These images
have, of course, themselves long since disappeared.[31]

Heretics at Carcassonne, in 1247, not only destroyed much of the Dominican
monastery there but attacked the church as well, smashing all its stained-glass
windows. They were excommunicated and made to pay reparations.[32] Other
Catharist iconoclasm stemmed from a strong revulsion felt for the Catholic cult
of images. Some heretics in Southern France, in order to combat what they considered idolatry, made an image of the Virgin with only one eye and with other
repulsive features, arguing that out of humility Christ had expressly chosen to
be born to such a mother. The image promptly began to accomplish miracles,
whereupon copies were made, which in turn produced their wonders. Finally
the perpetrators of the fraud divulged their secret, causing consternation among
the faithful.[33]

Another false image used in this manner was a sculptured crucifix, on which
Christ's feet were crossed and one of his upper arms was missing. The reported
prevalence of similar unconventional iconographic forms in Northern Spain
would appear to lend support to the angry campaign of opposition to innovations
in church art conducted by the famous Bishop Luke of Tuy, who was considered
an expert in rooting out heterodoxical deviants. Luke used these artistic mon-
strosities to authenticate his argument for rejecting any changes at all. It is
extremely interesting that the Church in the main repudiated this contention,
endorsing just the opposite tendency, that of making art more effective in the
fight against heresy by enriching its iconography.

Despite the primitiveness of Cathar art, the question rises whether it might
not have developed more evolved forms if it had been able to establish itself
permanently in some area, free of the savage persecution to which it was subjected. Early Christian funerary art, such as could formerly be seen in the upper
gallery of the Lateran Museum, is hardly more sophisticated. Indeed, it often
offers striking resemblances to Cathar work.

As a matter of fact, a few pieces of heretical art have been found which
showed tendencies of the working out of more complex technics and subject-
treatment. One of these presents a low-relief portrait of a convent superior with
his staff and Bible, another a knight carved against a cruciform background and
gesturing with either hand to symbols of Good and Evil.[34] But this work is from
Yugoslavia, where the Bogomils were more deeply entrenched than were the
Cathars of France. A total of 40,000 funerary steles have already been recovered
in this area, which gives some idea of the immense number of people who had
not only accepted the heresy but were prepared to carry it to their graves.[35]

Still it would be hazardous to attempt to say what would have happened to religious art if the heresy had won out in the thirteenth century. Since this did not occur in Southern France or anywhere else at that time, we have nothing but the effects of the Reformation on such art to go by, and they were often woeful enough. In some countries of the North the old church art was almost totally rooted out and when, much later, an attempt was made to supply a substitute, the results were for the most part pathetic. Thus some English canons belatedly rued the loss of their old stained glass, which by all accounts was as beautiful as the French. But the nineteenth century was far past the time when great religious art could be produced and the English churchmen would have done better to have left bad enough alone.

In France Protestantism has remained a tiny minority though it is interesting that its nuclei often occupy areas once given over to the earlier heresies. It is as though the people had retained a kind of collective nonconformism, to say nothing of the old angers and animosities. My wife and I were the guests some time ago of a minister of the French Reformed Church in a small community of the Gard, where the Albigensian tendency had once been strong and where pockets of Protestantism still hold on stubbornly. It struck us as significant that across one whole wall of his church, painted in large letters, were the names of Protestant martyrs from this area. They only went back two hundred years but the souvenir of the countless other unnamed dead, from the thirteenth and seventeenth centuries, seemed to throb in the frigid air of the little chapel.

Such harrowing ugliness as was to be found inside, however, would have been impossible if not intentional. The bare wood and plaster seemed to proclaim aggressively that here was a locus where the soul's inner beauty must suffice. When it was apparent that no other comers would add to the small band of sixteen (including the preacher's wife and ourselves) in the church, the young preacher retired into the sacristy and reappeared in a minute, after having slipped a short rabato over his head that reached only a few inches down his chest and ended in a narrow border of lace. The latter modest decorative feature somehow startled me.

Services began immediately, consisting mainly in the reading of a long series of selected short passages from the Bible, whose interrelationship, I must confess, escaped me. After each reading a hymn was sung and I cannot say for certain if it was planned or merely the effect of the poor technic of the preacher's wife, who unaided by a pitch pipe led the singing, but as they came out not one of the hymns had a recognizable melody. Our hostess had earlier impressed us as of mild and sweet disposition but her strident tones seemed to reveal unsuspected depths of embattled militancy.

The subject of the sermon had been selected from Paul's Epistle to the Romans: "I beseech you therefore, brethren, by the mercies of God, that ye present your bodies a living sacrifice, holy, acceptable unto God, which is your reasonable service." Typically French, our friend opened his talk with a troubled discussion of the word "therefore" ("donc," which in the French version heads the sentence). "What a bad beginning," he commented. "One thinks immediately, 'Aha, another exhortation'." And he almost smiled.

This struck me as a promising beginning, reassuring under the ascetic conditions. But rather than proceeding to soften the evangelical message, our host launched into an impassioned defense of it. He not only approved of, he proclaimed this harsh enunciation of the Apostle, that God would be satisfied with nothing less than all. Giving oneself to Christ, wholly, completely, body and soul, this was the Christian's "reasonable service." I half-imagined that I was listening to a Cathar "perfected one," calling on his disciples for ultimate self-denial, by which alone the soul's salvation could be accomplished.

The sermon ended abruptly and the surrounding ugliness, for a few minutes held at bay, surged back. The preacher's wife led the brave little band in a final discordant hymn and he retired again to the sacristy to remove his collar. Doubts assailed me painfully. I purged my mind quickly, however, of its posture of arbitration. Beauty was, after all, only an accidental, irrelevant feature of the great religious conflicts which had twice torn this country apart!

Besides, I realized, the quarrel was long since ended insofar as my own point of interest was concerned. The old art, done or undone, could never be repeated and I could now only verify the fact that the partial Catholic triumph had permitted the preservation of a major portion of the most marvelous body of art ever created. Indeed, much of it had been realized during the extraordinary conditions of the heretical challenge itself and the Church, while committing every atrocity in fighting the Albigensian threat, had at the same time amazingly refined its esthetic instrument in the process.

CHAPTER VII
ANTI-SEMITISM IN
MEDIEVAL ART

THE VISITOR to Beaulieu-sur-Dordogne is told by the guidebooks that the principal attraction of its abbey church is the tympanum, which presents what is possibly the earliest monumental interpretation of the Judgment Day [Pl. 95]. What one finds, at first view, is familiar enough. Christ is seated on his throne, his arms stretched wide to either side, reminiscent of their position on the Cross. He is surrounded by the twelve Apostles, presented in conversational pairs, and a somewhat smaller, enigmatic figure, far over to the left, who "could be Moses," it has been suggested.[1] Two angels blow the warning trumpets and four others bear the Cross and the nails of the Crucifixion and Christ's Crown.

Certain other details, on the other hand, do not fit into the usual pattern, probably due, it has been said, to the early dating of the work, which was done before conventions had had time to petrify.[2] An example is the very curious Hell, which occupies the double lintel and is tended by a variety of apocalyptic monsters, which purvey the torments to the Damned without the intercession of demons. It looks more like a wide band of decorative imagery than a place of terror. Or, as in Byzantine art, it may picture Earth giving up its victims. Even more surprising is the absence of the customary trappings of the celestial court: the Archangel Michael, Satan, and the scales on which the souls of the risen dead are weighed.

Right by the opening graves are seven clothed figures, three on the left and four on the right, in the places conventionally reserved for the Blessed and the Damned. Indeed, this is the characterization that has been universally assigned the little men by scholars, an error that prevented their ascribing to them a more interesting and, probably, a more correct role.[3] At times, what might be called the "persistence of the already seen" has caused writers to describe things that were simply not there. One suggested, for example, that the seven figures represented "corteges" of the Risen, supposedly after Judgment, when they would be passing on to Heaven and Hell.[4] But there is no unity of movement among these figures; indeed, they are engaged in no movement at all but are standing still and merely gesturing. Another writer described the little men as staring at the "terrible apparatus . . . of their judgment,"[5] which is the purest imagination. And a third proposed that the seven "already know their fate,"[6] which is equally fanciful.

The ascription by scholars of the roles of the Blessed and the Damned to the little men runs into obvious contradictions. It would, for example, be most unusual to find all such individuals belonging to a single sex, as they do here. Even the woman-hating monastic world of the twelfth century (the date of the Beaulieu tympanum is generally set at around 1130) did not exclude women from the final court scene. Besides, there is a great spread in the apparent ages of the seven, whereas according to accepted Christian doctrine of the time all mankind would assume the age of thirty at the Rising.[7] Finally, it should have struck scholars as strange that all seven of the already supposedly judged men were clothed. For in the early twelfth century it would have been rare indeed to present the Damned in this fashion.[8] Nothing in fact about the dress or appearance of the seven indicates any distinction in their fate.

I have been able to find only one group of recent writers who seem to have taken a fresh look at the little men. They refer to the "exoticism" of their headgear, concluding that the sculptor had by its means meant "to suggest the universality of the peoples called to Salvation."[9] For them, moreover, the seven figures represent "the wise men of all nations," who are engaged in "pointing out Christ and the Cross to each other."[10] Further than this they did not carry their observation of the seven men and it must be assumed that they considered them all to be the Blessed.

The reason for all this confusion, I submit, is that the little men are not the "risen dead" at all but are individuals who happen to be alive on Judgment Day. What is more, several of them are Jews. The assumption of the latter identity is not based on the obvious fact that two of them are wearing pointed or Phrygian-type hats. For the association of this kind of headdress with Jews did not become virtually exclusive until the thirteenth century. The fact that at least six of the seven are bearded cannot be regarded as determinant either since in the twelfth century the beard might also be worn by Christian prelates.

The conclusions alluded to are based entirely on the gestures of the seven little men [Pl. 96]. Three of them are doing nothing out of the ordinary, either pointing to Christ or tipping their hands in prayer. But a fourth has an index finger directed at his own head and the movements of the other three are more unusual still. In one way or another they have taken hold of the bottoms of their robes and are in the act of lifting them. It is only the beginning of a gesture as yet, a kind of suggested, fragmentary pantomime. But the fact that it is re-

Beaulieu-sur-Dordogne, Abbey Church: 95. Tympanum (12th century). The Judgment Day.
96. Detail of the tympanum. The four little men are at the right of the feet of Christ.

peated three times eliminates any chance of accident. One is somehow reminded of the brusque and vulgar movement that the son of Noah is sometimes shown making while his father lies drunk—"exposing his nakedness"—for which irreverent maneuver Ham (and his supposed descendants, the Negro people) was assigned to eternal degradation: "a servant of servants . . . unto his brethren" (Genesis 9:21–25) [Pl. 97].

But what would Jews be doing offering to expose *their* nakedness over the portal of a twelfth-century Christian church? And why especially on Judgment Day? What indeed would be the status of the Hebrew people, according to Christian belief, at that final milestone? There is a conflict of authorities on this point, which became the subject of a lively discussion toward the end of the twelfth century. According to the doctrine upheld by St. Gregory the Great and largely followed throughout the Middle Ages, unconverted Jews and other infidels who were already in their graves would be banned from the final judgment. This view was actually in contradiction to the New Testament, which held that all mankind must be judged, the dead as well as the living, Jews as well as "Gentiles," the former being tried by Mosaic Law, the latter by "the law written in their conscience" (Romans 2:12–16). St. Thomas Aquinas finally settled the controversy by affirming the more humane outlook of the Bible.[11]

At the time of the carving of the Beaulieu tympanum, however, the harsher viewpoint prevailed, at least in regard to Jews already dead on Judgment Day (hence, once again, the Jews at Beaulieu and, by association, their Christian companions, could not have been meant to figure the "risen dead"!). St. Bernard, for example, agreed that Jews already in their graves "will remain in death," in a letter that he wrote "To the English People," during the anti-Semitic violence that surged through Western Europe during the Second Crusade. However, in that same letter he fervidly cautioned that "The Jews are not to be persecuted, killed or even put to flight" for "we are told by the Apostle that *when the time is ripe all Israel shall be saved.*"[12]

97. *Bourges Cathedral.* Detail of façade frieze (13th century). Ham "exposing the nakedness" of his father, Noah.

If this prediction by St. Paul had not been fulfilled *before* Judgment Day (which in St. Bernard's time was still considered to be imminent), it would have to occur on that solemn occasion itself, when all living Jews would have to appear before the divine tribunal. This, it must therefore be assumed, is what is happening on the Beaulieu tympanum. The seven little men must represent those who are still alive on Doomsday and the Jews among them are excitedly anticipating the trial to which they will soon be called. That is the meaning of their strange gesture, by which they are referring insistently to the fact—are prepared to prove it by an anatomical demonstration, indeed—that they should be placed among the Blessed. This is, they are asserting, their right as sons of Abraham, who by his circumcision had sealed his people's covenant with God!

It would appear contradictory that such a certification should be put in so prominent a place on an abbey church. Clearly, however, the Jews' presence on Beaulieu tympanum is not an assertion but a question. The relationship of circumcision to salvation is to be considered in dispute and this is reflected in the agitated dumb play of the seven little men. Those among them who are not offering, through their gestures ("the language of the hands"), the morphological argument must be showing other reasons why they are to be considered among the Chosen. Their movements should link them to Christ. This is clear enough for those who point to him reverentially or pray to him. But what is the meaning of the act of the man who points his finger to his head?

The explanation of this gesture could possibly be supplied by the famous early Christian polemic—*De Altercatione Ecclesiae et Synagogae Dialogus*—which in the twelfth century was read as a sermon and also performed during Easter Week in churches all over France. In its simplest form the liturgical play took on the character of a long-winded discourse between Church and Synagogue (the latter, at times, could be represented by a group of Jews) as to which had the stronger claim to salvation. At the climax Synagogue vaunted circumcision as the ultimate proof in her behalf: It was the mark of preference ordained by God himself in his pledge to Abraham. To this Church replied that the sanctity of circumcision had been abrogated since the advent of Christ, and that it was no longer a sign of blessedness but of shame. "But my people carry the proof of salvation upon their forehead!"[13]

The influence of liturgical drama on medieval iconography has been too solidly documented to require further discussion here. Besides, it was not only in drama that Christian spokesmen inveighed against circumcision—it was one of the themes, for example, of a famous polemic by Lyon's Archbishop Agobard against the Jews.[14] In particular cases (like the one at Beaulieu) proof of the relationship between an enacted scene and a plastic work must of course remain entirely circumstantial. With this in mind, when Synagogue in the play next demands what that special sign might be on which Church bases her superior claims and the latter replies dramatically, "The Cross!" it fits into the pattern that there is a featured presentation of the Cross at Beaulieu, along with the nails that riveted Christ's body to it, and that our seventh little man should likewise be referring to it, beyond his "forehead" and over his shoulder. There is even an oblique reference to Moses in the Easter play, where the ultimate rejection of the "Mosaic Law" is set forth.[15] And in our tympanum the great Hebrew emancipator is presented as a pathetic, lonely figure far out of range of primary interest, apparently speaking but winning no listeners.

This then would seem to be the meaning of the little drama on Beaulieu façade, describing the manner in which the millennial debate between Christianity and Judaism would be decided on that final day when all humanity was to be judged. At a time of raging anti-Jewish feeling, it is remarkable that the dispute was given so mild a plastic form in this instance. In other cases, as we shall see, the confrontation is far more violent, far less subtle. However, a large number of the contemporary Christians would hardly have been content to let this controversy be conducted in any abstract or figurative manner, however brutal. The result was one of the sadder pages of human history.

Sculptured medieval polemics against the Jews are by no means rare. In a recent article elucidating the remarkable Bury St. Edmunds cross, acquired a few years ago by the Metropolitan Museum of New York, Thomas Hoving has analyzed the theological arguments underlying the dense iconography of this twelfth-century ivory masterpiece as being "the same as those used continually in the Disputes between Christian and Jew" during the Middle Ages. In the particular instance, he explains, the polemic was associated with Abbot Samson of the Benedictine monastery at Bury, "who was swept up in a harsh crusade against the Jewish people that made itself manifest in England during the last decades of the twelfth century. . . . It is against this poor alien people and their Synagogue . . . that the text of the cross directs itself with wrath. . . ."[16]

It is not surprising that the *De Altercatione* was long attributed to St. Augustine since that great Father of the Church had devoted much effort to convincing Jews of his time about the truth of Christianity. Indeed, it was a permanent preoccupation imposed by Christ's origin and by his declared messianic role, which established the Old Testament as the foundation of the new faith. Christ himself had given repeated emphasis to this dependency, and the Evangelists had followed it all too sedulously, giving their narratives at times the naïve character of ex post facto inventions. The tradition set in this manner was unabatingly continued by Christian scholars until the Old Testament seemed to consist of little besides prophecies of Christ and Mary and symbolic prefigurations of their acts.

This exegetical process was graphically illustrated in medieval church art by the figure of St. Paul who was shown grinding, in the mill of the New Testament, the grain brought to it by the old Hebrew Prophets. A magnificent ex-

98. *Vézelay, Church of La Madeleine* (12th century). Capital relief: St. Paul grinding out the grain of the Old Testament in Christianity's "mystic mill."

ample of this subject is presented in a capital relief at Vézelay [Pl. 98]. Another, in a stained-glass window ordered by Abbot Suger for his abbey church at Saint-Denis, though now lost, is known by his descriptive poem:

> By working the mill, thou, Paul, takest the flour out of the bran.
> Thou makest known the inmost meaning of the Law of Moses.[17]

Suger underscored the interpretive relationship between the Old and New Testaments in another stained-glass lancet showing a veil being taken from the eyes of Moses, which the abbot explained in a famous line: "What Moses veils the doctrine of Christ unveils."[18]

Among the Old Testament Prophets, highest honors were reserved for Isaiah, whose predictions were associated with the central events of Christianity: the Birth of the Virgin, the Annunciation, the Birth of Christ, and Judgment Day. These have constituted the nucleus of Christian iconography. The ancient Patriarchs and Kings likewise furnished incidents which Christian scholars interpreted as having symbolic reference to Jesus or his mother. Many of these strike us as forced today while others are more felicitous. Among the latter is the story of Jonah, who sojourned for three days inside the whale's belly before being ejected, alive—which is interpreted as a reference to Christ's confinement in his tomb for three days and his ultimate Resurrection.

Another effective image, this one referring to the Virgin, "who had received in her womb the divine flame without being consumed,"[19] is the burning bush in which Moses saw God. And Gideon's fleece, which let pass the dew without being moistened, is an effective, if somewhat indelicate, figure of the virginal conception of Christ by Mary.[20] But however these interpretations may strike us today, the important point to remember about them is that they had the most authoritative acceptance in the Middle Ages, as the art of every old church can demonstrate. At times the entire iconographic program of a façade was devoted to what has been called the "reconciliation" of the Old Testament with the New,[21] which is a euphemism for what would be a more appropriate term: absorption. For the early Fathers sought in this manner to tear the Old Testament out of the hands of the Jews and to appropriate it for Christianity.

Yet for them this approach to the Old Testament was an inescapable solution to a most disturbing paradox. For though the Jews rejected Christ, they had nonetheless been God's chosen people, in whose veins ran the same blood that Jesus had poured out on the Cross. This unforgettable fact established a basic tension in the Christian attitude toward Jews, which Pope Innocent III, one of their bitterest antagonists, expressed thus: "Although the Jewish perfidy is in every way worthy of condemnation, nevertheless, because through them the truth of our own faith is proved, they are not to be severely oppressed by the faithful."[22] This counsel of tolerance was issued during a period of sharply increasing persecution of the Jews and it must be said that it had little enough effect.

The position of the Jews within the Christian community had been steadily deteriorating from its relatively favorable status earlier in the Middle Ages. Under Charlemagne and especially his successors, Jews had large acceptance in the social order. They were permitted to build synagogues and Christians were even said to have visited their services while priests discussed the Old Testament with rabbis.[23] In Southern France likewise the position of the Jews was excellent, stemming here, too, from the early friendliness of Charlemagne, to whom they had rendered important services against the Saracens. As a reward the emperor granted them one third of the city of Narbonne, from which they eventually operated a fleet. The Jews' right to own land in Languedoc—with full hereditary privileges—is documented as far back as the tenth century[24] and was still referred to with pride, in 1170, by Benjamin da Tudela, the famous traveler and diarist, who told of one wealthy Jew of Narbonne, who owned landed property "of which nobody can deprive him by force."[25]

This situation in Southwest France continued into the thirteenth century though the Albigensian "crusade" was fated to cause a drastic deterioration. Jews in this area served as administrative officers for prelates and counts, enjoyed rights in the secular and ecclesiastic courts, and in contractual proceedings were allowed to take their oath on the Book of Moses.[26] Their culture flourished. They founded schools of their own and together with Moslem physicians established France's first medical faculty, at Montpellier. Even in Northern France Jews owned land and vineyards and ran their own communities in the towns by elected provosts. They were admitted to the royal court and were befriended by scholars, Abélard telling in one of his letters to Héloïse of consulting a rabbi on the meaning of an obscure passage in Kings.[27]

Though theological reasons are usually emphasized for the rise of medieval anti-Semitism, there is little doubt that strong economic and even political motives were also at play. In Carolingian times, when Western Europe was all but landlocked, the Jews had an essential economic role, serving as virtually the sole trading tie with the outside world. The swift economic development of the West beginning in the eleventh century radically changed this situation. In manufacturing and commerce, the Christians, who represented the overwhelmingly dominant segment of the population, everywhere began to take the lead. Wherever Jews had an entrenched position, as in Italian silk manufacturing, they were assailed by discriminatory taxes or simply confiscated out of competition. Their participation in the fairs and markets of Northern France was finally restricted to money changing and selling old clothes.[28]

This steady attack on the Jews' economic position was accentuated by the Crusades. The enormous cost of these undertakings caused the eyes of their leaders to turn almost automatically to the Jews, who possessed much liquid wealth. In England, in preparation for the Third Crusade (1189–1192), they were asked to contribute the then immense sum of 60,000 pounds; the whole of the rest of the country, only 70,000.[29] The violently anti-Semitic sentiments stirred up during each Crusade furnished the appropriate setting for this spoliation. During the Second Crusade Pope Eugene III had ordered a moratorium on interest payments for debts owed to Jews by those taking the Cross. Peter the Venerable, abbot of Cluny, urged rulers to go even further and despoil Jews of all their property "so that the money of those cursed ones may at least serve a useful purpose in helping to combat the Saracens."[30] But Peter himself was not above borrowing from the Jews when he was in financial straits, giving them as security "precious objects from the sacristy, in particular the gold plate coverings of a crucifix."[31]

Philippe-Auguste followed Peter's counsel to the letter, declaring debts owed to Jews forfeit, but he charged the debtors twenty per cent for their deliverance. In 1181 he expelled the Jews from the royal domain, confiscating all their real property, including their synagogues, which he turned over to Bishop Maurice de Sully. One of these, consecrated to Mary Magdalene, served for hundreds of years as one of Paris' leading churches. After this expulsion the Jews paid for their reentry some years later, thus beginning that pathetic cycle of confiscation, expulsion, and paid readmission that served the kings for generations until their victims were mulcted of their substance.

In certain areas of Western Europe, particularly along the main pathways of the Crusades, violent physical attacks on the Jews were added to their expropriation. This came close to genocide in West Germany, where during the First Crusade (1096-1099) within a few days an estimated 12,000 Jews were massacred.[32] Many more died by their own hand. In the Second Crusade (1147–1149) a Cistercian monk, Raoul, organized mass pogroms, inciting his followers with the cry: "We are marching a great distance to . . . take vengeance on the Moslems. Lo and behold, there live among us Jews whose forefathers slew [Jesus] and crucified him for no cause. Let us revenge ourselves on them first. . . ."[33] Raoul's mob incitement brought a blistering condemnation from St. Bernard, for which humanitarian act Jews are said to have expressed their gratitude by naming many of their sons after the great ascetic.[34]

The social status of those Jews who remained alive was profoundly degraded during this period. The walled ghetto became generalized and the Jews' confinement inside it during important Christian holidays was as much protective as it was discriminatory. Even so, Christian youngsters were allowed to climb the ghetto walls on Good Friday and throw stones at the Jews, a "right" that Bishop Guillaume of Béziers remitted, in 1160, in return for the payment of an annual tax. The "droit du soufflet," or privilege of slapping Jews on Easter, was also bought off in various places, as in Toulouse, by payment of an impost and the "gift" of forty-four pounds of wax for Good Friday candles at the church of Saint-Étienne.[35] The Jews at Arles, in 1178, won protection by pledging to finance the building of a bridge.[36]

Discriminatory practices against the Jews were formalized, under the encouragement of Pope Innocent III, at the great Lateran Council of 1215, where a special mode of dress and an identifying emblem were prescribed for them. Thus originated the infamous yellow wheel, which was to be worn for six centuries.[37] If the yellow wheel was left off by Jews, St. Louis had the clothes confiscated and given to the person who reported the violation. Philippe-le-Hardi, his son, added the pointed hat to the prescribed attire, bringing the Jews further insults and attacks. Not daring to go on the road thus clothed, they were eventually allowed to buy off the requirement when away from home.[38]

This broad program of isolation and eclipse ended by almost completely divorcing the Jews from the Christian community. They had been merchants, vintners, coiners, innkeepers, masons, tanners, bakers, tailors, butchers, goldsmiths, glaziers. In the East Benjamin da Tudela had found them manufacturing handicrafts in Salonika, silk cloth in Constantinople, and the "far-renowned Tyrian glass" at New Tyre. The Jewish communities in the Holy Land, now quite small, almost all practiced the dyer's trade, this careful observer reported.[39] But most of this variety in Jewish economic activity was to disappear before the end of the Middle Ages and the status of the petty usurer was imposed upon the Jew. Reflecting this trend, he was depicted in art as point-hatted and bearded, hook-nosed and meanly clad, his recognizable image that continued to be used all the way into modern times.

As the tide of anti-Semitism swept through Western Europe during the twelfth and thirteenth centuries, it was reflected in all media of religious art and liturgy. In manuscript art, reports one authority, the inimical confrontation of Church and Synagogue intensified with the outbreak of anti-Jewish violence in real life and the gracelessness of Synagogue's image "increased in the same proportion as did hatred against the Jews."[40] Most commonly she was shown with a veil across her eyes, a falling crown, a drooping banner, and the tables of the Law of Moses slipping from her hand. But as the spirit of animosity heightened other props were added to her portrait. She would be crowned with the conical bonnet, shown riding on a goat or an ass, symbol of stubbornness, or accompanied by an owl, which could not stand the light, or by a scorpion, emblem of treachery.[41]

The anti-Semitic occurrences in manuscript art exceed those in monumental works both in number and virulence, as can be gathered from a recent author who made an exhaustive study of the former. In his monograph,[42] Bernhard Blumenkranz also includes a number of examples of the use of the conical hat without pejorative intent, in one of which even Christ is shown wearing it. This is as the "Pilgrim of Emmaus," whom the two Apostles fail to recognize, considering him just another Jew. The author points out, however, that the "innumerable decidedly anti-Jewish" illustrations are by far preponderant.

In monumental art, the anodyne use of the conical hat is also quite frequent. But its purpose (as also in the manuscript field) is always purely identificatory and not to be compared with the inimical intention that is attached to it when associated with hateful acts. This becomes sharply clear, for example, when cone-hatted Jews are shown stoning St. Stephen in a carving at Rouen (see Pl. 109), and St. Paul, who was present and "was consenting unto his death" (Acts 8:1), is the only Jew depicted as bareheaded though he was still at the time the greatest persecutor of Christians of them all.

In monumental art, anti-Jewish emphasis was somewhat more refined than in the manuscripts but no less categorical [Pl. 99, Pl. 100]. Viollet-le-Duc's conjecture[43] that the sculptured confrontation of Church and Synagogue was featured only in cities with a Jewish population has been recently partly confirmed by the as yet incomplete findings of Bernhard Blumenkranz. Of fifty known towns where such figures existed, thirty-five have already been shown to have harbored Jews. "Actually," the writer comments, "we have here an anti-Jewish polemic expressing itself in art, and this presupposes the existence of the adversary against whom the polemic is directed."[44]

The implication of a mounting antagonism toward Jews and Judaism in real life comes through in the form of violent acts being more and more applied directly to the person of Synagogue, in works of art. Even Christ, otherwise so passive and aloof, began to be made the agent of some angry outburst, like tearing the veil from Synagogue's eyes, seizing the Book of the Law out of her hands, or pushing her roughly away [Pl. 101]. Usually an angel took the place of Christ in these indelicate roles, however, knocking the crown off Synagogue's head or striking her to the ground, as occurs in a magnificent swirl of wings in a carving at Saint-Gilles [Pl. 102].

Indeed, one finds in this church various other illustrations of the Jewish-Christian "dispute," a considerable part of the façade being pervaded by it. Presented in intermittent scenes, it is set forth through personifications that are contrasted in striking human terms. The opposition is between what might be called "good Jews" and "bad Jews," since Christ's drama itself took place in a kind of Jewish microcosm. The central character among the latter group was, of course, Judas, who is shown in various execrable dealings with other Jews of his type. Thus the conspirators confer on how much money should be offered him and the amount is whispered into Caiaphas' ear by his treacherous little servant, Malchus. The apostate then comes before the high priest, urged on for appearance's sake by one of his co-conspirators. But his hollow palm is ready to receive the coins which Caiaphas pays out [Pl. 103].

Playing off Judas and the large segment of the Jewish microcosm he symbolized, whose rejection of Christ led them to iniquity, are the smaller band of "good Jews." Featured among them are the members of that highly favored group of disciples whose love for Jesus is so tenderly described in the Evangels. The full story of the Three Marys and Lazarus is told at Saint-Gilles, from the high point of the sensational miracle of the Raising of Lazarus to that charming bit of folklore showing the three women stopping to shop for spices and ointments on their way to Christ's grave.

Other scenes at this church in which "good Jews" figure always emphasize their acceptance of Christ, which ranged them on the side of virtue. One of these is the quiet little drama to which we have already alluded (see Ch. VI and Pl. 90), in which the young disciple of Jesus draws his older companion toward the Savior. It is part of the great panorama representing the Entry of Christ into Jerusalem, where other Jews who have responded to his appeal appear. Among these none is as astonishing as the small boy who tries to climb the palm tree, the better to see Jesus as he approaches the city gates. His strong little hands grasp the palm branch and he looks straight out at the observer with eyes that are radiant with faith and inner goodness. His is one of the sweetest faces in all of medieval art [Pl. 104].

Can it be a coincidence that Malchus, the high priest's servant and trusted advisor, should be presented as a young boy also, of about the same age and stature as this other boy? By his features and conduct, however, Malchus is the antithesis of Jesus' bright young convert. Hard eyes, thin lips, twisted little

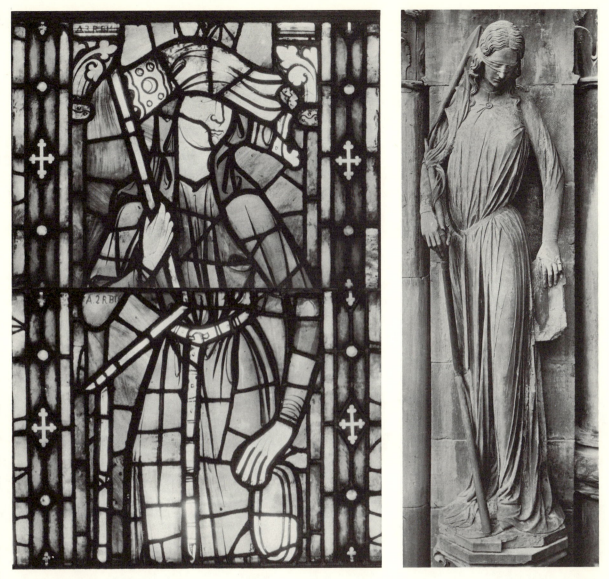

99. *Troyes Cathedral.* Stained-glass lancet (13th century). The Synagogue. She is blinded by her own banner, whose staff is broken in several places, as the plaque containing the "Law of Moses" slips from her left hand.

100. *Strasbourg Cathedral.* South porch (13th century). The Synagogue. Now at the Musée de l'Oeuvre.

mouth, his malevolence is the more terrible for being found in a child. The Devil himself is not needed when this boy can pour his poison into the high priest's ear. There is indeed ample provocation for St. Peter to draw his sword against him, on the Mount of Olives. For he personifies the very spirit of evil: the Christ-killing Jew [Pl. 105].

101 (above, left). *Former Church of Sainte-Larme de Sélincourt*. Relief from baptismal font (12th century). Christ crowns "Ecclesia" while he veils "Synagoga's" eyes. Now at the Amiens Museum. *Saint-Gilles*, *Abbey Church* (12th century): 102 (below). West façade, tympanum of south portal. The Crucifixion. At right Synagogue (head missing) being struck to the ground by an angel (head also missing). Note the falling Temple, which Synagogue had been wearing as a headdress. 103 (above, right). Detail of façade frieze. At left, two Jews discussing how much Judas should be paid; at right, the high priest paying off Judas.

The Jew was rendered repulsive in medieval art either by physical distortion or by his role, or by both. His caricatured stereotype goes far back in Christian annals, the early Greek Father, St. John Chrysostom, having devoted eight virulent sermons to this purpose in the fourth century. He accused the Jews of sacrificing their sons and daughters to devils and of committing other unspeakable outrages, for which God rejected them. "When it is clear that God hates them, it is the duty of Christians to hate them, too," he declared. It has been said that Chrysostom's savage description of the Jews was meant to discourage Christians from being friendly with them, and this seems to have been a perennial preoccupation with ecclesiastics.[45]

It was later on in the Middle Ages that the actual plastic image of this caricature began to take form, such as we find it in Hildegarde of Bingen's famous manuscript or in the Forest Roll of Essex, where a Jew is presented in a sketch as a hooded, mean, bearded little man with a hooked nose that arches over to his lip. He is handled in much the same way in editions of the *Biblia Pauperum*, the popular Bible in Pictures that began appearing in the late thirteenth cen-

Saint-Gilles, Abbey Church (12th century):

104. Detail of the procession greeting Christ on his Entry into Jerusalem. A little boy tries to climb a palm tree, the better to see Jesus.

105. West façade frieze. Detail of the Taking of Christ on the Mount of Olives. St. Peter cutting off the ear of the boy, Malchus.

106. *Saint-Gilles, Abbey Church*. West façade (12th century). The Taking of Christ on the Mount of Olives.

107. *Strasbourg Cathedral* (13th century). Detail of the Carrying of the Cross. Christ at left and conical-hatted Jew in center. The blacksmith's wife holding the nails in her hand is at right.

tury.[46] More important, however, was the art in the churches which was open to the gaze of all.

The story of Christ presented a number of other episodes in which animosity to the Jews could be underscored. In his Expulsion of the Tradesmen from the Temple, for example, a Jewish money changer is often shown (as at Saint-Gilles) raising his coin bag jeeringly toward the Savior. In the Taking of Christ on the Mount of Olives, Judas is not the only Jew accompanying the Romans to their prey. There are others, too, with murder in their wild eyes [Pl. 106].

When Christ is conducted before Caiaphas and the high priest of the Jews asks him: "Art thou the Christ, the Son of the Blessed?" and Jesus replies: "I am," Caiaphas tears his clothes in repulsive anger. Jesus is then mocked and buffeted, his tormentors spitting into his face their "stinking spittle."[47] Through the rest of this terrible and pathetic account frequent opportunity is given artists to picture Jews as vile and craven. And legend has added to Scripture, as in one amazing story about the smith who was asked to forge the nails for the Cross. When he refused, his wife undertook the odious task and it is reported that she sang gayly while working at it. She is shown in a relief at Strasbourg cathedral, standing beside Christ, on the road to Calvary, the nails ready in her evil hands [Pl. 107]. The reader may be surprised by the handsome appearance of this woman. However, as has already been pointed out, esthetic beauty need not to have been intended as reflecting virtue, church thinkers holding that all creatures, including even those associated with the Devil, shared to some extent in the beauty of their divine maker.[48]

One of the most popular stories in medieval art is that of Theophilus, a church official who sold himself to the Devil in exchange for worldly advancement (see Pl. 10). It was an early version of the Faust legend, in which the medieval artist often made a Jew play the role of mediator between the vidame and Satan. In a lancet at Le Mans, for example, Theophilus is shown handing over a bag of money to the Jew in payment for this service. In the French written version of the story, when the meeting with the Devil takes place the Jew greets him as "my king and my lord," "my master and my companion."[49] The plastic arts succeed in showing this intimate relationship of the Jew with the powers of evil by other means [Pl. 108].

Jews are, of course, often portrayed as usurers in medieval art and the classical example of the Jewish usurer is Dives, the Unjust Rich Man, whose parable is presented in countless churches (see Pls. 38, 79). The linking of Dives with the "Jewish people" and of Lazarus, the Just Man, with the "Gentile people" was a later adaptation. Christ certainly made no such identification in the original parable. But a number of authoritative Christian writers accepted its authenticity and when Honorius d'Autun narrated the story, telling of Lazarus at death being taken up into Abraham's Bosom while Dives tumbled down to Hell, he added: "And thus will the perfidious Jews be cast into outer darkness."[50]

Jews are sometimes shown playing key roles in the martyrdom of saints and, of course, are the chief actors in the murder of Christendom's first martyr, St. Stephen. This story, one of the most popular in all church art, was something like a brilliant résumé of the great dispute which medieval Christians conducted with the Jews. Only Stephen's words are reported in the Acts of the Apostles, which an angel whispers to him, as the artists often showed it, while a devil inspired his adversaries. In the end the gentle saint's calmness dissolves and he shouts at the Sanhedrin, calling them "stiffnecked and uncircumcised in heart and ears" and accusing them of having killed not only the "Just One" but all the prophets who had predicted his coming. Beside themselves with confusion and rage, the Jews "gnash their teeth at him" and stop their ears with their hands, rush him out of the city and stone him to death in one of the most violent scenes of violence-filled hagiography (Acts 7:51–58) [Pl. 109].

The charge of the desecration of the host by Jews, like the accusation of the ritual murder of Christian children, originated during the surge of anti-Semitism released by the Crusades. It was of course the body of Christ that was once more crucified in this manner, the blood that flowed from the wafer as the Jew sought to destroy it proving not only his eternal depravity but also the true sacredness of the host. Jews were likewise accused of attacking holy images and crucifixes and of making wax effigies, which they then proceeded to desecrate.[51] These charges were also laid to the heretics of the time. But, anomalous as it may seem, the Church regarded Jews as virtually heretics, "as men who had known the truth and deliberately rejected it."[52]

Most prominently incorporating this accusation in medieval art is Simon the Magician, who is often shown engaged in a spectacular contest with St. Peter and St. Paul. As this Jew and relapsed Christian convert and heretic prepares to prove the superiority of his supernatural powers, the two saints are presented as bereft of all visible support, armed only with their prayers. Their redoubtable opponent, in contrast, has on his side not only the Emperor Nero but the Devil as well and often one or more conical-hatted Jews, who may also be seen with this baleful crew at the Apostles' martyrdom [Pl. 110].

108. *Notre-Dame de Paris.* North wall relief (early 14th century). Theophilus sells himself to the Devil. In the background is a Jew with a pointed hat, who has acted as intermediary.

109. *Rouen Cathedral* (12th century). The Stoning of St. Stephen. Note the Jews wearing conical hats as St. Stephen's executioners. The figure at the left (St. Paul before his conversion) is not given a conical hat out of consideration of his later role.

Among the most popular of medieval art subjects concerning Jews were those involving conversion stories. They reflected an important fact of contemporary life, a great fever of conversion characterizing most periods of intense anti-Semitism. But the Jews largely remained attached to their faith or apostatized merely to escape death or destitution. Then, the danger past, they returned to their "former errors."[53] Pope Gregory the Great had, back in the seventh century, set down the Church's basic opposition to enforced baptism.[54] However, in the paroxysmal conditions of the Crusades, this wise counsel often went unheeded. The frequently avowed goal was to wipe out Jews completely and it was considered a grace to offer them the choice of conversion in place of death. At Rouen they were baptized with a poniard at their throat.[55] In one city of Germany the whole Jewish community was driven into the river and given a mass baptism.

But simultaneous efforts to convince the stubborn hearts of the Jews were not neglected. In the Good Friday liturgy the leitmotif, *"Jerusalem, Jerusalem, convertere te!"* was repeated over and over.[56] Liturgical plays often ended with the Jews accepting baptism. The Church's leading minds applied themselves to this goal. St. Bernard, when defending the Jews against persecution during the Second Crusade, gave as his reason the biblical promise of their "eventual conversion." Those that converted were received with marks of appreciation. In London and other English cities a *domus conversorum* was set up.[57] St. Louis also showed the highest solicitude for converts, establishing a sort of dole for them. The sainted king is said to have loved to hold them over the baptismal font himself, showing a penchant for "Blanche" (his mother's name) and "Louis" when renaming them.[58]

Often in conversion scenes the artist forgot or disregarded the aimed-at goal and presented only antecedent parts of the account, in which the Jew was shown acting hatefully. Thus, incrusted in the wall on the north side of Notre-Dame de Paris, is a relief (early fourteenth century) of Mary's funeral procession, which a Jewish rabbi has the temerity to attack, trying to overturn the coffin. The Archangel Michael swoops down and cuts his hands off with his sword,

110. *Poitiers Cathedral*. The Crucifixion stained-glass window (12th century). Detail of martyrdom of SS. Peter and Paul. Note the association of Nero, the Devil, and a Jew.   111 *Notre-Dame de Paris*. North wall relief (early 14th century). Detail of the Virgin's funeral procession. Note the rabbi whose hands have been cut off and remain attached to the coffin. He himself is extended on the ground.

which remain plastered to the bier. In the original story the Jew prays to Mary for forgiveness and wins her grace. His hands are restored and he is converted. But in the relief hatred of the Jew apparently submerged this denouement, which would have presented him in a laudable posture [Pl. 111].

The story of the Jewish moneylender who left a picture of St. Nicholas to watch over his fortune is equally ambivalent. Two thieves come and make off with his hoard, the saint's image failing to prevent this crime. On his return the outraged usurer delivers a beating to the painting. But this malicious act brings on a curious outcome. The saint appears suddenly before the thieves and frightens them into returning the treasure. Whereupon the Jew is converted. In this naïve legend, charmingly told in a stained-glass series at Le Mans, as well as in another conversion story there, it is noteworthy that the apostatizing Jew is convinced by an incident involving what he was believed to have loved above all else: money.

One is seemingly given a more generous choice in still another stained-glass story at Le Mans cathedral, this one presenting the legend of a Jewish glazier who throws his converted son into his blazing furnace. But the dramatic contrast between the repugnant father and his charming son could have been expected to win affection for the Jews only in the eventuality that they, too, accepted conversion. The boy, accompanied by his Christian school chums, is shown raptly prepared to receive the glowing wafer. And he comports himself with the grace and courage of a martyr when his infuriated father throws him into the fire. His magnificent faith causes Mary herself to enter the flames and to shield him with her cloak [Pl. series: 112, 113, 114].

The curious circumstance about much medieval conversion art is that it was created and displayed inside churches. Hence, unless we can assume that Jews were frequent visitors to them, we must conclude that these works were directed to the Christian audience. What, then, could be their purpose? Aimed at proving the superiority of the Christian faith, this art reflected the continuing polemic which all through the Middle Ages Christian thinkers felt called on to conduct with Judaism and the Jews. This controversy found a spectacular expression in the thirteenth century, when great public debates were arranged in Paris, Narbonne, and other places, between Christian savants and Jewish rabbis.

Often the most amazing freedom of speech characterized the reported arguments of the Jews during these disputations. In the great four-day debate at Barcelona between Pablo Christiani, a converted Jew, and the rabbi Nahmani, the latter to disprove the claim that Christ was the Messiah argued that the prophets had promised that all wars would cease at the messianic epoch and men would live as brothers. Turning to James I, king of Aragon, he said: "It seems to me, O king, that you and your knights would find it hard to have to submit to the demands of the messianic age and renounce all war making!" The

other Jews present were frightened by this boldness but the king admired Nahmani's courage, it is said, telling him in private later that he had never heard a
bad cause so brilliantly defended and plying him with gifts as a sign of his
esteem.[59]

But the disputations were not meant to bring about mutual respect and tolerance. St. Louis, under whose auspices a great debate was held at Paris, in 1240,

Le Mans Cathedral. Stained-glass panels in upper choir triforium representing the legend of the Jewish boy of Bourges (13th century). Sequence of the story: 112 (opposite page). The Jewish boy, accompanied by his Christian school chums, prepares to take Communion. The priest's right hand (obscured by leading) extends a wafer to the boy. With his left, he raises a chalice. Behind him, on the altar, is a cloth-covered ciborium. 113. Hearing of his son's conversion, his infuriated father (a glazier) throws him into his blazing furnace. The boy's courageous adherence to his new faith is symbolized by his composure and by his tipped hands. His mother's sorrow is implied by her bowed head and by her hands placed against her breast. 114. The boy's faith is rewarded by the Virgin's coming to his help. She enters the furnace herself and covers him protectively with her cloak.

later declared regarding these disputations that there was only one way to answer blaspheming Jews—with a sword, "in the belly, as far at it will go."[60] In the Paris contest the situation had actually been set up for an easy Christian victory, the dispute being confined to the Talmud, from which a few isolated passages had been selected out of context to prove that it was dangerously subversive.

Nevertheless, while the debate lasted, all Paris prayed and fasted, asking God to "turn away the danger that threatened her." The archbishop of Sens, who at the time had ecclesiastical jurisdiction over Paris, was impressed by the replies of Rabbi Jehiel, the Jewish spokesman, and ordered that the Talmud be spared. But St. Louis' Dominican advisors, who had demanded a condemnation, accused the archbishop of having been bought off by the Jews. This charge was proved to everybody's satisfaction when the prelate was struck down by illness a year later and died. And twenty-four wagonloads of Talmuds were confiscated under pain of death and burned.[61]

Tolerance for the "crimes" of Judaism did not characterize the Church during the Middle Ages. Whatever the views held as to the ultimate fate of the Jews nothing could erase from Christian consciousness the belief that they had been responsible for the Savior's sufferings and death.[62] Church art and liturgy certainly never allowed the faithful to forget this. Even when accepting the doctrine that the Jewish people must be preserved so that they could illustrate "the living words of the Scripture,"[63] the idea might be advanced that only "a few" of them were needed for this purpose. And the Jews were not to win honor by this consideration, moreover, but rather only "to give living witness of their own shame and their crime in spilling the divine blood of Christ."[64]

This terrifying accusation, which runs like a black thread through so much of medieval Christian thought, was given a strong contemporary accent at sessions of the recent Ecumenical Council. A Church spokesman there, Cardinal Bea, while calling for the formal abandonment of this accusation, referred candidly to "the old and extremely strong anti-Semitic tradition in the Church," which had allowed Nazi propaganda to insinuate itself "even among Christians," thus facilitating the murder of "hundreds of thousands of Jews."[65]

Among the various elements that have had a share in fostering these anti-Jewish sentiments among Christians, the role of medieval art has been far from negligible. Much of it is great and moving art in other respects but the anti-Semitic content is often so familiar, so taken for granted, that it is easily overlooked, contributing in this manner to those automatic responses, which have for many centuries remained tragically unchanged.

CHAPTER VIII
ICONOCLASM AND ITS
RATIONALIZATIONS

THE DESTRUCTION OF ART is often productive of feelings of self-righteousness, particularly when it occurs in periods of social conflict or in countries considered backward. Actually art has been ravaged by all peoples and at all times, in the West as much as anywhere. An inventorist of 1724 reported that there were over three hundred "old" churches in Paris.[1] Today there are but twenty-one of these still standing. Only a part of those that have disappeared were victims of France's series of revolutionary upheavals. The remainder were martyrs to religious conflicts, to the change of taste, to royal vanity, to urban expansion, or simply to indifference.

The Revolution of 1789 especially is a familiar whipping boy for French outrages against art monuments. It undoubtedly had its inglorious share of such vandalism but its role was not nearly as exclusive as guides and sacristans describe it. The Reformation was at least as ruinous as the Revolution, as a scholar discovered recently when he catalogued French artistic devastation, period by period.[2] And these two were by no means the only major annihilators of medieval art.

Whether in creation or destruction, religious art has seldom left people indifferent. Some have held to it with passion; others have abjured it just as fervidly. At times its content and even its form have been fought over with extraordinary vehemence, many people having lost their lives in one such controversy. Whatever else was involved and whichever side had merit, the conflict itself was an attestation of the importance of its subject. Imbued as it is with the power to sway man's thoughts, to rouse his emotions, we should not be surprised that at times of social contention religious art has often become a target.

It has been shown elsewhere how the Saint-Gilles abbey church suffered at the hands of the Huguenots. Whatever of architectural value was left by them was finished off during the Revolution of 1789. Nor is it surprising that Albi cathedral, that "lair of the inquisitor," was not forgotten by the Protestants. However, they were successfully driven off by a doughty prelate, after having penetrated into the sanctuary where one soldier emptied his bowels on the altar —he was burned alive for this crime—but the flamboyant art of the enclosure did not suffer greatly. This unfortunately was not the case with a number of other medieval edifices. The mutilation of sculpture by the Reformists was often so thorough—as at Meaux, Auxerre, Charité-sur-Loire, Périgueux—that it is virtually impossible to identify the surviving stumps.

It is on record that Calvin sought to restrain his followers from iconoclasm. But his declared opinion that "images in a temple are an abomination, a defilement,"[3] would hardly be calculated to encourage moderation. Luther was more consistent in frankly asking that monasteries be reduced to heaps of ashes, a course of action which the Swiss Protestant Zwingli explained brutally: "When we destroy their nests, the storks do not return."[4] Little regard for the esthetic merits of art works was shown by these men, but the painting by the Dutch artist, Frans Francken, showing Protestant iconoclasts with the heads of asses was a gross distortion. These men were far from stupid. It was the Catholic content that they frankly aimed at. Only the French Jansenists hated beauty on principle, their famous Mère Angélique, whom Philippe de Champagne painted so sympathetically, being quoted as saying: "I love all that is ugly. Art is nothing but lies and vanity. Whoever makes concessions to the senses takes away from God." She had the portal sculpture of her chapel at Port-Royal defaced to alleviate the pain that the sight of beauty caused her.[5]

Protestants at the abbey of Saint-Savin-sur-Gartempe, in 1562 and 1568, obedient to the Lutheran doctrine of devastation, destroyed all its conventual buildings, set fire to the bell tower, burned the choir stalls and threw the miraculous image of the Virgin into the river. It is beyond comprehension why they should have spared the church frescoes, the finest medieval mural painting in France [Pl. 115]. The ruined abbey became the headquarters of a brigand, the notorious Baron des Francs, who married the abbot's sister. When returned to the Benedictines, the monastery was in such a state of decrepitude that repair seemed hardly worthwhile. And the monks were too poor to undertake anything beyond whitewashing the frescoed walls and trimming them in floral designs.[6]

As it turned out, this probably saved the great Saint-Savin frescoes from destruction during the Revolution. Repeatedly we meet up with fortunate accidents of this kind, where temporary oblivion has helped preserve old art—a sad enough commentary in itself. Prosper Mérimée, the celebrated author, whose services in salvaging medieval art rendered over many years as Inspector of Historic Monuments are not too well known, gets credit for resurrecting the Saint-Savin murals. Due to his efforts likewise a number of other medieval

115. *Saint-Savin-sur-Gartempe*, *Abbey Church*. Fresco (beginning of
12th century). God appears to Abraham.

116. *Chartres Cathedral*. Sculpture from the former roodscreen (13th century).
The Nativity. Now in the cathedral crypt.

paintings were rediscovered, most of which had been blotted out by churchmen who had found them unbearably offensive or naïve.*

Unfortunately the methods used to obliterate much religious art during the fastidious eighteenth century were not always reversible. Nor were the reasons for destroying it uniquely esthetic ones. It is suggested, for example, that the effigies of St. Christopher that used to be prominently displayed at churches so that Christians could say a quick prayer to him and thus assure their living through that day were the victims of Voltaire's barbs.[7] The canons aimed at blunting the satirist's irony by demolishing its object. It would have seemed more reasonable if they had left the art and abolished the legend.

It was also under the sign of the Enlightenment that the declared war was

*In Sweden, when modern technics permitted the uncovering of medieval paintings which had been whitewashed, the clergy were at times embarrassed by so much splendor—often nude—which they claimed drew the attention of the faithful away from their sermons.

conducted against the old roodscreens that closed the sanctuary off from the nave in many churches. Thus incidentally disappeared some of the finest of Gothic sculpture. Various offices had been held in this private enclave of the clergy, who now expressed the desire of opening these services to the people: an admirable intention, if the screen sculpture had been preserved. This rarely occurred, however, except in a few instances where the excellent base stone was used, in reverse, for church pavement. Those at Chartres, dug up long after, are as beautiful as any other sculpture of the same period at this cathedral [Pl. 116].

It is understandable that a period so self-conscious about intellectual clarity as was the eighteenth century should have regarded light with fervor. But it is harder to appreciate why so logical an age should have considered it indispensable that churches be bathed in the sun's pure rays. This passion for bright church interiors resulted in the destruction of a great part of France's marvelous stained glass. Even at wondrously preserved Chartres some of the great upper windows of the choir were pulled out so as to light up a marble composition newly carved for the main altar. And Notre-Dame de Paris lost all its old lancets at this time. The man assigned this task has left a detailed record of its execution coupled with much self-praise for the grisaille that he substituted for the medieval glass.[8] It was around this time too that the interior of the cathedral was painted white and that Germain Soufflot, king's architect and builder of the Paris Panthéon, tore a large swath out of its central tympanum to allow for the passage of great royal processions.

One would think, to heed Goethe, that men of the eighteenth century suffered from real anguish when inside edifices illumined by medieval colored glass. To Faust it gave the sense of being in a dark and horrible prison:

> Weh! steck ich in dem Kerker noch?
> Verfluchtes, dumpfes Mauerloch,
> Wo selbst das liebe Himmelslicht
> Trüb durch gemalte Scheiben bricht!*[9]

If sculpture was to be obliterated for esthetic reasons, one would hope that the method used on Autun's façade in the eighteenth century would have been more widely applied. Here the great tympanum was simply plastered over. Seventy years later, when the local priest surmised that the old sculpture might still be intact beneath the mortar, he had to go back to a document of 1482 to ascertain the subject of the muffled tympanum. So swiftly had this work, surely among the very greatest of Romanesque monuments, been forgotten.[10] The plaster covering was removed and the sculpture found to be in excellent condi-

---

*Ah, am I still stuck in this cell? / Curséd, musty dungeon hell, / Where Heaven's cherished rays must pass / Through murky panes of painted glass!

tion. Only one arch of saints' figures had been chopped away: Evidently they had been too salient to be covered over. And the head of the great central Christ had also disappeared—undoubtedly for the same reason.

More than fifty years after the uncovering of the Autun façade the local Musée Rolin was the recipient of five pieces of medieval sculpture, one of which was identified by the historical society of the area as possibly being the missing Christ head. But the problem of acquiring a ladder sufficiently long to try it out proved too arduous. It was not until another half century had passed, in 1948, that enough interest was finally stirred up to make the test. The head was found to fit "exactly, almost to the slightest sinuosities of the break." And the local savants announced triumphantly that "the Christ of the tympanum has regained all its majesty."[11]

The unearthing of Autun's famous reclining Eve (see Pl. 127), one of the finest of unclothed twelfth-century sculptured figures, was the prize of an independent accident. It was discovered during the demolition of a house for which the back surface of the carving had served as face stone. Old descriptions of the north façade from which this figure had been taken when most of the cathedral's medieval sculpture had either been covered over or destroyed tell of the great matching forms of Adam and Satan that completed this truly unique presentation of the Temptation. Are they too reposing somewhere, immured in some eighteenth-century house? One hopes in any case that hereafter the tools of Autun's demolition squads will be used with circumspection.

Whatever has been said on the positive side about the Revolution's cultural accomplishments through the organization of some of the nation's great museums, the fact remains that these collections were in the bulk made up of objects rescued from iconoclasm. Rarely have the reasons for the destruction of art been more honestly acknowledged. The communal council of Paris, in a decree adopted October 23, 1793, declared that it was its duty "to cause to disappear all monuments that could feed religious prejudices and which recall the hated memory of the kings." It consequently ordered the sacrifice of the famous row of the "Kings of France" high up on the façade of Notre-Dame.[12]

It is ironic that this loss (the statues to be seen on the cathedral's front today are modern restorations) and others like it in many churches were the result of an iconographic error. For scholars have proved that these crowned figures were not the founders of the royal dynasty, as had been assumed for centuries, but were actually the Kings of Judah, a sort of genealogical representation of the ancestors of Christ. The correct attribution might not have spared the great figures in any case, since the revolutionaries often made no great distinction between mundane and heavenly monarchs.

There was nevertheless something almost animistic in the way any feudal symbols were attacked during the great upheaval. Anything bearing the fleur-de-lis was scratched, scraped, chopped, chiseled. One would wonder conse-

quently at the amazing preservation of Chartres, which swarms with the royal
coat of arms. It would almost seem as though a special grace did indeed protect
this most marvelous of all of France's medieval monuments. As a matter of
fact, the cathedral was at one point threatened with extinction and was saved
only by a ridiculous circumstance. Its lead roof had already been removed—to
be melted down into revolutionary bullets—and the weather coming in through
the timberwork began promptly to attack the vault. The district administrator
soon began to complain about the high cost of keeping the church in repairs and
suggested that it be destroyed in a "patriotic demolition." The fate of Chartres
hung in the balance until some architect offered the countering viewpoint that
the debris caused by an explosion would too much obstruct traffic around the
cathedral.[13]

It should be said that only two years later the national Commission Tempo-
raire des Arts called for the repair of the damage done to the cathedral by the
removal of its lead roof-covering, calling it "one of the most beautiful monuments which the republic possesses." But this was a strictly minority opinion,
judging from what happened to other medieval edifices. Sainte-Chapelle became
a flour warehouse,* Saint-Germain-des-Prés a saltpeter refinery. Notre-Dame
was put up for sale and might have gone over to private ownership but for a legal
controversy. Moissac church was likewise placed on the block but found no
buyers at 6,000 livres. Its beautiful cloister, on the other hand, was purchased
for the city by the communal secretary—for 300 livres.[14]

And much of what the Revolution left intact of France's medieval heritage
disappeared in the nineteenth-century's version of a demographic explosion and
the great push of urbanism that was associated with it. Progress seemed often
to have been inseparable from destruction of the old—in reality it was esthetic
indifference that often dictated disastrous solutions of civic problems. That
fabulous innovation, the railroad, proved a formidable peril to medieval beauty.
Its iron cowcatcher crumbled many superb monuments such as the Alyscamps
of Arles and Carpentras' old wall. Prosper Mérimée, by eloquence and vitupera-
tion, was able to save Avignon's papal enceinte and the Moissac cloister. But
there were countless other victims to modernism, including the three beautiful
twelfth-century cloisters of Toulouse. It is surprising that in this case some of
the pillar capitals of La Daurade, Saint-Étienne, and Saint-Sernin were put
aside, thus sparing scholars the task of proving that here, in the brilliant capital
of Languedoc, twelfth-century French carving reached its most exquisite
mastery.

The spirit of conservation, which would have seemed so normal, was nevertheless rare enough in the early nineteenth century. In the destruction of the

---

*It later was used to store old court records from the Palais de Justice and this important
function, Louis Grodecki has told the author, probably saved its precious glass, since the leading
had to be kept in good repair so that the papers would not be damaged by the weather.

great abbey church of Cluny, for centuries Christendom's most imposing edifice, whose radiating influence profoundly marked Western art, no such care was taken. First a big hole was gouged out of the nave, to make way for a market. The following year demolition of the entire structure was decreed— by the quickest method. The towers were blown down and the vault came tumbling with them. Thereafter the great mound served as a quarry until its stone was gone. Somehow a few bits of rubble were spared from the ruins: The marvel of this art reveals only too sadly to us our irretrievable loss [Pl. 117].

And so the disgraceful story of devastation has continued, right down to the present day, with the "well-intentioned" mayor of one of France's charming medieval towns having had to be argued out of the demolition of an enclave of two hundred houses recently on the grounds that "tourists would no longer come to Saumur."[15] But it is becoming more and more generally accepted at last that the problems of hygiene and decent living quarters in an old setting, formidable though they may be, can be solved without resort to measures of artistic desolation.

This was by no means the constant concern of the nineteenth-century city-planner Haussmann, who tore down a mass of medieval edifices around Notre-Dame, avowedly to provide an unobstructed view of the cathedral, and chopped façades and apses off medieval churches that stood in the way of his boulevards. However, Napoleon III's prefect had an imperious supplementary reason for much of his artery-expansion program: to rid Paris of those twisted, narrow streets which the insurrectionists of 1830 and 1848 had barricaded to such advantage. Haussmann himself said it as plainly as could be desired: "The execution of these diverse operations . . . opened up Old Paris, the quarter of revolts and barricades. . . . Assuredly the Emperor, in planning these broad avenues, which are so unsuited to the habitual tactics of the local insurrectionists, was not thinking primarily of their strategic importance . . . but it is undeniable that this was a very happy consequence of these operations. . . ."[16]

The farther one goes back in time the more candid become the reasons given for the sacrifice of art. This frankness stemmed from the acceptance, challenged only in modern times, of its enormous sociopolitical role. Art-as-propaganda is no invention of the Marxists. A spokesman of the Revolution of 1789 had already said: "Since painting speaks to the imagination of the people, it is up to the legislator to see to it that it gives them only useful lessons."[17] And one thousand years prior to that, at the Church Ecumenical Council of Nicea, held in 787, exactly the same conception of the control of art was expressed in a celebrated decree, beginning: "The composition of religious images is not left to the initiative of the artists. . . ."[18]

The occasion was the great "quarrel of images," which for over a hundred years engaged the two leading centers of Christendom, Constantinople and

Rome. An amazing feature of this conflict was the fact that it was launched by one of Christianity's great champions, Emperor Leo III, who fifteen years before the epochal battle at Poitiers had stopped the Moslem surge onto the European continent from the East by the successful defense of Byzantium. Such a man must have had serious reasons for opening a campaign that quickly transformed the Church into two warring camps. Leo's initial act—removing the image of Christ from the palace front and substituting a cross for it—was grounded on theology, as was explained by an inscription that was put up at the time: "The emperor cannot tolerate an image of Christ, without voice or breath, and Scripture itself prohibits his reproduction by his human side alone."[19] However, there is considerable evidence that the controversy entailed a number of other motives.

A revealing indication is that the extreme decision of banning man's image categorically from all art was never adopted by the Byzantine iconoclasts. It appeared, for example, in murals painted on public buildings, though always in strictly lay subjects, triumphal processions, and the like. Even when religious works were painted out, the human figure was not absent from the secular pieces that were often substituted.[20] On the other hand, we must not lose sight of the fact that strong anti-image trends had always existed in the East. Leo himself stemmed from a section of Asia Minor where the Catholic bishops were determinedly iconoclastic.

Historians have also pointed to Leo's imperative desire to establish the imperial power as preeminent, which purportedly caused him to look askance at any division in his subjects' loyalty.[21] He is presumed to have seen the most dangerous challenge as coming from the monastic orders, whose sway over the masses derived largely from their miracle-working images.[22] Moreover, the Byzantine emperors who destroyed images also took over church possessions, breaking up monastic colonies, deporting many monks, simply murdering others.[23]

Rome's response to the Byzantine iconoclasm was passionate and varied. It proclaimed the image-destroyers to be outright heretics and countered the charge of idolatry by mustering tradition in support of the holy images and by arguing their utility as a medium of religious discipline over the uninstructed masses. It also began a systematic collection of stories of miracles caused by the images and fostered their cult. Finally, after more than a century, Rome was able to break permanently into the iconoclastic dynasty itself when the throne fell to a woman, Empress Irene, who turned out to be image-faithful, reestablishing their cult—and the authority of Rome—in the Empire.

This important accomplishment was consecrated by the great Council of Nicea, which, while considering a number of problems of a broader social and political nature, did not hold esthetic questions as less worthy of attention. The role of art and its manifold relations within the social structure were meticulously studied and the most detailed rules laid down regarding its creation. This, it was decreed, was to take place strictly according to Church "principles" and "tradition" and under close supervision of clerics, who were empowered not only to dictate the subject matter but the very arrangement of figures in a composition. Only the "art" was left to the artist, and this was meant in the narrowest technical sense.[24]

A strong tincture of antagonism to images continued to color clerical thought nevertheless all through the Middle Ages, in the West as well as in the East. There is a famous story about two young clerics from the cathedral school of Chartres proving that it was still strong as late as the eleventh century. While on a pilgrimage to the South, the young men stopped at the church of Aurillac where they expressed righteous indignation before a statue of Saint Géraud, which was decorated in gold and precious stones. One of the scholars is reported as saying to his companion, "with an ironic smile: 'Brother, what do you think of this idol? Would not Jupiter or Mars find themselves content with such a statue?' "

The chronicle goes on to tell about another image-hating monk, who three days later, at Conques, passed off some sarcastic remarks about the mass of pilgrims prostrated before the gem-incrusted image of Sainte Foy, which can still be seen at this church [Pl. 118]. The blasphemer was struck dead. Whereupon the narrator saw the light. This was no "vile idol," he acknowledged, but a pious commemoration of the saint, meant to make her intercession in behalf of those who prayed to her the more efficacious.[25]

The impassioned campaign that St. Bernard conducted against the "excesses" of church building and ornamentation, while not usually looked upon as iconoclastic, nevertheless fits largely into this pattern. An understanding of this qualified iconoclasm, inspired by twelfth-century Christendom's leading figure, would be impossible if one did not take into account the contemporary conditions and problems of the Church. Gregory VII had died without accomplishing his major reforms. The papal power was still a football of secular forces. The Cistercian movement was in effect an attempt to carry out the program that Gregory had outlined but failed to realize.

Though Cîteaux grew rapidly, the heresies of the twelfth century spread with greater speed. With admirable clarity St. Bernard saw the social basis of this massive revolt against the Church. This consciousness vibrates throughout all of his great *Apologia*, that bitter, brilliant stricture of the extravagances of ecclesiastic living and art. "The Church's walls are dazzling but her poor are needy. Her stones are clothed in gold but her children are abandoned in their nudity. The eyes of the rich are regaled at the cost of the poor. The curious find their pleasure there but the needy do not find the means of sustaining themselves."[26]

117. *Former Abbey Church of Cluny* (12th century). Capital relief: The Third Tone of Plain Song.
The Cluny capitals are now in the Musée Lapidaire Farinier.

118. *Conques-en-Rouergue, Church of Sainte-Foy*. Statue of Sainte Foy (10th century). In church treasury.

Bernard's descriptions of the gastronomic excesses of many convents seem to have been extracted from a gourmet's handbook. How many different ways were necessary to serve mere eggs? "What pain and care were not taken to disguise them, to turn them, to make them soft, to make them hard, to chop them? Here they are fricasseed, there they are cooked over the fire; they are stuffed, they are scrambled, and at times their parts are separately served." As for wine, in some convents three or four different ones had to be tasted before one could be chosen for a meal. And what could be said of food and drink could be equaled by other lavishness. Some churchmen had grown accustomed to being surrounded by cavaliers and servants with "curled perukes." They could not travel twelve miles without carrying linens, glassware, even chandeliers. He had met one abbot who had more than sixty horses in his suite.[27]

The saint was not solely concerned about the poor when castigating such luxury. Fundamentally he was interested in the Church and in the image that it presented to the faithful, which he wanted to be identified with Christ of the Evangels, friend of the poor, of the suffering, and of the humble. And he saw the monks as sort of shock troops in the great battles that the Church was engaged in. Austerity was more than a display of Christian virtue, it was the very condition of good soldiership. It must be said that Bernard himself gave an uncompromising example of the asceticism that he advocated. He vomited so frequently that he had a special hole dug in the ground near his place at table. In every way imaginable he mortified his physical self, demanding the same kind of discipline from his companions. Once he rebuked a monk for snoring, sleeping "according to the flesh," as he disdainfully described it.[28]

Bernard's attacks on the excessive splendor of much monastic art cannot be understood except in the context of these other anxieties. He exempted buildings meant for the cult in his criticisms of church construction and decorative splendor, thus differentiating himself from the out-and-out iconoclast. For he recognized the Church's enormous educative role and the importance of figurative illustration for an illiterate population. The bishops, he acknowledged, were answerable for "the foolish as well as the wise." They had to "excite the devotion of vulgar people by carnal means, not being able to do so sufficiently by spiritual ones."[29]

But while making allowances for churches devoted to the cult Bernard was uncompromising on art destined for the gaze of the religious alone, fearing for them what has been termed the "concupiscence of the eyes."[30] These were all men who had left the world for the love of Jesus Christ, "who see all that is most striking, most charming, as so much dung." And thinking of the refulgent art at the convents of Cluny, Vézelay, Saint-Remi of Reims, and other Cluniac churches, he demanded: "Whose devotion, I beg you, do we mean to excite? What benefit do we expect to draw from all these things? Is it the admiration of fools or the satisfaction of simpletons?"[31]

One can appreciate Bernard's viewpoint as having great inner-Church importance while giving fervid thanks that his impassioned efforts were not more successful. Kingsley Porter has called him "beauty-hating."[32] Certainly it would be hard to call him "beauty-loving." As a matter of fact, he was usually quite blind to his external surroundings, his contemporary biographer attributing this to his having "mortified the sense of curiosity." He further narrates that Bernard lived at Cîteaux for a year without noticing that the novices' room was vaulted or that it had three windows. For a whole day he traveled along the lake at Lausanne without even seeing it. And when on another occasion he was reproached for the fine livery of his mule, he was amazed, demanding: "What harness, what mule?"[33] His abstraction protected him from the temptations and disturbances which he wished to spare the religious communities. Several books in the Clairvaux library that have been preserved teem with the kind of monsters Bernard flayed in his *Apologia*,[34] and one of them, a manuscript of the Song of Songs, contains illuminated initials, one "O" showing a man and woman in a close embrace.[35] The ultimate irony: After his death, St. Bernard's body was wrapped in an Oriental cloth that was richly decorated with woven illustrations of those very same monsters against which he had so passionately inveighed.[36]

St. Bernard's ban on curiosity extended to intellectual matters also. He had a glittering example in Abélard of how a far-ranging inquisitiveness of mind could lead even the strongest brain astray. Cistercian monks were permitted to read only the Fathers and Scripture. They were not allowed to conduct classes for lay students for such worldly contacts were replete with danger, physical and mental.[37] As late as 1198, when the interest in ancient learning was everywhere bursting medieval intellectual bonds, a Cistercian monk was punished for having secretly learned Hebrew, the language of the Old Testament. The following year, it is recorded, another monk was disciplined for writing poetry.[38]

Yet such taboos were all part of a wholly consistent program. It is known that St. Bernard looked askance at the wide artistic and literary activities of the Cluniac convents. Though he defended spiritual work as being of higher excellence than manual, he would have been the last to suggest that his own convents shift from their physical labors to the Cluny curriculum of manuscript-writing and psalmody. Actually the Cistercian monasteries were developing rapidly into great agricultural-productive units. Clairvaux itself was to build up to a mammoth community of three hundred monks and four hundred lay brothers, all toilers. Economics may have had nothing to do with St. Bernard's initial program, but the hard work and abstemiousness he prescribed were bound to prosper just as they would help keep the morals of the monks intact.

The influence of Bernard's artistic admonitions was profoundly felt on Cistercian structures. An oratory built at Clairvaux in 1136, when the saint and his order had already attained the kind of fame which in the Middle Ages placed fortune at his beck, has been described as bare and "dismal."[39] Bernard's biographer bursts with virtuous pride when describing Pope Innocent II's visit to this convent and the rigorous asceticism that "the Romans" (the pope's suite) saw there: "nothing that could tempt their cupidity, no furnishings to attract their eyes by their richness, and in the chapel they saw nothing but empty walls. These monks could be envied only for their saintly morals." The table offered the visitors was as forbidding: In the bread chaff was mixed with the flour, beans were the great delicacy, and there was no flesh served. By exception a fish plate was brought out on one occasion—but only for the pope: "all the others had nothing but the look of it."[40]

The order early issued decrees rigorously limiting the amount and kind of church and vestmental ornamentation. All painting and sculpture were banned, storied pavements also, for had not Bernard expressed horror at once seeing a passerby spit into an angel's mouth?[41] Stained-glass windows, which were just then beginning to fill churches with glory, were held in especial horror by the Cistercians, undoubtedly because of their rich colors. When certain abbeys disobeyed the ban and installed them anyway, they were ordered to destroy them. Eventually painting church windows in grisaille was considered to be acceptable. Sculpture was not even allowed on the high pillar capitals. And there was to be but one crucifix in any church—at the main altar. As for the exterior, stone towers were prohibited as tending to "violate the modesty of the order." And the bells were limited to two, their chimes carefully regulated.[42]

Though these measures were mainly restrictive there is some evidence that destruction of art works, and even iconoclasm, were encouraged by the Cistercians. When Bernard counseled his friend, Comte Thibaut de Champagne, to combat adversity by acts of increased piety and abnegation, the latter took two huge vases, gifts of his uncle, King Henry of England, "admirably worked and encrusted with precious stones of the greatest value," and had their gems torn out and their gold broken up and sold. With the money he let tabernacles be built, Bernard's biographer boasts, "more precious than gold and diamonds in the Lord's eyes."[43]

Pressure by St. Bernard on other orders for the simplification of their lives and trappings was persistent. After his death the same influence was attempted by his disciples, as is illustrated by the celebrated *Dialogue between a Cluniac and a Cistercian Monk*, which appeared in the second half of the twelfth century. In it Bernard's apostle reproaches his opponent with the excessive luxury of Cluny's paintings, tapestries, silks, and sumptuous ornaments. He even scolds him for the great number of its bells and "the subtlety of its chants."[44]

Into the thirteenth century the program of militant austerity was pressed by Cîteaux, deeply engaged as it was in the fight against heresy, which was coming to its zenith at the time. More than ever the Cistercians were conscious of the vulnerability of the Catholic clergy because of the extravagance of their lives. Their efforts to sway members of other orders is illustrated by the account of the visit some Cistercian monks made at the Premonstratensian abbey of Vicogne. They were horrified by the brilliant murals that their hosts had just had painted in their chapter house and church and demanded that they be effaced immediately. Far from complying, the Premonstratensians engaged in further extravagances, buying two great bells and one small one, a hanging candelabrum of gilt metal, two silver candlesticks, a new censer, and the vestments to go with all of this.[45]

There does not seem to have been unqualified enthusiasm in the rest of the Church for Cîteaux' bleak program. Indeed, even the latter lost much of its early militancy by the fourteenth century. But unfortunately by this time the great period of ecclesiastic building was ended and the loss caused by Bernardine austerity irretrievable. Happily there was, even in the saint's time, a countering conception of the place of art within the Church, responsive to the liberating currents released by the profoundly changing socioeconomic order. The Church reflected these developments most strikingly through its urban bishops and some of its great abbots, who were among the most energetic and able businessmen of their time. The moneymaking enterprises of such men as Suger of Saint-Denis, San Domingo of Silos, and Robert de Torigini of Mont-Saint-Michel would have beggared the activities of even the most successful of the contemporary merchants.

The renowned abbot of Silos has been described as "a modern saint in his time, not a martyr or pure ascetic" but one who "established the power of his abbey as the kings established their secular power."[46] As for Abbot Robert, between the years of 1155 and 1159, he had to take business trips to England and the Channel Islands, to the king's assizes at Gavrai, Domfort, Caen, and Carentan, to the espiscopal courts of Avranches, Coutances, and Bayeux, and to that of the archbishop of Rouen. In these various sessions he was engaged in "proving his rights, exchanging, purchasing, receiving by gift or royal charter; acquiring here a piece of land, there a mill, a vineyard, a tithe, a church to add to the lands and rents, mills and forests, markets and churches and feudal rights which the abbey already possessed."[47]

These men also found time to write and to encourage letters and art and particularly art that added to the luster of their own monasteries. Robert created a great façade for his church and Abbot Suger's accomplishments in his abbey church are legendary. The characteristic element in this stupendous work, most of it done in the incredible span of thirty-nine months, was the way every detail, small or great, was guided personally by the abbot. He led carpenters to the woods in search of vault beams of proper length, finding the required twelve—not eleven and not thirteen—certainly by grace of a heavenly dispensation. He supervised the cartage of stone from the quarries and the acquisition of the best ingredients for his stained-glass windows. He provided the geometric instruments needed to line up the new apse with the old nave and concerned himself especially with all the ornamentation, discussing their work with the goldsmiths and devising the iconography of the lancets. No wonder he put his name everywhere [Pl. 119]. He must have felt in the most active sense that "*Sugerius hoc fecit.*" For without him it probably would not have been done, surely not in the way it was.

The historical image that has come down to us of a great dramatic contest between the two most eminent French churchmen of the twelfth century—St. Bernard and Abbot Suger—is doubtless highly colored. Nevertheless, these men did represent sharply variant tendencies within the Church, whose primary political aspect was their relationship to pope and king. Bernard everywhere pushed the temporal claims of the papacy and other members of the hierarchy. He even sided with a notorious simoniac, Archbishop Henri de Sens, when the latter was brought before a court of bishops presided over by Louis VI. The prelate claimed that only the pope had jurisdiction over him, which St. Bernard passionately seconded in letters to the pontiff. "Let a judgment come from your mouth," he wrote Honorius II, "that will rescue innocence and preserve equity.

119. *Saint-Denis, Abbey Church* (12th century). Detail of stained-glass lancet. Abbot Suger lies prone at the Virgin's feet. His name is prominently inscribed (above his head), as it was in other places in the church. The figure of Suger was rather freely repaired in the 19th century.

Otherwise, to refer this case to the king's authority is nothing less, alas, than to turn a man over to the hatred of his enemies."[48]

Abbot Suger, boyhood companion and lifelong friend of Louis VI and regent for his son, Louis VII, during the latter's absence at the Second Crusade (1147–1149), served the royal interest loyally. A fortunate circumstance allowed him to identify closely his two greatest attachments, the crown and his abbey. This was made possible by the fact that the latter's founder, St. Denis, was the patron saint of France, which made the abbey church a kind of national shrine. Moreover, the abbot's devotion to the throne proved less embarrassing than it might otherwise have been because of Rome's strong reliance on French support during its protracted struggles with the German emperors.

It was in fact during France's conflicts with Germany that Suger's patriotism shone most brilliantly, displaying a nationalistic spirit that was far ahead of its time. When invasion by the Germans threatened, Saint-Denis was the center at which rallied the nation's united resistance, to whom the abbot delivered the fighting watchword: "Let them feel the reward of their affront, not in our land but in theirs which, often conquered, is subject to the Franks by the royal right of the Franks." For him the English too were "destined by moral and natural law to be subjected to the French" for France was "the mistress of the earth."[49]

It would be difficult to conceive of such a man as following the ascetic prescriptions of St. Bernard. All the ideas, all the projects of the abbot, by his nature and position, led to worldliness. He was the incomparable showman, to whose great church galas the whole population swarmed, even "the synagogue of the Jews of Paris."[50] What a difference in his reception of Pope Innocent II at Saint-Denis and that given him at Clairvaux! Suger himself described it, in his obsequious pride of the poor peasant's son "lifted up from the dunghill."[51] The pope and his cardinals were dressed in their "richest ornaments," the pontiff with a miter on his head "circled by a golden diadem." He rode on a white horse, "richly caparisoned," preceded by his cardinals, two by two, also mounted, on colored palfreys. The barons went on foot, "like humble servants," leading the pope's horse by the bridle, throwing handfuls of coins to the crowd to help clear the passage. All this culminated in the celebration of mass by the pope, whose golden crown glittered with brilliant stones and pearls. Then all the notables retired to the cloister for a sumptuous meal, the mutton for which had been supplied at the last minute by one of those frequent "miracles" that brightened the abbot's enchanted life.[52]

Suger's recorded views regarding the proper place and character of church art seem a directed reply to the Spartan ideas of St. Bernard. In his *De administratione* he explains the function of splendor in a sacramental sense: "To me, I confess, one thing has always seemed preeminently fitting: that every costlier or costliest thing should serve, first and foremost, for the administration of the Holy Eucharist. . . . The detractors also object that a saintly mind, a pure heart, a faithful intention ought to suffice for this sacred function. . . . [But] we profess that we must do homage also through the outward ornaments of sacred vessels, and to nothing in the world in an equal degree as to the service of the Holy Sacrifice, with all inner purity and with all outward splendor."[53]

When rebuilding the tombs of the founding saints at Saint-Denis, he narrates, his intention was to adorn them with gilt panels of cast copper, "lest the place be disfigured by the substance of unconcealed stones." Considering the "generosity" of these saints to the faithful, he adds, it was no more than proper to cover their ashes "with the most precious material." As for the altar, he had thought of a golden "but modest" panel. However, the holy martyrs themselves intervened to shame him for his diffidence, as though to say to him: "Whether thou wantst it or not, we want it of the best." Their intercession made itself known in the form of bounteous gifts! Even popes donated priceless gems from their pontifical rings to be encrusted in the panel and kings and princes gave "precious pearls of diverse colors and properties."[54] On another occasion, when work on his great crucifix was proceeding and jewels for it ran out, "lo and behold" another "miracle" occurred. Some monks came with a batch of shining stones which the Comte Thibaut had given them as alms. The heaven-favored Suger pushed a good bargain and got them for four hundred livres, "though they were worth much more."[55]

It would be hard to separate rationalization from naïve credulity in much of this. However, what appears to have been an above-normal sensitiveness in Suger to external color and magnificence was seconded by a coincidence that could have struck him as nothing short of predestined. According to the doctrine of his patron saint, Dionysius the Pseudo-Areopagite (St. Denis), whose fifth-century manuscript was in the abbey library, it was only through the contemplation of material objects, presented to man by reflected light, that he could attain to God, the source of all light. This was the so-called "anagogical" concept, which the abbot illustrated by describing the effect on him of beautiful gems. They carried him, he explained, into "some strange region of the universe which neither exists entirely in the slime of the earth nor entirely in the purity of Heaven." Basically this was a materialistic doctrine, entirely consistent with the abbot's worldliness and which John the Scot, when he translated Dionysius' manuscript into Latin, about 858, had put into less fanciful outline: "It is impossible for our mind to rise to the imitation and contemplation of the celestial hierarchies unless it relies upon that material guidance which is commensurate to it."[56]

When rebuilding the church at Saint-Denis and endowing it with shining ornamentation and sacramental gear, Abbot Suger seemed always to have color and light in mind. He had a mosaic put into a façade tympanum—though this form of art was by then anachronistic in Northern France—solely because he could not resist the variegated brightness of its glass. No man could have been better chosen to give the art of stained glass its great impulsion, consecrated at Saint-Denis by fourteen windows and by the first appearance anywhere of a great rose in the west façade. He himself has described the way he saw his reconstructed church "pervaded by the wonderful and uninterrupted light of most sacred windows."[57] And long before the seventeenth- and eighteenth-century canons, he pulled down the old roodscreen of the sanctuary "lest the beauty and magnificence of the church be obscured by such a barrier."[58]

It was by its luminousness more than by its dimensions that Saint-Denis marked itself as the pioneer of Gothic churches. It was the brightness of its "modern" spirit that impressed itself on the eyes and minds of the large part of the French hierarchy that attended its consecration, accomplished with usual Sugerian pomp: a brilliant procession outside the church, a separate mass celebrated in every chapel by a different prelate, the king and his retinue helping to keep order at the doors "with canes and sticks."[59]

But whatever the illustrious visitors carried away from Saint-Denis in the way of new ideas on church architecture and adornment, they had actually contributed to it in its elements. It was only the combination that was entirely new. For Suger had gone into every corner of France, and indeed outside the country as well, to gather his artists and ideas. During its rebuilding Saint-Denis became the foremost artistic marketplace of its time. It is fairly certain that many of the innovations, in form and iconography, for which the abbot is often solely credited, came out of the creative ferment that was established here. Thus, most appropriately, at its royal abbey, was created France's first truly national style, which, it has been said, proved to be a significant factor in the centralizing policy of its kings.[60]

In the great esthetic contest during the first half of the twelfth century, between the Abbot of Clairvaux and the Abbot of Saint-Denis, it was the latter who ultimately triumphed. It is fortunate for the fate of Western art that it did not happen the other way around for the loss would have been immeasurable. Some eminent historians have been able to isolate the Cistercian architectural accomplishment to reach an abstract judgment about it, as in the case of one eminent scholar, who held that its rigorous restrictions, far from destroying the feeling for "beauty, grandeur, and nobility," forced the architect "to seek out simple and logical solutions . . . that led him to perfection."[61]

But such verdicts have been reached in the context of the total legacy of the Middle Ages, which somewhat distorts them. What has followed the Sugerian doctrine is so resplendent that the Bernardine variant, however denuded, may be calmly appreciated for its own unique qualities. But what if it alone had persisted as the type of Western art? How sad and drab our esthetic world would have been! And it is questionable besides if the Church itself, with the support merely of such a "pure" and "perfect" art, could have continued to belong to the whole people in the explosive dynamism of Western life.

By a surer instinct Suger aimed at and reached the masses. His immediate motives did not, it is true, take this goal very clearly into account. Devoted to royalty, he meant also to serve the Church, not by retreat and isolation, however, but by an ever greater involvement in the world. This primary drive vitalized everything he did and helped translate his theological-esthetic concepts into artistic forms of rare effectiveness and appeal.

CHAPTER IX
THE MEDIEVAL ARTIST
AND THE BUILDING BOOM

OVER THE MAIN PORTAL of the church of Saint-Pierre at Moissac, at the bottom of either side of the outer arch, can be seen two tiny figures that are outside the range of the door's major sculpture. In fact, they can easily be passed over by the hurried visitor for they are not mentioned in guidebooks and have no apparent relationship to the iconographic story. Yet the little carvings *are* important, representing, it seems evident, the self-portraits of the two sculptors who collaborated on this portal.

Far from being posed, the two men are frantically active, their bodies twisted in what are clearly purposive movements. The one at the right gives up his identity more readily because of the mason's mallet in his right hand, which he has swung far back and down, prepared to deliver a blow on the head of a chisel which he is holding with his left. He is apparently in the process of finishing off the last of an alternating series of ornamental imagery—the same bird pecking away at the same plant—that goes all the way to the top of the arch and then down again on the other side [Pl. 120].

The other figure is engaged in the same operation though his hammer has disappeared. He is sharply differentiated from his co-worker in appearance, the intention of the sculptors having clearly been to say: "There were two of us who did this." The second man is clean-shaven, the broad movement of his arm having brought him face to face with the viewer. He is a younger man, whereas his companion is a person of maturer years, as his beard indicates. But the powerful muscles of the latter's uncloaked torso and of his arms reveal a prideful insistence on the vigor of his body.

Medieval artists have often attached self-portraits to their work. Even artist-clerics were not above doing so. The notion of the anonymity of early craftsmen, a hoary clerical legend, was uncritically accepted until the nineteenth century. Theophilus Presbyter, a monk who was an artist and a compiler of a

120. *Moissac, Church of Saint-Pierre.* Tympanum of south portal (12th century). Christ in majesty, surrounded by angels, the symbols of the Evangels, and the twenty-four Elders of the Apocalypse. The two tiny figures at the lower ends of the outer arch are the sculptors of the tympanum, their "signature."

famous early arts manual, expressed the kind of idea about this that used to be universally credited: "God is mindful of the humble and quiet man, the man working in silence and in the name of the Lord."[1]

The nineteenth-century art historian, A.-N. Didron, was one of the first to express doubts about the idea that medieval artists had remained voluntarily anonymous and, as the accepted legend went, "completely unselfish in their labors, working only for the love of God and their art."[2] He called on scholars to gather evidence to the contrary and within three years over 3,000 names of medieval artists were supplied from a wide variety of sources.[3]

But the pious notion managed to hang on, anyway. Several writers took up the question again in this century, adding masses of new names to Didron's list.

As for the supposed humility of medieval artists, for this, too, we have only the word of the clerics. It was, it is true, still too early for the Cellini type of personal apotheosis. But there is plenty of evidence proving that medieval artists had a healthy self-esteem. A charming example among many is the inscription that the twelfth-century sculptor, Natalis d'Autry-Issard, put on one of his carvings: "God has created everything. Man has remade everything. Natalis made me." With less fantasy Gilabertus de Toulouse simply reminded people that he was a "well-known man." Martinus d'Autun referred to himself forthrightly as a "celebrated sculptor," while the scribe "Eadwine" of the Canterbury Psalter offered a triple self-identification: his name, a full-page portrait, and his self-characterization as the "prince of scribes"![4]

As indestructible as the notion of anonymity has been the idea that most artists, certainly those before the thirteenth century, were monks or other clerics. Viollet-le-Duc alleged that this idea was consciously fostered by contemporary churchmen, who suppressed attributions to lay artists while trumpeting the work of clerics.[5] The *"fecit"* attached to ecclesiastics' names on medieval inscriptions was deliberately misinterpreted so as to mean, not "had done," but "created."

Modern scholars, particularly the English, have done much to correct this error. One of them has brought forward evidence to the effect that even tenth- and eleventh-century churches were built by "lay masons and stonecarvers, not by monks."[6] Another, L. F. Salzman, has pointed out that "Even as far back as the thirteenth century Matthew Paris expressly warns us that the attribution of a building to a particular abbot only means that he arranged for it to be built and provided the funds." And he adds: "It is hardly necessary to stress the fact that the stone buildings of the Middle Ages were erected by professional [lay] workmen," who were under the control of one master mason, as could be shown by "hundreds of building accounts."[7]

When the clerics did their own building, it was because of extraordinary conditions. They were in an isolated site or had no funds to hire professional labor or had moved to a new place and were eager to create a shelter before the cold set in. Where monks were mentioned as working it was usually as unskilled helpers of professionals "and one is inclined to suspect that they were often more of a hindrance than a help," another English authority has observed. In nine of ten cases when the aid of an enthusiastic novice is vaunted in chronicles, he notes, it is because he fell off some scaffolding or suffered some other mishap![8]

It is instructive to compare the manual of Theophilus with another artist's sketchbook dating from the Middle Ages, that of Villard de Honnecourt, who was an architect—and a layman. The monk's handbook, composed over a century earlier, is spotted with prayers and other pieties, typical of the cleric-artist's attitude toward his work. Let no man glorify himself for his skill, he declares, "or hide . . . in the closet of a grasping heart . . . what has freely been given . . . by the divine condescension." For practice of his craft gave the artist the chance to redeem himself from original sin. And Theophilus asks all his readers to "pray to Almighty God to have mercy on me."[9]

With what contrasting self-assertion does the lay artist write, introducing himself in the manner of an actor stepping out on the stage apron, decorously lifting his hand and announcing: "Villard de Honnecourt salutes you and asks all those who will work in the various categories spoken of in this book to pray for his soul *and to remember him*" [Pl. 121].[10] Here is the profoundly typifying element in the man: the frank desire to be known, to be properly regarded by his contemporaries and by posterity.

The architect seems clearly to be addressing himself constantly to workers in the trade, indeed to the men who are working under his supervision. And there is ample proof that his sketchbook was used, passed from hand to hand.[11] It is amazing that in so slim a book, with only thirty-three parchment sheets (the original was perhaps twice as large), so much is contained for the stone-mason and the carpenter, for the sculptor and the architect: a selection of decorative flora and fauna as well as human models in various postures and activities and drawings of architectural details and of machinery indispensable to the builder. He also has a section on geometry and it is strictly practical, showing the mason how to find the radius of a pillar, for example, an essential guide for matching sections. Not even the formula for a wound-healing balm is missing, which, considering the frequency of accidents in medieval building, was very much to the point.

Though Villard's eye was always strictly on business, nevertheless he has revealed much about himself, at times inadvertently. We know from the peculiarities of his language that he was a native of Picardy and an attempt has been made, from the edifices whose details he sketched, to propose where he may have studied and worked.[12] His models were some of the finest buildings that Northeastern France had to show, around 1235, when the sketchbook was presumably prepared: Laon and Chartres, Cambrai and Reims. It has been suggested that he gathered his drawings for a job in Hungary, to which he was assigned by the Cistercians. One may assume that he convinced his distant hosts for he was with them for a protracted stay though it is not known what he built for them. And we learn much about the man's esthetic tastes, from the selection of his models, from the very adjectives he uses.

We can, finally, sense something of the relationship between an artist and his patrons in those early days from Villard's book. He was not above carrying along with him a bag of tricks on which he counted to impress his employers: how, for example, to install a lectern eagle which at the appropriate moment would snap around to attract the eyes of the drooping faithful to the pulpit.[13] And in regard to a handwarmer which he recommended to the comfort of prelates he had this to say: "This instrument is good for a bishop. He can boldly participate at high mass, and as long as he holds it in his hands and as long as the fire lasts, he will not be cold."[14]

The medieval artist, therefore, was neither voluntarily anonymous nor very humble and he was more often than not a layman. To what extent, then, was he able to express his own ideas in his work? Émile Mâle has upheld the traditional conservative view on this score: "No, the artists of the Middle Ages were neither rebels, nor 'thinkers,' nor forerunners of the Revolution. . . . They were the docile translators of a great thought, which required all their talent to understand. It was rarely permitted them to originate ideas and the Church conceded to their fantasy hardly more than the element of pure decoration."[15]

Viollet-le-Duc, on the other hand, maintained that medieval artists played fast and loose with the subjects assigned to them. "Art in the cities," he said, "became . . . a kind of freedom of the press, an outlet always ready to react against the abuses of the feudal state. The civilians saw in art an open book in which they could boldly project their thoughts, under the mantle of religion. . . . If one examines with great care that secular [*sic!*] sculpture of the thirteenth century . . . one finds there something entirely different than religious sentiment. One finds there, above all, a democratic sentiment expressed in the manner of treating the given themes, a hatred of oppression which explodes everywhere, and, what is nobler yet, . . . the freeing of man's intelligence from its theocratic and feudal swaddling clothes."[16]

This viewpoint is doubtless highly colored but it is as erroneous to ignore the considerable amount of freedom of expression enjoyed by the medieval artist. This fact comes through, for example, in the campaign that Bishop Luke of Tuy conducted against artistic innovation. He quoted the supporters of novelty as arguing: "Since the aim of religious art is to arouse the emotions of the spectator, the artist must have liberty to compose his works, so as to assure to them the greatest effectiveness. . . . In order to avoid the dullness of accustomed formulas, the artist needs freedom to devise unusual motifs and to invent new ideas . . . [which] serve to deepen love for Christ through the emotions they arouse."[17]

121. *Villard de Honnecourt's Sketchbook* (13th century). At right, presumed self-portrait of the architect.

This quotation, which strikes the modern person as so entirely reasonable as to have almost a contemporary ring, was of course anathema to a reactionary like Bishop Luke. Yet it would have made no sense for him to be so exercised about it unless many churchmen of his time (the thirteenth century) did actually hold to it. But the campaign against this trend was not fated to succeed. The new, emotion-provoking iconography was to spread its influence until it completely captivated Christian art. However, this did not occur without a fight and the phenomenon of Bishop Luke is important in that it reveals that the medieval Church was not nearly as monolithic as is supposed. Variation in artistic ideas and expression was possible and indeed frequently occurred.

As to the extent to which the artists contributed their own ideas, this varied greatly even within the time-span we are considering. They early had a negative kind of influence, in any case, due to the gap in their own and the clerics' intellectual background. Not all "orders" could be given them with the confident expectation that they would be carried out. How could the cleric, who in the twelfth century might be reading works of the ancients, commission an artist, who might be illiterate, to carve a portrait of Aristotle that would do him justice? One is reminded of the capital relief at Vézelay presenting the disciple whom John the Baptist had sent to inquire of Jesus if he were indeed the true Christ. He is a leering, pigeon-toed country bumpkin [Pl. 122].

True, medieval artists learned swiftly and it was not long before their work would take on depth and subtlety. But this could only occur if they were given an ever-increasing degree of creative freedom. Otherwise, their efforts could never have attained the spiritual heights to which they soon soared. Another circumstance making for artistic latitude was the fact that churchmen were not trained to think in plastic images. It was inevitable for shrewd ecclesiastics to realize, as Bishop Luke has implied, that it was often best for the work itself—certainly for its popular appeal—if the artist was allowed a certain amount of creative free-play.

No cleric, unless he were a creative artist himself, could have thought out so striking a touch as occurs in the Parthenay Annunciation to the Shepherds, where the little shepherdess is shown suddenly frozen in the act of shearing when she hears the angel's voice. She stares with rapt gaze out on the void while her pause brings closer the miracle of this message [Pl. 123]. Such also is the gesture of Mary at Gabriel's awesome tidings, on the façade at Arles. She reaches up to her distaff, as to the first familiar object coming to hand, whose touch will quiet her terrible agitation. So too on this same portal is the figure in the line of the Damned, who turns just before being claimed by the flames to look back: a look that contains more of horror and vain regret than would any melodramatic outburst [Pl. 124].

But it is far more difficult to account for the work of such an artist as Gislebertus, the great sculptor of Autun cathedral. Was it merely because the canons

122. *Vézelay, Church of La Madeleine* (12th century). Capital relief: St. John the Baptist sends an envoy to query Christ.   123. *Parthenay, Church of Notre-Dame-de-la-Coudre* (12th century). Detail of the Annunciation to the Shepherds. The little shepherdess. All that remains of the angel is the wing, above at right. Now at the Louvre Museum.   124 (below). *Arles Cathedral* (12th century). Detail of the Judgment Day. At right, one of the Damned looks back in a final gesture of regret.

were well satisfied with him as a "docile translator" (Mâle) of their ideas that he was allowed to etch, into the center of the great façade, beneath the very feet of Christ, his proud claim of authorship: "GISLEBERTUS HOC FECIT" [Pl. 125]? There are reasons to believe on the contrary that, far from being a "simple, modest, sincere" (Mâle) translator of other people's thoughts, this man was by his intellectual authority and inventiveness able to impose his own ideas upon those who hired him. His energy alone must have awed those who saw him at work. Recent scholarship has attributed to his hand not only the gigantic tympanum but the side portal as well, which was destroyed in modern times, and fully fifty of the interior capitals. Working at white heat, he abandoned only a rare few pieces to assistants, preferring to leave important elements unfinished rather than turn them over to another's chisel.[18]

Before Gislebertus the Judgment Day scene had never attained the grandiose proportions and drama that he gave it. He originated, as far as we know, such

125. *Autun Cathedral*. West façade frieze (12th century). Detail of the Judgment Day. Separation of the Blessed from the Damned. Note the sculptor's signature.

126. *Autun Cathedral*. West façade frieze (12th century). Detail of the Judgment Day. One of the Damned.

important elements as the Virgin's intercession in behalf of the Risen, the Weighing of Souls, the angels' separation of the Blessed from the Damned.[19] But these themes might also have been contributed by a cleric. They have artistic significance only because of what Gislebertus did with them. His tympanum is like a high moment in a staged drama of stupendous amplitude, the actors vibrantly responsive to a masterly director's bidding. Yet there has been no rehearsal for *this* scene. The trumpets blow and each creature responds according to his fate. There is tension in all. Even the Blessed are seized by urgency, crawling, pulling, pushing to get aloft. And the terror of the Damned is an endless agony, suffered by each in isolation and with a subjective realness that is startlingly modern and convincing [Pl. 126].

And never, surely, in a twelfth-century relief, has there been such an Eve as this one at Autun. Presented in a languid horizontal posture, her body and breasts fully modeled, she whispers suggestively to Adam (unfortunately now lost but who was originally likewise in a reclining position facing Eve) as she

127. *Autun Cathedral*. Relief from former north portal (12th century). Reclining Eve, formerly part of a group representing the Original Sin. Now at Musée Rolin.

reaches back, in an almost hidden gesture, to pluck the apple from the branch which the Devil (also missing) bows down accommodatingly to her hand [Pl. 127]. Like the artist's unexampled treatment of the Sin of Unchastity, featuring the bewitched look of the young man before his naked temptress (see Pl. 17), this Eve of the Temptation is far ahead of her time in provocative sensuality.

Gislebertus brought renovation to almost every subject he undertook. His "Fourth Tone of Plain Song," which he adapted from Cluny abbey's "Eight Tones of Plain Song," assumed a more striking disposition in his hands. With bells hanging from the young musician's fingers and arms and even from his robe, with his assistants striking others with their hammers, the pealing melody fills the medieval air [Pl. 128]. But it is in dramatic insight and intensity that the artist particularly excelled. Mary in her Assumption is shown piercing the vault of her tomb as she soars to Heaven [Pl. 129]. Simon the Magician plummets to earth like a spent meteor when his wings have been melted by the Apostles' prayers [Pl. 130]. One can hear Cain's anguished outcry as he falls back mortally wounded, with Lamech's arrow in his throat. And what a dramatic confrontation that is when Dives appears before Abraham to plead for his drop of water. The Patriarch, closely embracing Lazarus in his cloak, calmly orders the Unjust Rich Man back to Hell in the clutches of his demon.

Even to the most circumspect of directing canons such marvelous "discoveries" must have proved irresistible. When Gislebertus went on then to

192

Autun Cathedral (12th century). Capital reliefs:
128. The Fourth Tone of Plain Song.
129. The Assumption of Mary.
130. Simon the Magician plummets to earth.

complete his work with the extraordinary Judgment Day tympanum, his employers may have been impressed to the point that they themselves suggested the crediting signature. Indeed, the name of Gislebertus must have by this time come to mean something in creative France of the twelfth century. Significant about these fresh outlooks is the fact that none of them actually affronted basic dogmatic concepts. Rather they merely represented deeper, more human approaches to allowed material. Nothing could indicate as yet that even this path was full of potential danger. As it presented itself to the alert cleric it had only positive features to recommend it. Only such distorted minds as that of Bishop Luke could see anything harmful in this trend. But for his kind all truth had been once and for always established and they would have been content to live with that, forever unchanged.

Gislebertus was only one artist whose force and originality broke through clerical convention. There were numerous others, in the twelfth century or even earlier, often relatively unknown or whose work has not been emphasized from this point of view. An example among many are the frescoes of Tavant, painted with a bold imaginativeness that exceeds even that of the more famous Saint-Savin murals (Pl. 131, Pl. 132, and see Pl. 115). Equally astonishing are the reliefs on the exterior wall at the rear of the church at Selles-sur-Cher. They have been described as "rough" ("grossiers"),[20] and primitive they are. Yet they are full of dramatic invention and excitement: the startling way the Angel of the Annunciation is jet-propelled toward Mary, for example, or the Devil's superb insouciance as he comes right into the dining room of the Last Supper to give Judas his cues! True enough, this artist was somewhat backward in technical proficiency. But he must have impressed his clerical employers with his other astonishing qualities [Pl. 133].

The liberating trend accelerated, as might be expected, in the thirteenth century, where bright new material can be found at every hand. This is by no means confined to sculpture but abounds likewise in the lancets, particularly in those given by the guilds, in their utterly novel signatures primarily but also frequently in their manner of handling traditional stories as well. This is strikingly illustrated in the Genesis window at Chartres—given by the shoemakers' guild—in the way God chucks Adam's heavy chin, looks him sternly in the eye as much as to say: "Come, lift up your head and—THINK" [Pl. 134]. He regards Eve mistrustfully as he calls her forth from Adam's body, foreknowing her sinful disobedience. And as the first couple crouch after their transgression, hiding from God's anger, the bushes and all about them suddenly turn red, portending that man's blood would thereafter flow from this unruly act: the blood of birth, of Cain's and all men's future crimes, which only the sacrificial blood of Christ would wash away.

Giving circumstantial support to the idea of the increasing creative freedom

Church of Tavant. Church crypt, frescoes (12th century):
131. The Vice of Unchastity.   132. Man dancing (King David?).

of artists in the twelfth and especially in the thirteenth century is the evidence
of steady improvement in their social position. At the end of the eleventh century, we recall, the serf of the abbot of Saint-Aubin d'Angers named "Foulque"
won his freedom and use of a vineyard through his skill as a painter.[21] Early in
the twelfth century the artist was not only usually a freeman, but his status was
superior to that of most other workmen. The Comte d'Anjou, Foulque V, in
1120, exempted all artisans, masons, and carpenters from all corvées and charges
due the seigniory of Montcontour. Between 1127 and 1137, the Duc d'Aquitaine, Guillaume VIII, decreed his special protection over workmen engaged in

133. *Selles-sur-Cher, Church of Saint-Eu-sice*. Relief at exterior of apse (12th century). The Annunciation.

134. *Chartres Cathedral*. The Genesis stained-glass window (13th century). The Creation of Adam.

building abbey churches in the various regions of his domain and explicitly for-
bade his officers to interfere with them or their families in any manner whatso-
ever. In 1187, the Comte de Toulouse, Raymond V, gave the master masons of
Nîmes such privileges as to render them "vassals of lower degree, with whom
the seignior arranged a sort of feudal fief."[22] It has been suggested that such
concessions were made to win and keep skilled workmen, for whose services
competition was sharp.

It is somehow strange to think of the medieval mason as having worked by
the piece but the proof of this is given by a number of documents.[23] And his
piecework marks, scratched out on the stone he cut, can still be seen on many
buildings, both religious and secular, one scholar having counted 4,000 of them
in all parts of France (and Germany).[24] The mason's conditions of work were
likewise strictly regulated. He toiled from dawn to dusk and though he had more
holidays than his modern counterpart, he lost much less time in winter than
might be supposed for the lodges were shut off and often heated. Harvest time
cut down the building crew (the unskilled men, in any case) more than the cold.
Since he did not work by artificial light, the mason put in fewer hours and was
paid less per day in winter than during the rest of the year.

Documents often show the mason's employer supplying him with gloves and
it was probably a required prerogative of his work. He might get a sun hat in
summer and boots against the autumn rains.[25] One source tells of all building
workers receiving doughnuts on Mardi Gras.[26] The medieval artist sometimes
even received sick benefits.[27] The masons in particular seem to have been very
jealous of their established working conditions, or of their rights, as they saw
them. There is a pertinent story about a group of men who were employed by
the abbey of Obazine during the twelfth century. The convent was evidently
consecrated to a vegetarian diet and the men got tired of the food that was
served them. One day they secretly bought a pig, cooked and ate it in the woods,
then hid what remained in jars for the next day's meal. But Abbot Étienne
learned of his workmen's gluttony, found the meat and threw it down the
latrine, while observing to his monks, it is reported: "We're just sending this
sow on the route that she would take anyway in a little while."

The workers were infuriated at the insult. Rejecting the abbot's placating
words, they cast down their tools, saying that for this affront not only would
they refuse to work but they would keep all others of their trade from taking
their places. Étienne replied confidently that he would find substitute workmen
and even if he did not, "it was better that the house of God remain unbuilt
rather than that the residence of his servants [the monks, supposedly] be soiled
by unclean meat." The account was written by a cleric so the outcome was a
"happy" one. The shamed workers ran after the abbot, he chronicled, threw
themselves at his feet and begged pardon for their "foolish words."[28]

In another chronicle, regarding the sanctification of Bishop Conrad of Pfullingen, it is disclosed that the churchman got into a quarrel, in 1066, with the lay architect who was building the cathedral of Utrecht over the pay he was to receive. Conrad fired the man, bribed his son for his "secrets," and undertook his functions himself. The architect took his revenge by killing the bishop.[29] Another labor dispute ending in a murder is described in the "chanson de geste," *Les Quatre Fils Aymon*. Renaud de Montauban, a knight wishing to expiate a sinful life, offers himself as a laborer at the building lodge of Cologne cathedral. However, at the end of the day when the workers receive their pay (each a different sum for they were paid by the piece),[30] Renaud will accept only a penny ("un denier") and a morsel of bread. The other men are enraged, fearing that this will endanger their wage scale. "The Devil must have brought him here," they conjecture. Finally they kill Renaud and throw him into the river. But the crime is revealed when the fish raise his body and float it on the surface, lighted by three candles.[31]

L. F. Salzman, in his authoritative work on medieval building, stresses this class consciousness of the workmen, noting that they controlled the conditions of their labor as jealously as do modern trade unions.[32] He tells of the bitter complaints on this score by the religious reformer, John Wycliffe, who charged that the workers "conspire together that no man of their craft shall take less for a day than they fix, though he should by good conscience take much less; that none of them shall do good steady work which might interfere with the earnings of other men of the craft, and that none of them shall do anything but cut stone, though he might profit his master twenty pounds by one day's work by laying a wall, without harm to himself."[33] Not only do the actions of these workmen seem strikingly familiar but the exaggerated accusations against them, in the mouth of this fourteenth-century employer, sound no less typical of today.

It is self-evident that this type of control of their working conditions by employees would be impossible without organization, secret or overt. We know in fact that by the fourteenth century workers already had their own associations as differentiated from the earlier guilds, which had taken in not only the masters but the workers ("valets") and apprentices as well. The earlier arrangement is repeatedly adverted to by the famous collection of guild charters published by St. Louis' provost, Étienne Boileau. The *Livre des métiers*, though collated in the middle of the thirteenth century (c. 1268), contains many statutes that date back to the twelfth. Indeed, it is thought that important trades, like the butchers, goldsmiths, shoemakers, and locksmiths, may have organized their associations back in the earlier centuries.[34]

One statute of the stonemasons, for example, claims that they had been excused from night-watch duty since the time of Charles Martel, in the eighth century.[35] Only a few trades, those regarded as "métiers de luxe," were exempt from this function. The pertinent regulation of the "Painters and Sculptors of Images" is couched in prideful terms, explaining that this disposition was made in their case because of their "service to Our Lord and to his Saints and to the honor of the Holy Church."[36] These artists were likewise freed of several taxes imposed on the other trades and were even excused of the feudal poll tax in the fourteenth and fifteenth centuries. They enjoyed other exceptional privileges, such as being allowed to hire any number of assistants that they needed and of working at night, if circumstances required it.[37]

As distinctions among the workers in the building industry became more pronounced, those at the top eventually broke away to form a group apart. In the eleventh and early twelfth century there was little difference in the condition of the mason and the so-called "maître-d'oeuvre," or architect. The latter worked and even lived with his men.[38] But by the thirteenth century the architect's position had become so exalted that he was sermonized for his vanity. A churchman, Nicolas de Biard, preaching in 1261, was quoted as saying: "The masters of the masons, carrying a rod and gloves in their hands, say to others: 'Cut it for me thus,' and do no work themselves; and yet they receive the higher wages."[39]

The differences in economic position between the architect and the men working beneath him at the end of the thirteenth century may be conjectured from the tax records that are available. The Paris poll-tax listings of 1292 show a "Jehan Pasquier le maçon" paying one "sou," the same sum that "Symon le verrier" (glazier) was taxed. The payments by architects are not specified in these records. They certainly did not reach the astronomic rate of 114 livres, 10 sous, paid by the merchant and banker, "maître Gandoufle de Lombard," which one author, in 1897, calculated would have given him an income of 458,000 francs and which would have to be further multiplied by a high integer to bring it up to date.[40] But French architects' earnings were on a level with those of their English confreres of the same period, which, it has been estimated, would have entitled them to the rank of knighthood.[41]

A number of representations of the architect in art works indicate that his role was fully appreciated. He is usually shown with square or compass and often actively engaged in his functions. A stained-glass lancet at Saint-Germer-de-Fly illustrates beautifully the entire medieval building hierarchy. The architect has his ruler, the abbot his key, the treasurer his moneybag, and the masons their tools. The "maître-d'oeuvre" or architect of the thirteenth century enjoyed a number of perquisites in addition to his monetary earnings. He could eat with the canons or at the abbot's table, had the use of a horse or even two, and got a fine robe every year while his functions continued. He often had a house assigned him by the chapter and is even known to have been granted a life's pension by his employers.[42]

But most important of all, by medieval standards, was the handling of the architect's mortal remains after his death. In the thirteenth century a number of builders were assigned the exalted privilege of burial in the church they had worked on. More than that, their resting place was often marked by a plaque with a commemorative inscription and even with an effigy of the kind that was otherwise reserved for important seigniors. Such was the case of Hugues Libergier, the builder of the Saint-Nicaise church at Reims, whose handsome tombal stone was moved to the cathedral after the destruction of his church during the Revolution of 1789. Here one can still see him, square in hand and censered by two angels [Pl. 135].

The first four architects of Reims cathedral itself had also once had their effigies in the church, together with inscriptions carefully crediting them with the part of the edifice for which each had been responsible. Formerly located in the pavement of the central labyrinth of the nave and known to us now only by an early engraving, these four striking memorials had formed part of a decorative design, whose central figure was, it has been suggested, none other than Albéric de Haubert, archbishop of Reims.[43] Greater honor was never granted to creative artists, not even in later, more secularized centuries. And Pierre de Montreuil, when buried in the Sainte-Chapelle at Saint-Germain-des-Près, got an inscription giving him a university master's honors—"docteur-ès-pierres."[44] More noteworthy still, his wife Anne was likewise buried in this church and given her own inscribed tombstone.[45]

The extraordinary improvement in status and conditions of creative artists in the twelfth and in the thirteenth century especially cannot be fully understood apart from the immense significance of their contribution to the society of their times. For the medieval church was, as we have seen, not only a religious but also a primary social and economic establishment, whose multiple functions and enormous prosperity helped create one of the greatest building booms in history. Surely there was never a larger construction program undertaken in proportion to the available resources. The inevitable result was that work often languished because the builders had overextended themselves financially. They did not wait, as is the practice today, until a large part of the anticipated expense had been accounted for. Consequently the landscape of medieval France was dotted with a multitude of building projects in all states of incompletion.

Work in the Middle Ages—particularly material handling—was slower than today and transport of building materials was especially time-consuming. This was the period, as Lefebvre des Noëttes has told us, when the introduction of the rigid horse collar and the nailed horseshoe had made possible the substitution of animal for human power in transport. But roads were still primitive and other factors continued to slow down this work inordinately. Thus one yoke of cattle could be expected to take a full day, going and coming, in delivering to Chartres from the quarry at Berchères, a distance of fifteen kilometers, a cubic meter of stone, weighing about 1,500 kilograms (about 1½ tons). And the transport of twelve column shafts and 168 large building stones from Tonnerre

135. *Reims, Former Church of Saint-Nicaise* (13th century). Tombal portrait of Hugues Libergier, the architect of the church. Now at Reims cathedral.

quarry to Troyes, fifty-eight kilometers away, required the help of twelve to twenty teams, each with three horses, over a period of seven weeks.[46] In the latter case, cost of the stone was quintupled by transport.[47]

Nevertheless, the determining element in the overall speed of building was undoubtedly the availability of resources. The almost total rebuilding of Saint-Denis abbey church by Suger, surely one of the greatest fund-raisers of all time, took less than four years. The Sainte-Chapelle required six and though St. Louis' royal chapel is small, this record for its construction is remarkable when one considers the enormous amount of sculpture and particularly of pictured glass (over 700 square yards) that went into it. After it was destroyed by fire, the rebuilding of Canterbury cathedral was undertaken by the French architect, Guillaume de Sens. Under his direction the work quickly took on an extraordinary pace.

"In 1175," an author reports, "he tore down the old choir and gathered his supplies. The following autumn he put up four pillars and two more in the spring of 1177, as well as two other supports. During that same year he built the great arcades, the triforium and the high windows. Finally, before winter he put up three keystones of the great choir vault near the transept. During the summer of 1178 the French architect erected ten pillars in the right section of the rond-point and tied them together with arches, put the vault on the ambulatory and raised the wall to the level of the cornice." All this remarkable activity was unfortunately truncated in the spring of 1179, when Guillaume fell fifty feet from his perch while supervising the placing of the upper ogival arches of the vault and returned disabled to France.[48] However, his plans were faithfully continued by his English successor.

In all the previous cases building resources were undoubtedly ample. In others, where they periodically lacked, work went on interminably. Thus in the cathedral of Troyes (a rather extreme case), while work on the apse, the surrounding chapels, and the sanctuary had started in 1208, it was almost a century (1304) before the choir was completed. Thereafter work went on rather rapidly again and by 1316 the transepts and the north lateral portal were completed. However, it slacked off again for many decades. The church was not dedicated until 1429 and even by that date only a portion of the nave had been completed. The remainder was not finished until 1492 and the great façade portal begun only in 1506, long after the early Gothic style had become outmoded. Again and again over these decades and even centuries, mass rallies had to be held to open the pockets of the faithful, one of those recorded being to raise enough money "to build a new pillar." Out-of-town preachers were often called upon for help as the fund-raising powers of the local churchmen were apparently repeatedly exhausted.[49]

Until the mid-twelfth century monastery churches predominated among those built in France. Kings and barons made land grants to these institutions for this purpose but just as important were the contributions, however modest individually, of the thousands of pilgrims that streamed to the convents to benefit from the curative properties of their saintly relics. Pilgrimages to the city cathedrals were more rare until the cult of Mary created the appropriate spiritual conditions that rendered many of her images efficacious. And as the huge crowds that responded to the fame of her miracles made urgent the enlargement of the sanctuaries and churches in which her favored images were kept, these same multitudes poured into the offertory boxes the treasure that was needed for this purpose.[50]

This is a basic secret of the enormous amount of church building that took place during the Middle Ages. In the aggregate, medieval churches may have earned more money than all the merchants of the time. As the thirteenth-century writer, Cardinal Eudes de Chateauroux, has noted, Notre-Dame de Paris was built mainly from the contributions for the Saturday vesper candles, paid for by the women of the city, a half-penny ("obole") at a time.[51] Other important sources of building funds for this cathedral were the ordinary altar offerings, delivered in produce as well as money; special offerings made on holidays; ex voto gifts; and indulgences. The story is told about a usurer who late in life repented and asked Bishop Maurice de Sully what he must do to win remission of his sins. The churchman did not tell him to give his treasure "to the poor" or to return it to those he had plundered but to donate it to the church-building fund.[52]

Some of the work that went into church building was either required in the form of corvées or was contributed voluntarily by the so-called "peace brotherhoods" or by other fervid believers who were usually rewarded by forgiveness of sins. But this could not have accounted for more than a small part of the total working effort. The greater proportion of church costs, whether in labor, materials, or transport, had to be paid in money. And indeed the records are rich in evidence regarding the frantic quest for funds by ecclesiastics in behalf of their churches.

An effective routine was to send relics out on exhibition tours, accompanied by rousing preachers. The relics would often work miracles during the journey and in one case a man who had been raised from the dead went along with the bones that had accomplished this great wonder, aiding in the collection of "a great deal of money."[53] At times a church was purposely left unfinished in some prominent part for long years, begging for funds.[54] Ecclesiastic seigniors even gave their burghers communal charters in return for donations to their building programs.[55] And many church institutions went into heavy debt to push their construction schemes. This was true even of the Cistercians of the twelfth century, though so opposed otherwise to ostentation, so that an order had to be handed down by the general chapter forbidding the undertaking of building loans by affiliates.[56]

Pride and self-display doubtless had their part in the building fever of such men as Maurice de Sully, Abbot Suger, and dozens of others like them. Often their successors complained bitterly of their overly ambitious plans, which frequently they could not continue without courting financial disaster.[57] But an alternative might have been denied them by the way the work had been started, the original builders at times even beginning their structures from both ends simultaneously in order to forestall later curtailment of their ambitious programs.[58] Some of the prelates' own associates would deplore their "sickness of building"[59] and St. Bernard, as we know, conducted an impassioned campaign against it. But actually a large proportion of churchmen were engaged in it.

The popes themselves repeatedly entered these fund-raising quests and both popes and Church councils set one fourth of the episcopal income as the proper proportion to be put away for building purposes.[60] But even this ratio was often exceeded. In Chartres, after the great fire of 1194, the bishop and chapter of what has been called the richest diocese in Christendom pledged to give the greater part of their enormous incomes for three years to the reconstruction of the cathedral. After that period, however, despite magnificent donations by the king, the count, and the people of Chartres, there was an acute crisis in the building fund and for a while there was not enough even to pay the workmen. This was the occasion, according to the author of the contemporaneous *Miracles Nostre-Dame*, for some splendid wonders to occur. But the canons and bishop depended upon more solid methods, sending a relic across the English Channel. The quest was very successful, Richard the Lion-Hearted insisting on carrying the reliquary in a procession and Stephen Langton, Archbishop of Canterbury, giving the money for one window.[61]

The method of indulgences was found to be extraordinarily effective in loosening the purse strings of the faithful. Near the end of the eleventh century Urban II issued a bull granting freedom from penance to those who visited the monastery at Figeac, which had been destroyed by the Moslems. It was doubtless assumed that visitors would make donations enabling the monks to rebuild their abbey. The pope also granted a remission of half a sinner's time in purgatory if he arranged to be buried at this abbey. This procedure was to have tremendous consequences in the history of the Church.[62] Often the most extravagant promises were made to win contributions, to the extent even of laying out real estate grants in Heaven, where donors were promised as much space as they gave on earth, thus assuring seigniors in eternity the pleasures—hunting and jousting—to which they were accustomed. Whatever else might be said about such undertakings they proved eminently helpful to the Church's building program.[63]

Considering the enormous amount of building—both religious and secular—that went on during the twelfth and thirteenth centuries, one finds it difficult to understand where all the money came from. It has been estimated that as many as seven hundred churches were built in France during each of these centuries—or seven a year![64] This figure may not be as exaggerated as it seems when one recalls that in Paris alone the inventorist of 1724 counted over three hundred "old churches."[65] A recent incomplete list of Burgundian Gothic monuments of the twelfth and thirteenth centuries totaled over one hundred such edifices in this province.[66] A "usually cautious historian" of the nineteenth century claimed that eighty cathedrals and nearly five hundred abbeys were built in France between 1180 and 1270,[67] while another authoritative source has listed as having existed "at one time or another" 1,300 units of the order of Cluny "within or near the borders of modern France," plus about an equal number of parish churches or chapels under that abbey's jurisdiction.[68]

At its height France's building passion, which lasted about two hundred years, must have engaged an incredibly large proportion of the country's total production. Though France was the wealthiest of Western nations and at the end of the thirteenth century had a population estimated at about one third the present,[69] its annual output was certainly only a fraction of today's. The industrial and commercial establishment of the two eras would be utterly incommensurable. Even in agriculture, production in the earlier period would hardly have compared with that of the present. Soils were poorer and were sowed only once every three years while little was known about the preparation of natural fertilizer. The poor means of communication reduced the incentive to overproduce and forced every group to satisfy all its own needs, though soil and climate might not be adapted to various of the products.[70]

There can be little doubt that France's feverish building program put a great strain upon its economy. This may not have been as much felt during the period between 1000 and 1250, when all of Western Europe was dynamically expanding its "internal and external frontier." However, when this closed down, according to one author, a real economic retrogression took place and "towns could no longer afford the building activity which seemed easy and natural a century earlier."[71] Amazement has often been expressed that small medieval towns could have erected their often enormous cathedrals. Chartres had only 10,000 inhabitants in the thirteenth century, when the cathedral was built, it has been pointed out with awe.[72] Though such calculations miss the point that so much of this construction depended upon other than local contributions,[73] these programs must nevertheless have frequently produced a real drain on the town's resources.

One author has even suggested that this outflow, which withdrew capital and manpower from essential industry and commerce, might have in some instances "irreparably blocked the growth of young cities."[74] He narrates how in one town near Boulogne, when the exhausted population stopped giving to the abbot's church-building fund, "It was necessary to wring out of them their casseroles and bronze cooking pots, their cauldrons and iron tripods."[75]

It is difficult, if not impossible, to calculate the cost of a medieval church in modern financial terms. Almost complete records of the church of Saint-Nicaise at Reims show that more than 25,000 livres were spent on it from 1231 to 1258.[76] A comparative notion may be derived from the fact that the total earnings of Philippe-Auguste's great royal domains and privileges in the fiscal year of 1202–1203 were barely eight times as much. And the French king's income was almost twice that of the English ruler for all his insular possessions![77]

Various attempts have been made to translate medieval money values into modern terms but all are admittedly undependable. An approximative working method used by two scholars seems reasonable: setting up the ratio of the earnings of an unskilled worker in early thirteenth-century France (six deniers) and in the present-day United States (eight dollars).[78] This would give a proportion of 1:320, meaning that the value of one livre tournois would be $320. At that rate the builders of Saint-Nicaise would have spent the equivalent of $8 million. J.-B.-A. Lassus, the architect and associate of Viollet-le-Duc, estimated that it would have cost 125 million francs to rebuild Chartres cathedral in his day.[79]

This figure (which would translate into about $250 million today) is not as excessive as it at first appears since to build a church in the thirteenth century meant not only raising its walls and arching its vaults but also filling its open spaces with storied glass and crowning its portals with dense statuary. Fully 1,200 figures were carved at Notre-Dame de Paris, twice that number at Chartres, and a fantastic 3,000 at Reims cathedral. The glass paintings at Bourges and Reims and Chartres cover hundreds of square yards (over 2,000 square yards at Chartres alone). All of France lived in the flush of this creativity. Even those dwelling in remote rural areas did not escape the intoxication. And in cities, where several churches might be going up simultaneously, the feeling of excited participation must have been very great as the people saw their oboles miraculously transformed into shining glass and stone.

It can be safely assumed that the phenomenal expansion of medieval building far outpaced the training of competent artisans. This would account for the acute competition for their services that often took place as well as for the rapid improvement in their economic position and status. Early in the twelfth century the canons of Notre-Dame-des-Doms at Avignon and those at Saint-Ruf had disputed the services of a crew of carpenters and of a young cleric who had learned the art of painting. It is also recorded that when Abbot Geofroy of the Benedictine convent of Trinité at Vendôme loaned one of his monks to Hildebert de Lavardin, bishop of Le Mans, to help him build his new cathedral, the latter would not let him go and the abbot had to resort to excommunication to get Monk Jean back into his monastery.[80] The kings of England often impressed building artisans into their service. This practice was not as current in France, but special inducements were used there to win skilled artisans for building projects of the king and of the great seigniors.

The young man of talent often went on the road, perhaps carrying a batch of drawings to show to prospective clients. We even know from one document that he could replace some local artist, provided he impressed the right people. This occurred at the cathedral of Troyes, where a roodscreen was being planned. The sketch of the local man had already been accepted by the canons when Henry de Bruxelles appeared and drew another, which the churchmen greatly preferred. The matter was understandably delicate and the chapter considered it advisable to call a meeting "of the bourgeois and workmen of the city" to help them out of the dilemma. Here the new drawing was endorsed and Henry was hired, together with another master mason, at a higher salary than that received by their predecessors.[81]

There is every reason to believe that work went on in a general environment of great interest and appreciation. It is recorded that Henry de Bruxelles and his colleague were taken to a church in another town to get ideas from its "masonry work."[82] It is also known that a visit to Saint-Gilles to study the celebrated screw staircase in the choir was considered obligatory for every master mason. The practice of such learning-visits must have been widespread: The similarity of architectural and sculptural ideas spreading over half the continent was not due exclusively to the vocational mobility of the medieval builders. And the artists themselves knew how to value their own work. A charming picture of this has come down to us, in the donor medallion of the sculptors' lancet at Chartres (see Pl. 44), showing one of a two-man team, who has just been relieved by his companion, contemplating the work that is nearing completion. The young sculptor studies the king's figure and assumes the traditional pose of appreciation: fingers on temple, the solemnity of attitude before a work of merit.

Everything points to a great ferment of artistic ideas existing at the time, together with an intense intercommunication among creative workers and amateurs alike. We have a tendency to credit single individuals with architectural and iconographic innovations that often had a widely shared source. Thus it was once suggested that Abbot Suger was the first to revive the typological symbolism of the early Fathers on the concordance of the Old and New Testaments, when he worked out the subject program for his great crucifix. But evidence is available now that this idea had been brought to Saint-Denis by the artist of the crucifix himself, Godefroid de Claire, from his native Rhineland, where the tradition of this subject went back at least two centuries and where Godefroid had already done similar works.[83]

Modern ivory-tower ideas of originality are utterly misleading when applied to the Middle Ages. When Villard de Honnecourt traveled to Hungary to undertake his job for the Cistercians, his great concern was not to prove to his hosts how novel and unique his own concepts were but to present to them the most advanced architectural forms that creative France had to offer. And he kept making additions to his sketchbook on the way. We also know that Guillaume de Sens, when hired by the canons of Canterbury after a stiff competition with other masters, brought not only ideas with him but also some material-handling equipment, which occasioned the greatest admiration among his English hosts.[84]

Similarly Theophilus Presbyter was very explicit in attributing the ideas contained in his book to their proper sources. They stemmed from every corner of the world, he pointed out: the "kinds and blends" of colors, from Greece; "workmanship in enamels or variety of niello," from Russia; "repoussé or cast work or engravings in relief," from Arabia; "gold embellishments" applied to vessels or to carved "gems and ivories," from Italy. His highest credits went to two countries: to his homeland, Germany, for her "subtle work in gold, silver, copper, iron, wood, and stone," and to France, in an appreciation that we ourselves can treasure, for "her precious variety of windows."[85]

The progress in Gothic architectural technics, which was so swift that

Viollet-le-Duc found it impossible at times to follow transitional evidences, was all the more remarkable in view of the elementary stage of the existing engineering know-how. The work of medieval architects was largely empirical and was often "unscientific and uneconomic."[86] It was very common for churches to fall soon after their construction and if they did not crumble, their pillars would turn, their walls buckle. Buttresses had to be added frequently to Gothic structures to avert disaster, until they became a constant preventive element. Or foundation piles would have to be bulwarked, as was required at Saint-Denis scarcely fifty years after Abbot Suger's reconstruction.[87]

The technical aids of twelfth- and thirteenth-century architects, it is true, did include building sketches (though not drawn to exact scale), and there were patterns for moldings and other parts that made the rounds of the lodges. Yet perhaps the most striking attribute of medieval architects was not their technical brilliance but their courage. It is certain that modern builders would never hazard into the unknown, in equivalent situations, as recklessly as did these early predecessors, armed with the comparatively primitive methods and equipment at their disposal.

A study of medieval sculpture in stone reveals a similarly dazzling evolution. After the fall of the Roman Empire and the virtual closing off of Western Europe during the period of massive invasions, stone carving all but disappeared, along with many other advanced technics in the arts and sciences. The building surge during and just following Charlemagne's reign was short-lived and was productive of primitive sculptural forms. Even the work of the late tenth and early eleventh century was for the most part extremely backward, remaining exemplars of this period being more graved than modeled.[88]

Toward the end of the eleventh century, however, stone-carving technic suddenly took a remarkable spurt. It has been suggested that advanced examples of this period, such as the apse sculpture at Saint-Sernin, in Toulouse, were copied from Gallo-Roman models.[89] But such models had been available to earlier sculptors as well! From that time, in any case, progress was breathtaking, with the Cluny choir and Moissac cloister sculpture (both coming near the turn of 1100) already demonstrating the high quality and originality that would thereafter mark the art of France.

Then followed swiftly the work of Autun, Vézelay, Saint-Gilles, the Moissac porch, the Chartres façade, and the unending outpouring of other exalted creations continuing through the twelfth century and into the thirteenth, where it pinnacled at Notre-Dame de Paris, Amiens, Reims, the side porches of Chartres, and countless other Gothic masterpieces, all of which has made this country, despite the later widespread destruction and mutilation, the most astonishing repository of old art still in place in the Western world.

This fantastic creativity was not just an accident of esthetic effusion, as some authors continue to suggest, nor the result of an overwhelming surge of piety.

The churches of France and their marvelous art represent truly the richest element of the life of the whole people, who during the centuries of their creation were undergoing the profoundest social and economic change and development.

And the artists themselves were an intimate, inseparable part of this great current. The art they produced was a public art in the deepest sense. Always elaborating widely shared concepts concerned with man's most elevated thinking of the time, they turned out work that was destined for a total audience—and by all evidence they reached it. For though its concentrated symbols were meant basically to serve the interests of the upper classes, it was also addressed to the masses, whose seething desires and needs it took into account. It was this universality that gave this art its unparalleled strength and richness, qualities which still reach and thrill us today over the gap of the better part of a millennium.

CHRONOLOGY

A CHRONOLOGY sins chiefly by omission. This one makes no pretension to being complete. It seeks merely to give the reader a general sense of the sweep of contemporary events accompanying the creation of France's great medieval monuments.

1049–1109: St. Hugues (born at Semur, 1024), abbot of Cluny. One of an almost unbroken line of remarkable leaders during the 250 years of this order's ascendancy (founded 910), who play a role of primary importance in secular and religious affairs as well as in fostering the arts. Under Hugues, the great abbey church at Cluny is begun.

c.1050: Raoul Glaber, monk, dies. His chronicles, which cover the period, 900–1046, are full of catastrophes, superstitions, and somber forebodings. But they also describe movingly the great surge of church building that spread through Western Europe after the fears of the world's end in the "Year Thousand" were proved groundless.

1060–1108: Reign of Philippe I, king of France, at that time a small area centered on Paris, hardly more than one twentieth of its present size. Period of rapid development of the monumental form of Romanesque architecture; productive of a number of splendid structures.

1063: Crusade launched to win Spain to Christianity. First of a series conducted during the following two hundred years, usually entailing a complex of political and commercial as well as religious motives.

1066: Battle of Hastings. Defeat of Harold II by William the Conqueror, duke of Normandy, who becomes king of England (1066–1087).

c.1068–1121: Guillaume de Champeaux, theologian, bishop, teacher. One of his students is Pierre Abélard, who quickly outshines his master. In 1108, Guillaume founds the famous school of Saint-Victor, near Paris, where a mystical theology is taught which has a great influence on the thinking of churchmen of the time.

1070: People of Le Mans undertake a punitive campaign against pillaging lords of the area. Sometimes considered a pioneer example of a commune, the effort more properly fits into the "Truce of God" movement, which probably originated at Le Puy, around 990, when armed peasants under clerical leadership forced ravaging lords to make a solemn "pact of peace."

1073–1085: Term of Pope Gregory VII, leading animator of campaign to correct clerics' morals, establish Church control over investiture.

1076: Communal movement as such (i.e., a sworn grouping to foster burgher interests) in an early manifestation at Cambrai, Flanders. Repeatedly crushed, it rises again and again. In other cities of the commercially active North, the impulse gathers strength, spreading to Saint-Quentin (1080), Beauvais (1099), and intensifying especially in the twelfth century, as at Noyon, Mantes, Laon, Amiens, Reims, Soissons, Saint-Riquier, etc.

1077: Henry IV of the Holy Roman Empire journeys to Canossa to offer "honorable amends" to Pope Gregory VII in quarrel over investiture.

1079–1142: Pierre Abélard, teacher, philosopher, brilliant, original thinker. Advocates a critical examination of patristic writings and fosters the concept of nominalism, forerunner of modern realism. Marries Héloïse (1101–1164), niece of a canon of Notre-Dame, whom later he leaves; their famous exchange of letters. After an agitated career, is charged by St. Bernard, at Council of Sens (1140), with expounding heretical ideas; is condemned.

1081–1151: Suger, abbot of Saint-Denis. Counselor of Louis VI and VII, regent of the latter during his absence on Second Crusade. Rebuilds his abbey church almost completely in the new Gothic style, describing the entire procedure in precious diaries. Great administrator, innovator. Writes important early biography, *La vie de Louis VI.*

1084: Antioch falls to Turks. Pilgrimage route to Jerusalem closed.

1085: Christians take Toledo from Spanish Moslems.

1086–1127: Guillaume IX d'Aquitaine, one of the earliest of the great troubadours of Southern France, the most famous of whom was Bernard de Ventadour, who writes in the court of Aliénor d'Aquitaine (1122–1204), Guillaume's granddaughter.

1090–1153: St. Bernard, a towering figure of medieval Christianity and one of the most influential men of his time. Strongly supports the Church's reform movement as well as its political ambitions. Writer of theological treatises and letters, one of which is famous for its opposition to "excesses" in church building and decoration.

1092 (4)–1156: Peter the Venerable, the last of the great abbots of Cluny (1122–1156), who comes at a time when the order is already in decline. Very influential in the affairs of his time. Author, scholar, friend of music and the arts.

1095: Under impulsion of Pope Urban II (1088–1099), First Crusade to the Holy Land is approved at Council of Clermont. Led by a monk, Peter the Hermit, the first expedition (1096), after massacring Jews all along its route, is itself annihilated by the Turks. The second expedition (1097) is better organized, a large professional army.

1096–1141: Hugues de Saint-Victor, native of Saxony, mystic philosopher and theologian. Comes early to abbey of Saint-Victor, where he helps initiate the mystical theology for which this school becomes famous.

1099: Crusaders take Jerusalem. The Holy Land is parceled out among Christian barons.

c.1100: Theophilus Presbyter, a monk of possibly Greek origin who settles at convent near Paderborn, writes the *Schedula diversarum artium*, a most important and detailed treatise on the technics of medieval arts, particularly painting, stained glass, and metal work.

fl. early 12th century: Adelard of Bath, English scholar, traveler. Visits Asia Minor, North Africa, Italy, Spain. Translates from the Arabic Euclid's *Elements*, which remains the West's textbook of geometry for centuries.

1100–1135: Reign of Henry I, fourth son of William the Conqueror. While king of England, he continues a major continental interest, holding Normandy and other parts of France.

c.1100–1125: *Chanson de Roland*, greatest of the French "chansons de geste." A national epic in heroic style, narrating the supposed exploits of Charlemagne and his associates in Spain, actually it reflects topically the contemporary Christian campaign to reconquer that country from the Moslems.

1108–1137: Louis VI ("le Gros"), king of France. He conducts never-ending series of small wars by which he consolidates royal power against the barons. Period of continuing economic growth, important church building.

1112: Revolt of burghers of Laon against their seignior, Bishop Gaudry, who frustrates their demands for commercial and social reforms. It is one of a long series of urban uprisings during this century against feudal obstructions to the explosive growth of industry and trade, ecclesiastical seigniors usually proving more retrogressive than secular lords in this respect.

1113: St. Bernard joins religious community of Cîteaux, launching one of the great monastic reform movements of the time; foundation of the Cistercian order. An often-forgotten element of this movement is its work of greatly increasing tillable land, setting new masses to work on it.

1114: First known document dealing with the famous Fairs of Champagne. Established at Troyes, Provins, Lagny, and Bar-sur-Aube, they are France's major commercial meeting places for merchants from Northern and Southern Europe. After opening of Straits of Gibraltar to regular maritime contact, in 1314, the Fairs of Champagne fall off in importance.

1119: Foundation of Knights Templars. Intended originally to protect pilgrims to the Holy Land, the order is soon deflected into banking activities, growing enormously wealthy, politically powerful.

1120: Foundation of Premonstratensian order by St. Norbert, another offshoot of the monastic reform movement, called forth by the softening of discipline in the older Benedictine and Cluniac establishments.

1120–1183: Robert Wace, Anglo-Norman poet, author of *Roman de Brut* and *Roman de Rou*, historical epics which at times contain descriptive passages of striking topical richness.

1124: Henry V, Holy Roman Emperor, in league with Henry I of England, invades France but turns back when that country's most powerful barons rally to the king's support. A high point of France's developing national spirit and royal prestige.

1125: Abbot Suger of Saint-Denis releases the entire town of its feudal obligation of mortmain, a pioneer action of its kind. In return, he receives 200 livres, which he needs for the "renovation and decoration of the entrance" (façade) of his abbey church.

c.1126–1198: Ibn Roshd Averroës, great Moslem physician and philosopher, of Cordova. Receiving wide acceptance at first, he later falls into disfavor because of his unorthodox ideas, is imprisoned, his fortune confiscated. Most famous for his commentaries on Aristotle, which play important part in latter's introduction to Christian scholars.

1130: Honoré (or Honorius) d'Autun, who died sometime after this date. Prolific writer, one of whose works, the *Imago mundi*, an encyclopedia of history and learning, is one of the most famous books of its time. Its influence on the iconography of art of the period is very great.

1135–1204: Moshe ben Maimoun, or Maimonides, born in Cordova, rabbi, physician, scholar. Compiler of the Talmud, author of many works, usually written in Arabic, including the *Guide for the Perplexed*, in which he seeks to reconcile faith and reason and which becomes the source of a great controversy among Jewish scholars.

c.1135–1190: Chrétien de Troyes, one of the outstanding poets of his time. Author of *Lancelot* (c.1168), *Yvain ou le chevalier du lion* (c.1170), *Perceval ou le conte du Graal* (c.1182), his works have had reverberations all the way into modern times, particularly with the Romantics.

1137–1180: Reign of Louis VII, king of France, marked by dynastic imbroglios complicated by marriages, through one of which Champagne is added to royal domain. But king shows friendliness to middle class, encourages developing commerce, establishes many new towns ("villes neuves").

1137: After decades of strife with their abbot-seignior, the burghers of Vézelay set up a commune in alliance with the abbot's peasant-serfs. Encouraged by the Comte de Nevers, who is himself involved in a controversy with the abbot, they are eventually abandoned by this baron and defeated.

c.1140: Pierre de Bruys, leader with Henri de Lausanne of an important heretical movement, is burned at the stake outside Saint-Gilles abbey church. He casts doubt on the mass, baptism of infants, authority of the Church, launches a cross-burning campaign. (Some authors place him earlier, his immolation at 1126.)

c.1140–1150: *Guide du pèlerin*, part of the *Livre de Saint Jacques*, a Latin work prepared with the probable aim of popularizing the pilgrimage to Santiago da Compostela, itself an important element in the Christian drive to repossess Spain.

1144: Fall of Edessa to the Turks endangers the Christians' position in the Holy Land. St. Bernard preaches the Second Crusade at Vézelay, 1146. Accompanying the resultant religious fervor is a new surge of anti-Semitism, which St. Bernard notably combats.

1144: One of a large number of "villes neuves" established during this century, Montauban is remarkable for being completely planned and laid out beforehand in the modern manner. These "new towns" were set up to accommodate the masses colonizing the new farm lands as well as those involved in the great spurt in industry and trade. Many feudal restrictions were often summarily abandoned in these centers.

1147–1149: The Second Crusade is undertaken under leadership of Louis VII and Emperor Conrad III. Result is almost a total failure but Abbot Suger makes his mark as able administrator of France during the king's absence, gaining the cognomen of "father of his country."

1147: Jaufré Rudel, seignior of Blaye, in Southwest France, a famous troubadour whose poems are written sometime before this date.

1154–1189: Reign of Henry II (nicknamed "Plantagenet"), king of England. By his marriage with Aliénor (Eleanor) d'Aquitaine soon after her divorce by Louis VII, he gains a position of challenging power in France.

1160–1180: Date of the *Magnus Liber Organi*, by Léonin, the great French composer and "maître de chapelle" of Notre-Dame de Paris. The *Magnus Liber* is a compilation of over 80 works (a few still extant) prepared for all feast days of the liturgical year. By its skilled use of two "voices," it contributes significantly to development of polyphony.

c.1160: Benjamin da Tudela, date of departure of this famous Spanish-Jewish traveler on his journey, which takes in all the countries of the Mediterranean world. His diary, remarkably detailed and exact, is a major historical source for this period.

1162: Henry II of England appoints his friend Thomas à Becket Archbishop of Canterbury, who soon after breaks with the king over the issue of the independence of the clergy (king's right of veto in elections of bishops and abbots; administration of justice). Thomas must flee the country, 1164. Returning in 1170 after a supposed reconciliation, he is assassinated soon after by royal killers. He is canonized in 1172. His cult becomes one of the leading devotions of the time.

1163: Council of Tours condemns the Albigensian (Cathar) heresy, which has been spreading throughout Southern France for some years. Of Manichean inspiration, Catharism is characterized by a revulsion to clerical extravagance and immorality, and is abetted by the conflicts of secular and ecclesiastic seigniors.

1170: Peter Waldo launches movement (Waldenses) to bring Church back to humble origins. Bent on reform rather than rupture, the "Poor Men of Lyon" are nevertheless excommunicated by Pope Lucius III, in 1184.

1174: Federation of peasants of seventeen villages near Laon is formed. The charter granted by Louis VII is soon after challenged by their seignior, Bishop Roger of Laon, however. At Comporté, in 1177, Roger and his allies rout the peasant militia in a horrible butchery. But agitation in this region continues for many decades.

c.1175–1253: Robert Grosseteste, bishop of Lincoln, one of the greatest medieval thinkers and teachers. Becomes Master (called Chancellor after 1215) of Oxford University. Is celebrated for his knowledge of sciences, mathematics.

c.1176: *Roman de Renard*, estimated date when composition of this great assemblage of popular fabliaux is started. Product of many authors, chiefly clerics or ex-clerics, whose work is often bitterly anticlerical, however. Important later additions include *Renard le Nouveau* (1288), by Jacquemard Gelée, called a "bourgeois epic"; and *Renard le Contrefait*, written by a "grocer" of Troyes sometime before 1322, which is likewise middle class in inspiration, anti-noble, libertarian.

1177-1236: Gautier de Coincy, author of the *Miracles Nostre-Dame*, which plays a key role in the development of the cult of the Virgin, as at Chartres cathedral.

c.1180–1230: Pérotin, successor of Léonin, is "maître de chapelle" at Notre-Dame. Revising the *Magnus Liber Organi*, he adds one or two "voices" to the original two, one of which might be instrumental. Also contributes importantly to musical notation.

1181: Philippe II ("Auguste") expels Jews from royal domain, confiscating their real property, including two synagogues at Paris. Later they are allowed to buy their way back, thus initiating a cycle that will only end with their total destitution.

1187: Jerusalem falls to the Turks and the Third Crusade (1190–1192) is launched. It ends disastrously despite the capture of Saint-Jean-d'Acre. Emperor Frederick Barbarossa drowns at Cilicia, 1190. Philippe-Auguste hurries back to France before the campaign has got underway. The English king, Richard the Lion-Hearted (1189–1199), also abandons the Holy Land before consolidating the victory at Acre.

1189: "Établissements de Rouen" is granted to burghers of this city by Henry II. A charter of broad municipal self-rule, it serves as model to the developing ambitions of the middle class.

1190: Before leaving for the Crusade, Philippe-Auguste draws up famous "Testament of 1190," naming his regents and also six burghers of Paris as guardians of the treasury and the royal seal, an act that illustrates the important posture being assumed by the middle class.

c.1190–c.1264: Vincent de Beauvais, whose *Speculum majus* is an important encyclopedia of the thirteenth century. A compendium of the natural sciences, history, theology, and philosophy, it is a primary source of medieval iconography.

1193–1280: Albertus Magnus, German-born Dominican monk, famed scientist, theologian, and teacher, one of whose pupils is St. Thomas Aquinas. Called *doctor universalis* because of breadth of learning, is preeminent for scientific contributions, based on interpretation of Aristotle's works, which he defends against Church conservatives.

1195: Herrade de Landsberg, abbess of Truttenhausen, date of her death. Author of famous encyclopedia, the *Hortus deliciarum*, the only known copy of which, beautifully illuminated, was destroyed at Strasbourg during the Franco-Prussian war of 1870–71.

1200: Paris masters and students receive first charter of "privileges" from the king, recognizing their special clerical status. In following years, the University (i.e., "Association") of Paris professors also receives official papal acknowledgment.

1201–1253: Thibaut IV, comte de Champagne, animator of a brilliant court, a renowned poet himself, author of "chansons," etc.

1202–1204: Philippe-Auguste delivers heavy blows to Plantagenets in France, taking over their provinces of Normandy, Maine, and Anjou. During his long reign (1180–1223), this king quintuples size of the royal domain, becoming the country's most important seignior. A consummate politician, he organizes a permanent army, establishes finances and administration on a firm basis.

1202–1272: Guillaume de Saint-Amour. Rector of Paris University, he becomes leader of the bitter opposition of the secular masters to the friars' attempt to dominate the university. Defeated in the end, he is expelled and exiled by demand of Pope Alexander IV.

1206: Foundation of the Preaching Order (Dominicans) by St. Dominic of Guzman (1170–1221), dedicated to fighting the Cathar heresy in Southern France. In 1232, the terrible weapon of the Inquisition is put into the hands of this order to aid it in its work.

1208: Murder of the papal legate, Pierre de Castelnau, allegedly by retainers of Comte Raymond VI of Toulouse, sets off the anti-Albigensian "crusade." Actually an invasion of the South by Northern barons (their leader, Simon de Montfort, is killed outside Toulouse in 1218), the war is one of the bloodiest in French history. It is described with verve in the *Chanson de la croisade albigeoise*, a 13th-century epic.

1209: Foundation of the Franciscan order by St. Francis of Assisi (1182–1226), a reform movement with initial ideals similar to those of the "Poor Men of Lyon," but which operates entirely within the Church.

1210: Jean Bodel, date of his death. One of the earliest of the "bourgeois" poets, famous for his fabliaux and especially for his *Jeu de Saint-Nicolas*, a pioneer (with the *Jeu d'Adam*) among semi-liturgical dramas, written partly in the vernacular, which were often acted on the public squares outside churches.

1214: Battle of Bouvines. Philippe-Auguste defeats coalition of Flemish, Germans, and English, the last under King John (1199–1216). A notable feature is the presence in Philippe's ranks of communal militia from several cities, a support symbolic of this monarch's extraordinary understanding of the increasing importance of the bourgeoisie.

1215: Soon after his defeat at Bouvines, King John is forced to sign the Magna Carta, a document containing historic concessions in individual and civic freedom as well as important commercial reforms.

1215: Lateran Council, Rome, where important decisions are taken regarding intensified prosecution of the anti-Albigensian "crusade." Strong measures of social isolation and degradation of the Jews also approved.

1215: Bertran de Born, who died before this date. One of the greatest of the troubadours.

1216–1250: Reign of Emperor Frederick II, during which relations with the papacy, traditionally inimical, deteriorate to low point. Innocent IV seeks St. Louis' military aid against Frederick but the French king opts for a Crusade to the Holy Land instead. Frederick is also noted for his scientific writings, particularly his remarkable observations and experiments on birds.

1220: France's first medical faculty established at Montpellier, largely staffed by Jewish and Moslem doctors.

c.1220–c.1292: Roger Bacon, English-born Franciscan monk. Inspired by Robert Grosseteste, he undertakes intensive scientific experimentation. Author of an encyclopedia, written with secret encouragement of Pope Clement IV. He has serious difficulties with traditionalists, being imprisoned toward end of his life. Emphasizing importance of testing accepted beliefs by experiment, he becomes one of the great forerunners of scientific research.

1221–1274: St. Bonaventura, theologian, cardinal, general of Franciscan order. Studies and teaches at Paris University.

1224–1317: Jean, Sire de Joinville, a favorite counselor of Louis IX, whom he accompanies on the Seventh Crusade. Writes the "Life" of the king (c.1309), after his sanctification. It is a spirited, intimate account of his "saintly words and good deeds."

1225–1274: St. Thomas Aquinas, most famous of Catholic theologians. Teaches at Paris University, 1252. Asked by Rome to reconcile Aristotle's writings with Christian doctrine, he produces the *Summa Theologica*, which will become the basic theological text of the Church.

1225–1235; 1275–1280: *Roman de la rose*, one of the most famous writings of the Middle Ages. First part, by Guillaume de Lorris (d.c.1235), is composed in the "amour courtois" style. The more brilliant second part, by Jean de Meung, or Clopinel (c.1240–c.1305), is far-ranging and often virulent in its attacks on clergy, nobility, superstition, women.

1226: At the death of Louis VIII (1223–1226), his widow, Blanche de Castille, becomes regent for her minor son, Louis IX (St. Louis, 1226–1270). She ably fights off challenges of powerful seigniors, proves resourceful ruler. Even after her son's majority, she continues to play an important part in the affairs of the kingdom, exert a strong personal influence on him.

c.1228–1298: Jacobus da Varazze (or Voragine), archbishop and author of the famous *Golden Legend*, a compilation of the lives of the saints, which serves as one of the major sources of medieval iconography.

1229: Treaty of Paris ends the military phase of the Albigensian war. A dynastic marriage is arranged and the great territory of the comte de Toulouse passes into the royal domain. One of the treaty's provisions is the founding of the University of Toulouse.

1229: Paris masters and students, in conflict with the bishop over control of the university, declare strike, abandon Paris for two years, joining faculties at Orléans, Toulouse, Cambridge, etc. Win papal bull, in 1231, upholding their cause.

c.1235: Villard de Honnecourt, architect of Picardy, whose famous album of sketches, done about this time, is the most informative firsthand source we have of the mode of working and thinking of medieval builders.

c.1240–1288: Adam de la Halle of Arras, Flanders. The first known trouvère to have developed into a sophisticated musician, writing motets and other polyphonic works.

1240: Public debate between Christians and Jews, at Paris, under auspices of St. Louis. Nicolas Donin, converted Jew, charges that the Talmud is subversive. Rabbi Jehiel defends it ably, wins some ecclesiastical support, but in the end all Talmuds are confiscated, burned.

1244: After several minor crusades fail to halt the continuing deterioration of the Christians' position in the Holy Land, their defeat at Gaza shuts off Jerusalem definitively. The Seventh Crusade (1248–1254), led by St. Louis, fails to reestablish the situation.

1244: Montségur, the last stronghold of the Cathars, falls to the Northern forces. The inmates are given the choice of recanting or death. Some accept the former but 200 of them, including their bishop, Bertrand Marty, choose the pyre instead.

1245: Strike of weavers of Douai, one of a number during this century, in various towns and industries. Defines emergence of a permanent proletariat on the one hand and rich capitalists on the other (e.g., Jean Boinebroke, Douai; Mathieu Lanstier, Arras).

fl.1245–1285: Rutebeuf, popular trouvère. Author of many works, some of which have surprising autobiographical reference. Champion of Paris masters in struggle with the friars. Also writes fabliaux and a miracle play, *Le miracle de Théophile*, one of the earliest dramatic pieces extant in the vernacular.

c.1250–1296: Philippe, Sire de Beaumanoir. Royal official and legist, author of the famous *Coutumes de Beauvoisis*, a pioneer compilation of French laws, which he assembles at the instance of Robert de Clermont, brother of St. Louis.

1251: "Les Pastoureaux," an amorphous movement of peasants rising ostensibly in reaction to news of Louis IX's troubles in the Holy Land, quickly turns revolutionary, terrorizing large areas of Northern France. In the end, they are exterminated by troops under Queen Blanche's orders.

1252: At death of Blanche, Louis IX assumes full power. He proves most able and equitable administrator, moving country farther on road to rule of law; modernizes judicial system, establishes royal investigators to check on local officials, suppresses baronial feuding. Despite great friendliness to Church, he astutely defends royal interests against powerful ecclesiastics.

1252: Masters of Paris University once again rise in defense of academic freedom, this time against increasing encroachment by Dominicans and Franciscans. Opposed by Rome on this occasion, they lose their fight and their courageous leader, Guillaume de Saint-Amour, is driven into exile, 1257.

1254: After expelling the Jews, in 1253, Louis IX readmits them the following year while curtailing their rights. He establishes on official basis the heretofore informal concept of "Juifs du Roi"—which gives them many obligations and few privileges. This concept is developed in following reigns to the point that when Jews leave kingdom voluntarily under Philippe-le-Bel due to his onerous taxes, he pursues them and forces them to return.

1257: Robert de Sorbon, Louis IX's confessor, founds "collège" for sixteen students in theology. By no means the first "collège" (there is one on record at the Hôtel-Dieu, founded in 1180), it eventually becomes the most important, lends its founder's name to the entire university.

c.1268: The *Livre des métiers*, published by Étienne Boileau, king's provost at Paris. A codification of work and trade regulations of the city's guilds, some of which were established much earlier (documents go back to 1121, but there are some guilds that existed even before that date), it is a work of extraordinary historical importance.

1270: After the fall of Caesarea, Louis IX leaves on the Eighth Crusade but is deflected toward Tunis, probably by the hope of converting the sultan there. He and many of his party, including members of his own family, succumb to the plague.

c.1270–c.1308: John Duns Scotus, Franciscan monk-scholar of Scottish origin, who with William of Occam (c.1300–c.1349), English Franciscan, is credited with developing the philosophical system of nominalism, forerunner of modern realism.

1274: *Les grandes chroniques de France*, its first official history, written at the abbey of Saint-Denis and in the French language.

c.1283: *Jeu de Robin et Marion*, by Adam le Bossu, a pioneer in the field of theatrical comedy. Is purely profane in subject matter and written entirely in the French language.

1285–1314: Reign of Philippe IV ("le Bel"), son of Philippe III ("le Hardi"), 1270–1285. He contests the Church's temporal power, assembles the first Estates General for support in this and other projects, among which is an exhausting war with Flanders.

1306: Revolt of the people of Paris against Philippe IV's debasing of currency, imposition of burdensome taxes. It is led by the city's artisans and tradesmen, but their chiefs are taken and hanged, their religious confraternities, charged with being centers of sedition, outlawed by the king.

1306: In desperate financial straits, Philippe IV has recourse to an old measure, expelling the Jews, confiscating their property. But soon after they are allowed to return, to help track down their debtors for the king.

1307: Philippe IV puts Knights Templars on trial on trumped-up charges, with aim of seizing their riches. Pope Clement V accommodatingly suppresses the order (1312) and its leaders, tortured into making "confessions," are burned at the stake.

1309–1376: At a low period of their centuries-long struggle with the Holy Roman Emperors, and due to other overwhelming difficulties, the popes are forced to abandon Rome, establishing their seat at Avignon.

1322–1328: Reign of Charles IV, third son of Philippe IV. Soon after the death of this king, the last male of the Capetian line, Edward III of England declares himself king of France and the dynastic setting for the Hundred Years' War is laid down. This catastrophic conflict (1337–1453) lays waste a large part of the country and sets France sharply back from the high point to which 250 years of extraordinary progress had carried it.

LIST OF MONUMENTS

THE FOLLOWING LIST is very incomplete, being made up largely of structures mentioned in the text. There are many other interesting or even important French churches (or those containing noteworthy art) that are not included, as for example: NORTH (Bayeux, Caen, Jumièges, Noyon, Saint-Georges-de-Boscherville, Soissons); EAST (Andlau, Dijon, Lautenbach, Marmoutier, Murbach); WEST (Angoulême, Bordeaux, Périgueux, Saintes, Tavant, Vicq); CENTER (Issoire, Limoges, Nevers, Orcival, Saint-Nectaire, Souillac); SOUTH (Elne, Narbonne, Saint-Bertrand-de-Comminges, Saint-Martin-du-Canigou, Serrabonne). Many of the dates given are still in controversy or simply represent good guesses by scholars.

1067: Saint-Benoît-sur-Loire, abbey church, rebuilding begun after fire. Porch-tower with important sculptured capitals is 11th century also; choir and transept sculpture, early 12th.

c.1075: Toulouse, church of Saint-Sernin begun. Historically important reliefs in choir done in last years of 11th century. Sculpture of Porte des Comtes and of Miégeville dates from first half of 12th. Nave rebuilt in Gothic style early in 13th; other later changes. Sculptor's name mentioned: Bernard Gilduin.

c.1077–1082: Bayeux Tapestry. Probably executed on order of Bishop Odo, uterine brother of William the Conqueror. While giving a highly prejudiced version of Norman conquest, the Tapestry is a precious source of other contemporary information.

c.1085–1118: Cluny, abbey church of Saint-Pierre, period when choir and transepts were completed. Though only a fragment of this famous Romanesque structure was spared when it was barbarously destroyed in the 19th century, its enormous pioneer influence lives on in other churches. A few of its sculptured capitals from ambulatory and nave have also been preserved, ascribed dates starting from 1089–1094 for ambulatory, before 1109 for nave.

c.1090–1100: Saint-Savin-sur-Gartempe, date generally assigned to its renowned frescoes. The church itself, built earlier in the 11th century, has suffered much from mutilation, especially during the wars of the religions.

1096–1151: Vézelay, church of La Madeleine, one of the finest of Romanesque structures. Built during peaceful gaps in the abbey's agitated life, which sputtered throughout half a century. One particularly tumultuous period was probably touched off, in 1106, by the burghers' refusal to pay taxes imposed for the new building. Famous sculptured tympanum is dated c.1125–1130; nave capitals somewhat earlier. All estimates are still in controversy, however.

c.1100: Moissac, church of Saint-Pierre, date of the oldest of its cloister sculpture (or slightly earlier). That of the famous south porch is estimated from c.1115 to c.1130, depending on the scholar.

c.1115–1125: Sculptured capitals of the former convent (willfully destroyed in 1811) of Notre-Dame-la-Daurade, of Toulouse. Dates are those of the largest number of the capitals, though a few go back to c.1075, others ahead to the end of the 12th century. This carving, among the most exquisite of Romanesque art, is matched by capitals of another vanished cloister of Toulouse, Saint-Étienne, done by Gilabertus, which are dated c.1125–1135.

c.1119: Saint-Gilles, date (in controversy) when abbey church was started, though little enough remains from this period. Remarkable 12th-century façade sculpture, albeit mutilated, is largely preserved, however. Dated early by some, others place the carving in the second half of the century. Pierre Brun, who worked here in 1171, signed two statues ("BRUNUS").

Many other churches of Southern France were either destroyed during the Albigensian troubles or had their building periods drawn out by more than a century of strife.

1120: Saint-Philibert de Tournus, date when this church was reconsecrated after a new choir, apse, and transept were built. However, major portions of this great pioneer structure date from before our period: the west façade, 1000; narthex, 1008–1019; nave, also early 11th century.

1120: Autun, cathedral of Saint-Lazare begun. It was consecrated in 1130 (a consecration date rarely means that a structure was completed at the time). Notable for work by one of greatest of 12th-century sculptors, who inscribed on the magnificent tympanum he carved: "GISLE-BERTUS HOC FECIT." Also did many of the superb interior capital reliefs. His work is estimated to have spread over ten years, c.1125–1135.

1125–1149: Angers, cathedral of Saint-Maurice, period when (under Bishop Ellger) rebuilding of an earlier structure on the same site was begun. Its single façade portal was sculptured, 1155–1165. Church partly rebuilt in Gothic style, at end of 12th century and during much of 13th. Its fine stained glass dates from second half of 12th century, in nave; 13th century, in choir.

c.1130: Conques-en-Rouergue, church of Sainte-Foy, probable date of its famous sculptured tympanum. Church itself was built earlier, begun under Abbot Odolric (1031–1065) and finished under Abbot Bégon III (1087–1107).

c.1130: Beaulieu-sur-Dordogne, abbey church, date of its famous sculptured Romanesque tympanum, one of the first in which a Judgment Day scene was presented.

1130: Clermont-Ferrand, church of Notre-Dame-du-Port, date when mention is made of a sculptor, Maître Robert, who was possibly responsible for the church's fine capitals. The building itself, begun earlier, was largely built in the 12th century, though parts were done up to the end of the 13th.

c.1135: Sens, cathedral of Saint-Étienne, date when this early Gothic church was begun; completed in third quarter of century. Associated with its building is the name of the famous architect, Guillaume de Sens, who after death of Thomas à Becket was called to England to initiate Canterbury cathedral, in 1175.

1137–1144: Saint-Denis, abbey church, the overall period of its reconstruction in the Gothic style, a pioneer in this form. Its great animator, Abbot Suger, had already had the façade redone, in 1125, but in Romanesque. The only name of a working artist to come down to us is that of Godefroid de Claire, goldsmith, who headed a group that did a magnificent Crucifixion, which was richly decorated with storied enamel work. The famed architect, Pierre de Montreuil, also worked here, but in the 13th century, when he made further changes in the church structure.

c.1140: Arles, church (former cathedral) of Saint-Trophime, date when rebuilding of an earlier structure was begun. The cloister, with excellent sculptured capitals, dates in part from the second half of the 12th century. The Romanesque façade was done late in the same century, a time when advanced Gothic work was already being produced elsewhere. Despite this anachronism, the sculpture is nevertheless often noteworthy.

1150–1158: Le Mans, cathedral of Saint-Julien, date when its early 12th-century Romanesque nave was revaulted in Gothic style. Choir was redone, 1217–1254; other parts later.

1153–1191: Senlis, cathedral of Notre-Dame, another pioneer in the Gothic style. Parts date from the 13th century and even later, however.

c.1157: Saint-Germain-des-Prés, date of its choir, which was redone in early ogival style. However, the main body of this church is much earlier, before our period. Begun around 990–1014; parts of its nave and tower are also 11th century.

1160–1180: Laon, cathedral of Notre-Dame, date when this early Gothic church was begun, at the choir. Rest of church completed, 1180–1225.

c.1160–1180: Lyon, cathedral of Saint-Jean. Though begun at this time, under Archbishop Guichard, the church was not completed until far into the 13th century, with some even later additions. Though choir is still Romanesque, its vault, done at the end of the 12th century, is Gothic, as is the rest of the church.

1162–1180: Poitiers, cathedral of Saint-Pierre, period when the major portion of this church was done, in Romanesque style. Part of it is earlier, however. The façade, on the other hand, is in Gothic style (1242–1271), as are other elements. The church has excellent stained glass in both styles.

Poitiers has the most extraordinary group of old churches in France: Baptistry of Saint-Jean (parts dating from 4th century); Saint-Hilaire (11th century, in considerable part); Sainte-Radegonde (begun at end of 11th century); Notre-Dame-la-Grande (12th century), with its remarkable sculptured façade.

1162–1181: Reims, abbey church of Saint-Remi, date when parts of this famous Romanesque church were reconstructed in early Gothic style. Its original nave and transept dated from 1039–1049. Its façade is also early Gothic.

1163–1245: Paris, cathedral of Notre-Dame. Built entirely in Gothic style from its inception (except the Sainte-Anne portal), the church underwent an almost complete reconstruction, 1235–1320, however: chapels and buttresses added, transepts lengthened, etc. Chief animator was Maurice de Sully (bishop, 1160–1196), but names only of second group of architects and artists are known: Jean and Pierre de Chelles, Jean le Bouteiller, Jean Davy, Pierre and Eudes de Montreuil.

Second half of 12th century: Le Puy, cathedral of Notre-Dame, period of its construction. It is one of the notable group of late Romanesque churches in the Auvergne–Haute-Loire region, including Saint-Nectaire, Brioude, Issoire, Orcival, Mozat, etc.

1181: Date of the enamel-decorated pulpit (later, altar) at convent of Kolsterneuburg (near Vienna), done by Nicolas de Verdun, famed goldsmith, a work of pioneer artistic and iconographic importance. A student of Godefroid de Claire, Nicolas is also known as the maker of a reliquary at Tournai, 1205.

c.1190–1275: Strasbourg, cathedral of Notre-Dame, period from when its Romanesque apse was begun to completion of its Gothic nave. Its façade, begun in 1276 or 1277, was largely the work of Master Erwin (1284–1318). The famed "Bible of the Poor" stained-glass windows in the south aisle were done 1331–1350. A few years before 1290, on request of the cathedral chapter, the municipality took over the fabrique.

1194–1220: Chartres, cathedral of Notre-Dame, date of its rebuilding after a disastrous fire. Sculptured transept porches added, 1200–1260. Remaining from the Romanesque structure after the fire is the famous west façade, including its exterior sculpture and interior stained-glass windows (1145–1155); also the towers (1134–1170), one of which was not completed until much later, however.

1195–1265: Bourges, cathedral of Saint-Étienne, built almost without interruption; choir, 1195–1220; nave and façade, 1220–1265. Lateral portals are from a former Romanesque period, however. Almost all the magnificent stained glass is 13th century.

c.1206–1223: Troyes, cathedral of Saint-Pierre et Saint-Paul, period when (under episcopacy of

Bishop Hervé) the church was begun. It continued very slowly, the nave being completed only in the 15th century, the façade in the 16th. Has fine 13th-century windows in choir and ambulatory, however.

1211–1240: Reims, cathedral of Notre-Dame, period when its choir, halted 1233–1236 by civil strife, was built. Rest of the church was done slowly, going on to the end of the 13th century and beyond. The west façade, done by Bernard de Soissons, was built 1255–1290. Names of all its important architects are known: Jean d'Orbais, Jean le Loup, Bernard de Soissons, Gaucher de Reims, Robert de Coucy. Of these, all but the last once had their portraits engraved in the labyrinth flagstone.

1214: Rouen, cathedral of Notre-Dame, date when new building was begun after old structure was destroyed by fire. Two portals remain from 12th century but greater part of church dates from 13th and 14th. Has notable sculpture and stained glass, the Joseph window bearing signature of Clément, painter-glazier of Chartres.

1215–1234: Auxerre, cathedral of Saint-Étienne, date when its choir was completed, under Bishops Guillaume de Seignelay (1207–1220) and Henri de Villeneuve (1220–1234), including excellent stained glass. Rest of church continued through 13th century and on into the 14th and beyond.

1220–1269: Amiens, cathedral of Notre-Dame, period when major work of rebuilding, after a disastrous fire, was done. Transepts completed 1270–1288. Lateral chapels added at end of 13th century and into the 14th. Names of its three architects were engraved, in 1288, in the labyrinth: Robert de Luzarches, who drew up the original plans, Thomas de Cormont and his son, Regnault.

c.1236: Tours, cathedral of Saint-Gatien, date when this church was begun, though work on it continued for centuries, in a medley of styles. But its 13th-century stained-glass windows are notable. Name of a glazier, Richard, is attached to some of them (1257–1270).

1243–1248: Paris, Sainte-Chapelle, built by Louis IX, to house the "Crown of Thorns." Architect was the famous Pierre de Montreuil, who also built a Chapelle de la Vierge (destroyed) at Saint-Germain-des-Prés and worked at Notre-Dame, Saint-Denis, and on other projects. He and his brother, Eudes, were both "maîtres-d'oeuvres" under Louis IX.

1247: Beauvais, cathedral of Saint-Pierre was begun. The choir, probably designed by Eudes de Montreuil, was completed and closed off in 1272, but the structure, too daringly vaulted, crumbled in 1284. Work was slowly resumed but, subject to many difficulties, including another accident, during the following centuries, the church was never completed.

1248: Clermont, cathedral of Notre-Dame was begun. It was not completed until the middle of the 14th century, however. Has fine stained glass of the end of the 13th century. The name of the architect, Jean Deschamps, is associated with the building of the choir (1286).

1262: Troyes, church of Saint-Urbain, date when work was begun. At first pursued with expedition, choir was completed in 1266, but a fire and other difficulties put off the church's termination indefinitely. It has remarkable stained glass of the 13th century.

1282: Albi, cathedral of Sainte-Cécile, date when reconstruction was begun after an earlier building was devastated by the Albigensian wars. Not finished until late in the 14th century, with further additions after that.

This structure (which has been called the "lair of the Inquisitor") appropriately closes off the great period of church building in France. Due to wars and other calamities and also because the commanding position of the Church began steadily to decline, no future period could approach the enormous output of great religious architecture and art that was produced during the 12th and 13th centuries.

NOTES

CHAPTER I

1. C. Sauvageot, "La porte des martyres à Notre-Dame de Paris," *Annales Archéologiques*, XXII (1862), 309–21.

2. Félix de Verneilh, "Les bas-reliefs de l'université à Notre-Dame de Paris," *ibid.*, XXVI (1869), 96–106.

3. *Bulletin Monumental de la Société des Archéologues de France* (1867), 52–70. This publication will hereafter be referred to as *Bulletin Monumental*.

4. Émile Mâle, *L'art religieux du XIIIe siècle en France* (Paris: Armand Colin, 1898), p.452, n.5.

5. Adele Fischel, "Die Seitenreliefs am Südportale der Notre-Dame Kirche in Paris. Ein Versuch zu ihrer Deutung und Datierung," *Jahrbuch für Kunstwissenschaft* (1930), 189–200.

6. François Gébelin, *Notre-Dame de Paris* (Paris: Éditions Alpina, 1951), p.35.

7. Pierre-Marie Auzas, *Notre-Dame de Paris* (Paris: Hachette, 1956), p.18.

8. Mâle, pp.375, 399.

9. Marcel Aubert, *Notre-Dame de Paris, architecture et sculpture* (Paris: Ducros et Colas, 1928), p.19.

10. J.-B. Hauréau, "Philippe de Grève, chancelier de l'église et de l'université de Paris," *Journal des Savants* (1894), 430.

11. Hastings Rashdall, *The Universities of Europe in the Middle Ages*, I (Oxford: Clarendon Press, 1936), 340–41.

12. Louis Halphen, *À travers l'histoire du moyen-âge* (Paris: Presses Universitaires de France, 1950), p.322. This publisher will hereafter be referred to as PUF.

13. *Ibid.*, pp. 290–91.

14. Hauréau, p.430.

15. Maurice Perrod, *Étude sur la vie et sur les oeuvres de Guillaume de Saint-Amour* (Lons-le-Saunier: L. Declume, 1902), p.30.

16. Rashdall, pp.335–38.

17. Rutebeuf, *Poèmes concernant l'université de Paris* (Paris: Nizet, 1952), editor's preface.

18. Jean de Meung, *Roman de la rose*, Verses 11492–11495, 11505–11508. Quoted in Gustave Cohen, Henri Focillon et Henri Pirenne, *La civilisation occidentale au moyen-âge, du XIe au milieu du XVe siècle* (Paris: PUF, 1933), p. 283. (English wording is author's.)

19. D. L. Mackay, "Le système d'examen du treizième siècle, d'après le *De conscientia* de Robert de Sorbon," in *Mélanges Ferdinand Lot* (Paris: Édouard Champion, 1925), p.494.

20. Perrod, p.30.

21. Célestin-Louis Tanon, *Histoire des justices des anciennes églises et communautés monastiques de Paris* (Paris: L. Larose et Forcel, 1883), p.139, footnote.

22. Dom Jacques Du Breul, *Les antiquitez et choses plus remarquables de Paris* (Paris: Nicolas Bonfons, 1608), p.355.

23. Tanon, p.42.

24. Johan Huizinga, *The Waning of the Middle Ages* (Garden City, N.Y.: Doubleday, 1954), Chap.I.

25. Rashdall, III, 437–38.

26. *Nouveau Larousse Illustré*, I (Paris: Larousse, n.d.), 89.

27. Albert R.-A. Lecoy de la Marche, *Saint Louis, son gouvernement et sa politique* (Tours: A. Mame et Fils, 1887), p.236.

28. Pierre Vidal et Léon Daru, *Histoire de la corporation des marchands merciers, grossiers, jouailliers, ...* (Paris: Honoré Champion, 1912), pp.204–5.

29. René Leblanc de Lespinasse et François Bonnardot, *Les métiers et corporations de la ville de Paris, XIIIe siècle. Le Livre des métiers d'Étienne Boileau* (Paris: Imprimerie Nationale, 1879–97), Introduction.

30. Jean de Garlande, *"Dictionarius,"* in Auguste Scheler, *Lexicographie latine du XIIe et du XIIIe siècle* (Leipzig: F. A. Brockhaus, 1867).

31. Benjamin Guérard et al., *Cartulaire de l'église Notre-Dame de Paris*, I (Paris: Crapelet, 1850). Preface, p.xcix, which paraphrases the Latin of Document CXCV.

32. Albert R.-A. Lecoy de la Marche, *La chaire française au moyen-âge* (Paris: Didier, 1868), p.419.

33. Achille Luchaire, *Histoire des institutions monarchiques de la France sous les premiers Capétiens, 987–1180*, I (Paris: Imprimerie Nationale, 1883), 228.

34. A.-L. Gabriel, *La protection des étudiants à l'université de Paris au XIIIe siècle* (Hull, Canada: Leclerc, 1950), p.10.

35. Dom Jacques Du Breul, *Le théatre des antiquitez de Paris* (Paris: Sociétés des Imprimeurs, 1639), p.434.

36. Du Breul, *Les antiquitez et choses plus remarquables de Paris*, pp.261–62.

37. Louis Courajod, *Alexandre Lenoir, son journal et le musée des monuments français*, I (Paris: H. Champion, 1878–87), Introduction.

38. Du Breul, *Le théatre*, p.21.

39. Luchaire, p.225.

40. Tanon, p.153.

41. *Ibid.*, p.135.

42. Du Breul, *Le théatre*, pp.802–6.

43. Tanon, p.9.

44. *Ibid.*, pp.101–2.

45. A.-A. Beugnot, Fils, *Essai sur les institutions de Saint Louis* (Paris: F.-G. Levrault, 1821), pp.377–78.

46. Tanon, p.175.

47. Abbé Jean Lebeuf, *Histoire de la ville et de tout le diocèse de Paris*, I (Paris: Féchoz, 1883–93), 38.

48. J.-A. Piganiol de la Force, *Description de Paris, de Versailles, de Marly, . . .*, II (Paris: Charles-Nicolas Poirion, 1742), 75.

49. Frantz Funck-Brentano, *La Bastille des comédiens: le For-l'Évêque* (Paris: A. Fontemoing 1903), p.308.

CHAPTER II

1. Eugène Viollet-le-Duc, *Dictionnaire raisonné de l'architecture française du XIe au XVIe siècle*, I (Paris: B. Bance, 1854), 182–87.

2. Victor Sabouret, "Les voûtes d'arête nervurées—rôle simplement décoratif des nervures," *Le Génie Civil* (March 3, 1928), 205–9.

3. Marcel Aubert, "Les plus anciennes croisées d'ogives—leur rôle dans la construction," *Bulletin Monumental* (1934), 5–67, 137–237.

4. Erwin Panofsky, *Gothic Architecture and Scholasticism* (Latrobe, Pa.: The Archabbey Press, 1951), p.54.

5. Sabouret, "Les voûtes d'arête nervurées."

6. Pol Abraham, "Viollet-le-Duc et le rationalisme médiéval," *Bulletin Monumental* (1934), 69–88.

7. Émile Mâle, *L'art religieux du XIIIe siècle en France* (Paris: Armand Colin, 1902), p.37.

8. R.-C. de Lasteyrie du Saillant, *La déviation de l'axe des églises, est-elle symbolique?* (Paris: C. Klincksieck, 1905).

9. K. J. Conant, *Carolingian and Romanesque Architecture* (Harmondsworth: Penguin, 1959), p.83.

10. François Deshoulières, "Les cryptes en France et l'influence du culte des reliques sur l'architecture religieuse," *Mélanges Martroye* (1941), pp.213–38.

11. Conant, p.79.

12. Abbot Suger, *"De consecratione,"* in Erwin Panofsky, *Abbot Suger on the Abbey Church of St.-Denis* (Princeton: Princeton University Press, 1946), pp.87–89.

13. Louis Réau et Gustave Cohen, *L'art du moyen-âge et la civilisation française* (Paris: A. Michel, 1951), p.55.

14. Mlle. Chatel, "Le culte de la vierge Marie en France, du Ve au XIIIe siècle," *Thèses-Sorbonne* (Paris, 1945), p.303.

15. Eduard Wechssler, *Das Kultur-Problem des Minnesangs*, I (Halle a. S.: M. Niemeyer, 1909), 285.

16. C. R. Cheney, "Church-Building in the Middle Ages," *Bulletin of the John Rylands Library*, XXXIV (1951–52), 26–27.

17. Francis Salet et Jean Adhémar, *La Madeleine de Vézelay* (Melun: Librairie d'Argences, 1948), p.29 and footnote.

18. Mâle, pp.358 ff.

19. Meyer Schapiro, "From Mozarabic to Romanesque in Silos," *Art Bulletin*, XXI (1939), 313–74.

20. Joan Evans, *Life in Medieval France* (London: Phaidon Press, 1957), p.79.

21. A. Kingsley Porter, *Romanesque Sculpture of the Pilgrimage Roads*, I (Boston: M. Jones, 1923), 205.

22. H. M. Smyser, *The Pseudo-Turpin* (Cambridge, Mass.: The Mediaeval Academy of America, 1937), Chap.II.

23. George Zarnecki, "The Contribution of the Orders," in *The Flowering of the Middle Ages* (London: Thames and Hudson, 1966), pp.67, 76.

24. *Le guide du pèlerin de Saint-Jacques-de-Compostelle*, transl. by Jeanne Vielliard (Mâcon: Protat Frères, 1938).

25. Porter, p.205.

26. Conant, p.104.

27. Porter, p.177.

28. Émile Mâle, *L'art religieux du XIIe siècle en France* (Paris: Armand Colin, 1922), p.297.

29. *Le guide du pèlerin*, Appendix.

30. Conant, Plate 46B.

31. Mâle, *L'art religieux du XIIe siècle*, p.293.

32. Meyer Schapiro, "The Sculptures of Souillac," in *Medieval Studies in Memory of A. Kingsley Porter*, II (Cambridge, Mass.: Harvard University Press, 1939), 382.

33. Mâle, *L'art religieux du XIIIe siècle*, p.385.

34. Louis Grodecki, Jean Lafond et al., *Corpus vitrearum medii aevi*, I (Paris: Caisse Nationale des Monuments Historiques, 1959), 83–84.

35. Ch. Ferrat, "L'autel d'Avenas (Rhône)," *Bulletin Monumental*, XCII (1933), 377–79.

36. Jeanne Vielliard, "Notes sur l'iconographie de Saint Pierre," *Moyen-Âge* (1929), 1–16.

37. Schapiro, "The Sculptures of Souillac," p.379, footnotes 21,23.

38. **Abbé Sainsot, "Le tympan du portail de Mervilliers,"** *Congrès Archéologiques*, LXVII (1900), 97-119. For a different interpretation see A. Lapeyre, *Bull. Mon.* (1936), 317-32.

39. Augustin Thierry, *Recueil des monuments inédits de l'histoire du tiers état*, first series, I (Paris: Firmin-Didot, 1850), 18.

40. Louis Bréhier, *L'art chrétien* (2nd ed.; Paris: Renouard, 1928), p.228.

41. Salet et Adhémar, p.130.

42. A. Kingsley Porter, *Spanish Romanesque Sculpture*, II (Firenze: Pantheon Casa Editrice, 1928), Plate 97.

43. "Saint-Benoît-sur-Loire et Germigny-des-Près," *La France Illustrée*, Paris (1961), 29.

44. Richard Hamann-MacLean, *Frühe Kunst im West Fränkischen Reich* (Leipzig: H. Schmidt und C. Günther, n.d.), p.10.

45. Sir Frank Stenton et al., *The Bayeux Tapestry—a Comprehensive Survey* (London: Phaidon Press, 1957), pp.9-11. See C. R. Dodwell's qualifying view in *Burlington Magazine*, Nov. 1966.

46. Roger Sherman Loomis, "The Origin and Date of the Bayeux Embroidery," *Art Bulletin*, VI (1923), 3-7.

47. Quoted by A. Levé, *La tapisserie de la reine Mathilde, dite la tapisserie de Bayeux* (Paris: H. Laurens, 1919), p.132.

48. *Ibid.*, p.133.

49. *Ibid.*, pp.200–1.

50. Cdt. Richard Lefebvre des Noëttes, *La tapisserie de Bayeux, datée par le harnachement des chevaux et l'équipement des cavaliers* (Caen: Henri Delesques, 1912), p.5.

51. *Ibid.*, p.23.

52. Lynn White, Jr., *Medieval Technology and Social Change* (Oxford: Clarendon Press, 1962), pp.24–25.

53. Richard Lefebvre des Noëttes, *L'attelage et le cheval de selle à travers les âges* (Paris: A. Picard, 1931), pp.12 ff.; and L. White, Jr., p.60.

54. Richard Lefebvre des Noëttes, "La nuit du moyen-âge et son inventaire," *Mercure de France* (May, 1932), 572–99.

55. L. des Noëttes, *L'attelage et le cheval de selle*, p.178.

56. L. des Noëttes, "La nuit du moyen-âge," p.575.

CHAPTER III

1. Saint Bernard, *Textes choisis et présentés par Étienne Gilson* (Paris: Plon, 1949), p.65.

2. Meyer Schapiro, "From Mozarabic to Romanesque in Silos," *Art Bulletin*, XXI (1939), 313–74.

3. *Le Jeu d'Adam et Ève*. Transposition littéraire de Gustave Cohen (Paris: Delagrave, 1936).

4. Lily Braun, *Le problème de la femme: son évolution historique, son aspect économique* (Paris: E. Cornély, 1908), p.43.

5. G. G. Coulton, *Ten Medieval Studies* (Cambridge, England: University Press, 1930), p.52.

6. Émile Mâle, *L'art religieux du XIIe siècle en France* (Paris: Armand Colin, 1922), p.373.

7. Émile Mâle, *L'art religieux du XIIIe siècle en France* (Paris: Armand Colin, 1925), pp. 337–38.

8. Alice Hurtrel, *La femme, sa condition sociale, depuis l'antiquité jusqu'à nos jours* (Paris: G. Hurtrel, 1887), pp.40, 43.

9. Albert R.-A. Lecoy de la Marche, *La chaire française au moyen-âge* (Paris: Didier, 1886), p.430.

10. Saint Bernard, pp.66–67.

11. Both poems quoted by Pierre Jonin, *Les personnages féminins dans les romans français de Tristan au XIIe siècle* (Gap: Éditions Ophrys, 1958), p.445 and footnote.

12. Mlle. Chatel, "Le culte de la vierge Marie en France, du Ve au XIIIe siècle," *Thèses-Sorbonne* (Paris, 1945), pp.151–52.

13. Quoted by Mâle, *L'art religieux du XIIIe siècle*, pp.273–74.

14. Mlle. Chatel, p.220.

15. *Ibid.*, p.203.

16. Marion Lawrence, "Maria Regina," *Art Bulletin*, VII (1935), 150–61.

17. Mâle, *L'art religieux du XIIe siècle*, pp.426–37.

18. Mâle, *L'art religieux du XIIIe siècle*, p.276.

19. Mâle, *L'art religieux du XIIe siècle*, p.431.

20. Gustave Cohen, Henri Focillon et Henri Pirenne, *La civilisation occidentale au moyen-âge du XIe au milieu du XVe siècle* (Paris: PUF, 1933), p.231.

21. Édouard de Laboulaye, *Recherches sur la condition civile et politique des femmes, depuis les Romains jusqu'à nos jours* (Paris: A. Durand, 1843), p.243.

22. *Ibid.*, p.443.

23. Hurtrel, p.43.

24. É. de Laboulaye, p.444.

25. *Ibid.*, p.441.

26. Edmond Faral, *La vie quotidienne au temps de Saint Louis* (Paris: Hachette, 1942), p.141.

27. Chrétien de Troyes, "Yvain ou le chevalier au lion," Verses 5298–5301, in Gustave Cohen, *Chrétien de Troyes: Oeuvres choisies* (Paris: Larousse, 1936), p.76.

28. "Women in the Middle Ages," *Blackwood's Magazine*, CII (1867), 613–34.

29. Auguste Bebel, *La femme et le socialisme* (Gand: Volksdrukkerij, 1911), p.119.

30. *La chanson de la croisade albigeoise*, ed. Eugène Martin-Chabot, III, § XXXV (205) (Nogent-le-Rotrou: Daupeley-Gouverneur, 1931), Verses 121–129 and 145–156.

31. J. de Lahondès, "Église Saint-Nazaire (Carcassonne)," *Congrès Archéologiques*, LXXIII (1906), 32–42.

32. E. de Lépinois, *Histoire de Chartres* (Chartres: Garnier, 1854), p.127.

33. Marc Bloch, *La société féodale* (Paris: A. Michel, 1940), p.40.

34. Quoted in Joseph Anglade, *Les troubadours, leurs vies, leurs oeuvres, leur influence* (Paris: A. Colin, 1908), p.77.

35. Gaston Paris, "Jaufré Rudel," *Revue Historique*, LIII (1893), 223–56.

36. Eduard Wechssler, *Das Kultur-Problem des Minnesangs* (Halle a. S: M. Niemeyer, 1909), pp.72, 94, 95, 140, 182, 206, *passim*.

37. Guillaume de Lorris et Jean de Meung, *Le roman de la rose*, ed. Pierre Marteau (Orléans: H. Herluison, 1878–79), Verses 9489–9490.

38. *Lettres complètes d'Abélard et d'Héloïse*, transl. from the Latin into French by Octave Gréard (Paris: Garnier Frères, 1886), pp.81, 96, 98, 110, *passim*.

CHAPTER IV

1. Marcel Pobé et Joseph Gantner, *L'art monumental roman en France* (Paris: Braun, 1955), p.13.

2. Francis Salet et Jean Adhémar, *La Madeleine de Vézelay* (Melun: Librairie d'Argences, 1948), p.23.

3. Achille Luchaire, *Les communes françaises à l'époque des Capétiens directs* (Paris: Hachette, 1890), p.242.

4. Agnès Humbert, "Les chapiteaux de Vézelay," *Arts de France*, IV (1946), 40–43.

5. Henri David, "Les signes avant-coureurs du réalisme dans la sculpture religieuse du moyen-âge en Bourgogne," *À Cluny, Congrès Scientifique*, Dijon (1950), 254–59.

6. Raymond Rey, *L'art des cloîtres romans* (Toulouse: É. Privat, 1955), p.58.

7. Salet et Adhémar, pp.134–35.

8. Léon de Bastard, "Recherches sur l'insurrection communale de Vézelay," *Bibliothèque de l'École des Chartes*, 3rd Series, II (1851), 339 ff.

9. Meyer Schapiro, "From Mozarabic to Romanesque in Silos," *Art Bulletin*, XXI (1939), 313–74.

10. *Ibid.*

11. C. A. Robson, *Maurice of Sully and the Medieval Vernacular Homily* (Oxford: Basil Blackwell, 1952), pp.110–12.

12. Luchaire, pp.106–7.

13. Charles-Edmond Petit-Dutaillis, *Les communes françaises* (Paris: A. Michel, 1947), p.89.

14. Achille Luchaire, *Philippe-Auguste* (Paris: Hachette, 1881), pp.183–84.

15. Claude-François Menestrier, *Histoire civile ou consulaire de la ville de Lyon* (Lyon: N. et J.-B. de Ville, 1696), pp.365–66.

16. Luchaire, *Philippe-Auguste*, p.122.

17. Jean, Sire de Joinville, *Histoire de Saint Louis*, ed. and transl. Natalis de Wailly (Paris, 1874), § CXLV.

18. Louis Grodecki, "Le vitrail et l'architecture au XIIe et au XIIIe siècles," *Gazette des Beaux-Arts*, XXXVI (1949), 5–24.

19. Abbot Suger, *On What Was Done under his Administration*, transl. from the Latin by Erwin Panofsky (Princeton: Princeton University Press, 1946), p.24.

20. Robert Branner, review of Pierre du Colombier, *Les chantiers des cathédrales*, in *Art Bulletin*, XXXVII (1955), 61–65.

21. Otto von Simson, *The Gothic Cathedral* (New York: Pantheon, 1956), pp.162–63, 166, 178.

22. Pierre Bonnassieux, *Histoire de la réunion de Lyon à la France* (Paris: A. Vingtrinier, 1875), pp.30–31.

23. Lucien Bégule, *Monographie de la cathédrale de Lyon* (Lyon: Mougin-Rusand, 1880), p.8.

24. Robert Branner, "Historical Aspects of the Reconstruction of Reims Cathedral, 1210–1241," *Speculum*, XXXVI (1961), 23–37.

25. Hans Reinhardt, *La cathédrale de Reims* (Paris: PUF, 1963), pp.183 ff.

26. René de Lespinasse et François Bonnardot, *Les métiers et corporations de la ville de Paris, XIIIe siècle. Le Livre des métiers d'Étienne Boileau* (Paris: Imprimerie Nationale, 1879–97), p.iii.

27. Geneviève Aclocque, *Les corporations, l'industrie et le commerce à Chartres, du XIe siècle à la révolution* (Paris: A. Picard, 1917), Appendix, pp.313–26.

28. Prosper Boissonnade, *Essai sur l'organisation du travail en Poitou depuis le XIe siècle jusqu'à la révolution*, II (Paris: H. Champion, 1900), 224.

29. Yves Delaporte, *Les vitraux de la cathédrale de Chartres*, I (Chartres: Durand, 1926), 230.

30. Louis Grodecki, quoting Eugène Hucher, *Calques des vitraux de la cathédrale du Mans* (1855–62), in *Congrès Archéologiques de France* (1961), 93.

31. Pierre Louvet et Jean Moura, *Notre-Dame de Paris, centre de vie* (Paris, 1932), p.21, footnote.

32. Abbé M. J. Bulteau, *Monographie de la cathédrale de Chartres*, I (Chartres: R. Selleret, 1887), 246.

33. Alfred Franklin, *Dictionnaire historique des arts, métiers et professions exercés dans Paris depuis le treizième siècle* (Paris: H. Welter, 1906), p.37.

34. Luchaire, *Les communes françaises*, p.33.

35. J.-J. Bourassé et Abbé F.-G. Manceau, *Verrières du choeur de l'église métropolitaine de Tours* (Paris: Veuve Didron, 1849), p.25.

36. Georges Ritter, *Les vitraux de la cathédrale de Rouen* (Cognac: Impressions d'Art des Établissements Fac, 1926), p.9.

37. Hans Haug et al., *La cathédrale de Strasbourg* (Strasbourg: Éditions des Dernières Nouvelles, 1957), pp.17, 19, 118.

38. Ferdinand-C.-L. de Lasteyrie du Saillant, *Histoire de la peinture sur verre d'après ses monuments en France* (Paris: Firmin-Didot Frères, 1853–57), pp.259–60.

39. Gustave Fagniez, *Études sur l'industrie et la classe industrielle à Paris au XIIIe et au XIVe siècle* (Paris: F. Vieweg, 1877), pp.50–51.

40. Georges Boussinesq et Gustave Laurent, *Histoire de Reims depuis les origines jusqu'à nos jours*, I (Reims: Matot-Braine, 1933), 348–51.

41. Arnold Hauser, *The Social History of Art* (London: Routledge and Kegan Paul, 1951), pp.261–62.

42. Lynn White, Jr., "Natural Science and Naturalistic Art in the Middle Ages," *American Historical Review*, LII (April, 1947), 425.

43. Gustave Cohen, Henri Focillon et Henri Pirenne, *La civilisation occidentale au moyen-âge du XIe au milieu du XVe siècle* (Paris: PUF, 1933), p.289.

44. *Ibid.*, p.290.

45. L. White, Jr., p.433.

46. *Ibid.*

47. *Ibid.*, p.425.

48. Denise Jalabert, "La flore gothique—ses origines, son évolution du XIIe au XVe siècle," *Bulletin Monumental* (1932), 181–246.

49. L. White, Jr., p.427.

50. Hans R. Hahnloser, *Villard de Honnecourt* (Wien: A. Schroll, 1935), Plate 48 and p.147.

51. Charles Homer Haskins, *The Renaissance of the Twelfth Century* (Cambridge, Mass.: Harvard University Press, 1933), pp.333–35.

52. Émile Mâle, "Les arts liberaux dans la statuaire du moyen-âge," *Revue Archéologique* (1891), 344–45.

53. Kurt Gerstenberg, *Die deutschen Baumeisterbildnisse des Mittelalters* (Berlin: Deutscher Verlag für Kunstwissenschaft, 1966).

54. Albert R.-A. Lecoy de la Marche, *La chaire française au moyen-âge* (Paris: Didier, 1886), p.483.

55. Henri Focillon, *L'art d'occident* (Paris: A. Colin, 1938), pp.230 ff.

56. Émile (V. E.) Bertaux, *Études d'histoire et d'art* (Paris: Hachette, 1911), pp.3–26.

57. Henri Focillon, *Gothic Art* (*The Art of the West*, Vol. II [London: Phaidon, 1963]), p.103, footnote.

58. William Koehler, "Byzantine Art in the West," *Dumbarton Oaks Inaugural Lectures* (Cambridge, Mass.: Harvard University Press, 1941), pp.84–86.

59. André Michel, *Sculpture gothique* (*Histoire de l'art*, Vol. II [Paris: A. Colin, 1905–29]), p.126.

60. L. White, Jr., p.432.

61. Pierre Francastel, *L'humanisme roman* (Rodez: P. Carrère, 1942), p.123.

CHAPTER V

1. Émile Mâle, *L'art religieux du XIIIe siècle en France* (Paris: Armand Colin, 1925), p.63.

2. Joan Evans, *Art in Medieval France, 987–1498* (London: Oxford University Press, 1948), p.90.

3. Jules-Charles Roux, *Saint-Gilles: sa légende, son abbaye, ses coutumes* (Paris: Bloud, 1910), p.70.

4. Evans, preface.

5. J. Banchereau, "Travaux d'apiculture sur un chapiteau de Vézelay," *Bulletin Monumental* (1913), 403–11.

6. James C. Webster, *The Labors of the Months in Antique and Medieval Art to the End of the Twelfth Century* (Princeton: Princeton University Press, 1938), p.101.

7. *Ibid.*, p.101, footnote. Quoting Archer Taylor, *The Proverb* (Cambridge, Mass.: Harvard University Press, 1931), p.115.

8. Mâle, pp.70–71.

9. Webster, pp.89 ff.

10. *Ibid.*, p.102.

11. *Ibid.*, p.57.

12. Gustave Cohen, Henri Focillon et Henri Pirenne, *La civilisation occidentale au moyen-âge, du XIe au milieu du XVe siècle* (Paris: PUF, 1933), p.65.

13. Charles Verlinden, *L'esclavage dans l'Europe médiévale*, I (Brügge: "De Tempel," 1955), 803.

14. Jacques de Voragine, *La légende dorée*, II (Paris: Éditions Rombaldi, 1942), 309–14.

15. C. A. Robson, *Maurice of Sully and the Medieval Vernacular Homily* (Oxford: Basil Blackwell, 1952), p.168.

16. Charles Lenient, *La satire en France au moyen-âge* (Paris: L. Hachette, 1893), p.398.

17. Marc Bloch, *La société féodale* (Paris: A. Michel, 1940), p.199. Quoting from *Cartulaire de Saint-Aubin d'Angers*, September 17, 1138, No. DCCX.

18. Bloch, p.201.

19. *Ibid.*, p.205.

20. *Ibid.*, p.208.

21. Robert Wace, *Le roman de Rou et des ducs de Normandie*, ed. Frédéric Pluquet, I, 2nd part (Rouen, 1827), Verses 6027–6034 and 6107–6108.

22. Prosper Boissonnade, *Le travail dans l'Europe chrétienne au moyen-âge* (Paris: F. Alcan, 1930), p.185.

23. Arnold Hauser, *The Social History of Art*, I (London: Routledge and Kegan Paul, 1951), 256–57.

24. Victor Mortet, *Recueil de textes relatifs à l'histoire de l'architecture et à la condition des architectes en France au moyen-âge, XIe–XIIe siècles* (Paris: A. Picard et Fils, 1911), Document LXXXVII, pp.264–65.

25. G. H. Crichton, *Romanesque Sculpture in Italy* (London: Routledge and Kegan Paul, 1954), p.66.

26. Mâle, p.201.

27. Jacques de Voragine, pp.210–19.
28. Johan Huizinga, *The Waning of the Middle Ages* (Garden City, N.Y.: Doubleday, 1954), Chap.I.
29. Mâle, p.215.

CHAPTER VI

1. Raymond Rey, *L'art gothique du midi de la France* (Paris: H. Laurens, 1934), p.48.
2. Georgene W. Davis, *The Inquisition at Albi, 1299–1300* (New York: Columbia University Press, 1948), p.50.
3. Émile Mâle, *La cathédrale d'Albi* (Paris: P. Hartmann, 1950), p.17.
4. Raymond Rey, *Les vieilles églises fortifiées du midi de la France* (Paris: H. Laurens, 1925), p.181.
5. Gustave Cohen et Louis Réau, *L'art du moyen-âge et la civilisation française* (Paris: La Renaissance du Livre, 1935), pp.149–50.
6. Henri Focillon, *L'art d'occident* (Paris: A. Colin, 1938), p.190.
7. Rey, *L'art gothique*, pp.40–41.
8. Victor Allègre, *L'art roman dans la région albigeoise* (Albi: Imprimerie Coopérative du Sud-Ouest, 1943), Introduction, Part I.
9. Rey, *Les vieilles églises fortifiées*, p.130.
10. Hastings Rashdall, *The Universities of Europe in the Middle Ages*, I (Oxford: Clarendon Press, 1936), 350.
11. Quoted by Émile Mâle, *L'art religieux du XIIe siècle en France* (Paris: Armand Colin, 1922), pp.421–22.
12. Charles-P. Bru, "Notes en vue d'une interprétation sociologique du catharisme occitan," *Annales de l'Institut d'Études Occitanes* (August, 1952), 67.
13. J.-L. Pène, *La conquête du Languedoc* (Nice, 1957), p.17.
14. Henry Charles Lea, *A History of the Inquisition of the Middle Ages*, I (New York: Harper, 1888), 127–28.
15. Augustin Fliche, *La réforme grégorienne* (Louvain: *Spicilegium Sacrum Lovaniense*, 1924), p.6.
16. Lea, p.165.
17. Mâle, *La cathédrale d'Albi*, p.14.
18. *La chanson de la croisade albigeoise*, ed. Eugène Martin-Chabot, II (Nogent-le-Routrou: Daupeley-Gouverneur, 1931), 220.
19. Lynn White, Jr., "Natural Science and Naturalistic Art in the Middle Ages," *American Historical Review*, LII (April, 1947), 421–35.
20. Canon Bertrand de Roffignac, "Le tympan de la porte Saint-Ursin à Bourges," *Mémoires de la Société des Antiquaires du Centre*, XXXVI (1913), 47–67; and quoted in Rashdall, p.48, footnote.
21. Edgar de Bruyne, *Études d'esthétique médiévale*, III (Brügge: "De Tempel" [Sinte Catherina Druk], 1946), 88, 110–11.
22. Pène, p.32.
23. Meyer Schapiro, "The Sculptures of Souillac," in *Medieval Studies in Memory of A. Kingsley Porter*, II (Cambridge, Mass.: Harvard University Press, 1939), 378–80.
24. Quoted by Mâle, *L'art religieux du XIIe siècle*, pp.422–23.
25. **Henry Kraus, "Christian-Jewish Disputation in a 13th-Century Lancet at the Cathedral of Troyes," *Gazette des Beaux-Arts* (September, 1968).**
26. Emile Mâle, *L'art religieux du XIIIe siècle en France* (Paris: Armand Colin, 1925), p.156 and footnote.
27. J. de Lahondès, "Église Saint-Nazaire (Carcassonne)," *Congrès Archéologiques de France*, LXXIII (1906), 32–42.
28. Raymond Dorbes, "Les stèles manichéennes et cathares du Lauragais," *Cahiers d'Études Cathares* (1949, No. 4), 3–6.

29. Maurice Denuzière, "Pèlerinage hérétique en Albigeois," *Le Monde* (September 10, 1963), 1.

30. Bernard Delmas-Boussagol, "Les monuments funéraires bogomiles à l'exposition d'art médiéval yougoslave," *Cahiers d'Études Cathares* (1950, No. 5), 31–37.

31. Mâle, *La cathédrale d'Albi*, p.18.

32. Aimé Champollion-Figeac, *Droits et usages concernant les travaux de construction, publics ou privés, sous la troisième race des rois de France* (Paris: A. Leleux, 1860), p.344.

33. Lea, p.103.

34. Delmas-Boussagol, pp.31–37.

35. O. Bihalji-Merin et A. Benac, *L'art des Bogomiles* (Paris: Arthaud, 1963), p. xviii.

CHAPTER VII

1. Eugène Lefèvre-Pontalis, "*À* quelle école faut-il rattacher l'église de Beaulieu (Corrèze)?" *Bulletin Monumental* (1914), 76.

2. Émile Mâle, *L'art religieux du XIIe siècle en France* (Paris: Armand Colin, 1922), p.178.

3. For the original discussion of this subject, see Henry Kraus, "A Reinterpretation of the 'Risen Dead' on Beaulieu Tympanum," *Gazette des Beaux-Arts* (April, 1965), 193–99.

4. Eugène Lefèvre-Pontalis, "Église de Beaulieu," *Congrès Archéologiques de France* (1921), 383.

5. Abbé J.-B. Poulbrière, "L'église de Beaulieu et son portail sculpté," *Bulletin de la Société Archéologique et Historique du Limousin* (1873), 41–103.

6. Joan Evans, *Cluniac Art of the Romanesque Period* (Cambridge, England: The University Press, 1950), p.31.

7. Louis Réau, *Iconographie de l'art chrétien*, II–II (Paris: PUF, 1957), 741.

8. *Ibid.*, p.743.

9. Marguerite Vidal, Jean Maury et Jean Porcher, *Quercy roman* (Abbaye-Sainte-Marie-de-la-Pierre-Qui-Vire: Les Presses Monastiques, 1959), pp.317–18.

10. *Ibid.*, p.292.

11. *Dictionnaire de théologie catholique*, VIII, 2nd part (Paris: Letouzey et Ané, 1925), 1759, 1823 ff.

12. *The Letters of St. Bernard*, transl. into English by Bruno Scott James (London: Burns & Oates, 1953), Letter No. 391: "To the English People."

13. Paul Weber, *Geistliches Schauspiel und kirchliche Kunst* (Stuttgart: P. Neff, 1894), pp.29 ff.

14. *Ibid.*, p.37.

15. *Ibid.*

16. Thomas P. F. Hoving, "The Bury St. Edmunds Cross," *The Metropolitan Museum of Art Bulletin* (June, 1964), 317–40.

17. Abbot Suger, "On What Was Done under his Administration," in Erwin Panofsky, *Abbot Suger on the Abbey Church of St.-Denis and Its Art Treasures* (Princeton: Princeton University Press, 1946), p.75.

18. *Ibid.*

19. Émile Mâle, *L'art religieux du XIIIe siècle en France* (Paris: Armand Colin, 1925), p.148.

20. *Ibid.*

21. Joan Evans, *Art in Medieval France, 987–1498* (London: Oxford University Press, 1948), p.129.

22. Joshua Trachtenberg, *The Devil and the Jews* (New Haven: Yale University Press, 1943), p.165.

23. Ibid., pp.159–60, *passim*.

24. Gustave Saige, *Les juifs du Languedoc antièrement au XIVe siècle* (Paris: A. Picard, 1881), p.64.

25. *The Itinerary of Rabbi Benjamin of Tudela*, ed. and transl. A. Asher (London and Berlin: A. Asher, 1840–41), p.32.

26. Saige, p.53.

27. J. G. Sikes, *Peter Abailard* (Cambridge, England: The University Press, 1932), p.30.

28. Israel Abrahams, *Jewish Life in the Middle Ages* (London: Macmillan, 1896), p.241.

29. Salo W. Baron, *A Social and Religious History of the Jews*, IV (New York: Columbia University Press, 1957), 81.

30. Hirsch Grätz, *Histoire des juifs*, IV (Paris: A. Lévy [A. Durlacher], 1882–97), 102.

31. Georges Duby, "Le budget de l'abbaye de Cluny entre 1080 et 1144," *Annales: Économies, Sociétés, Civilisations*, VII (1952), 155–72.

32. Grätz, pp.75 ff.

33. Baron, p.102.

34. *The Letters of St. Bernard*, No. 393.

35. Saige, p.11.

36. Victor Mortet et Paul Deschamps, *Recueil de textes relatifs à l'histoire de l'architecture et à la condition des architectes en France au moyen-âge, XIIe et XIIIe siècles*, II (Paris: A. Picard, 1929), Document LXI, 134–135.

37. Grätz, p.168.

38. Henri Sauval, *Histoire et recherches des antiquités de la ville de Paris* (Paris: L. Moette, 1724), p.523.

39. Abrahams, p.218.

40. Weber, p.68.

41. Réau, p.746.

42. Bernhard Blumenkranz, *Juden und Judentum in der mittelalterlichen Kunst* (Stuttgart: W. Kohlhammer Verlag, 1965).

43. Eugène Viollet-le-Duc, *Dictionnaire raisonné de l'architecture française du XIe au XVIe siècle*, V (Paris: B. Bance, 1861), under "Église," 155.

44. Bernhard Blumenkranz, "Pour une nouvelle Gallia Judaica. La géographie historique des juifs en France médiévale," *L'Arche* (December, 1965), 42–47, 75.

45. James W. Parkes, *The Conflict of the Church and the Synagogue, a Study in the Origins of Anti-Semitism* (London: The Soncino Press, 1934).

46. Joseph Reider, "Jews in Medieval Art," in *Essays on Anti-Semitism*, ed. Koppel S. Pinson (New York: Conference on Jewish Relations, 1946), p.100; and Trachtenberg, p.27.

47. Réau, p.447, footnote.

48. Edgar de Bruyne, *Études d'esthétique médiévale*, III (Brügge: "De Tempel" [Sinte Catherina Druk], 1946), 88, 110–11.

49. Trachtenberg, p.24.

50. Arthur Martin et Charles Cahier, *Vitraux peints de Saint-Étienne de Bourges* (Paris, 1841), p.237, footnote.

51. Trachtenberg, p.122.

52. *Ibid.*, p.174.

53. Raoul Glaber, "Chronique," in F.-P.-G. Guizot, *Collection des mémoires relatifs à l'histoire de France*, VI (Paris: Dépôt Central de la Librairie, 1824), 266.

54. Jacob R. Marcus, *The Jew in the Medieval World, 315–1791* (Cincinnati: Union of American Hebrew Congregations, 1938), pp.111–12.

55. Grätz, p.74.

56. Weber, p.26.

57. Margaret Schlauch, "The Allegory of Church and Synagogue," *Speculum*, XIV (1939), 462.

58. Albert R.-A. Lecoy de la Marche, *Saint Louis, son gouvernement et sa politique* (Tours: A. Mame et Fils, 1887), pp. 337 ff.

59. Grätz, p.204.

60. Jean, Sire de Joinville, *Histoire de Saint Louis*, ed. and transl. Natalis de Wailly (Paris: Hachette, 1881), pp.31–32.

61. Grätz, p.197.

62. Weber, p.63.

63. *The Letters of St. Bernard*, No. 393.

64. Glaber, pp.267–68.

65. Henri Fesquet, "L'attitude des chrétiens enver les juifs et envers la liberté religieuse à l'ordre du jour de Vatican II," *Le Monde* (November 21, 1963), 1.

CHAPTER VIII

1. Louis Réau, *Les monuments détruits de l'art français*, I (Paris: Hachette, 1959), 295.

2. *Ibid.*, p.104.

3. *Ibid.*, p.101.

4. *Ibid.*, p.100, footnote.

5. *Ibid.*, p.113.

6. Prosper Mérimée, *Notice sur les peintures de l'église de Saint-Savin* (Paris: Imprimerie Royale, 1845).

7. Réau, p.168.

8. Pierre Le Vieil, *L'art de la peinture sur verre et de la vitrerie* (Paris: L.-F. Delatour, 1774), pp.23 ff., 200–1, *passim*.

9. J. W. Goethe, *Faust*, 1st part (Basel: Birkhäuser, 1944), p.147.

10. George Zarnecki et Denis Grivot, *Gislebertus, sculpteur d'Autun* (Paris: Éditions Trianon, 1960), p.21.

11. Jean Berthollet, "Un événement, le Christ du tympan d'Autun recouvre sa tête," *Annales de Bourgogne* (1949), 142.

12. Réau, p.230.

13. *Ibid.*, p.309.

14. *Ibid.*, p.357.

15. M. de Sacy, in *Vielles Maisons Françaises* (October, 1963), 47.

16. Baron Georges Haussmann, *Mémoires du baron Haussmann*, III (Paris: Victor-Havard, 1893), 54–55.

17. Réau, p.404.

18. Émile Mâle, *L'art religieux du XIIIe siècle en France* (Paris: Armand Colin, 1925), p.397.

19. André Grabar, *L'iconoclasme byzantin* (Paris: Collège de France, 1957), p.133.

20. *Ibid.*, p.156.

21. Karl Schenk, "Kaiser Leons III Walten im Innern," *Byzantinische Zeitschrift*, Leipzig (1896), 257–301. Quoting Karl Schwarzlose, *Der Bilderstreit, ein Kampf der griech. Kirche um ihren Eigenart und ihre Freiheit* (1890), p.7.

22. Arnold Hauser, *The Social History of Art*, I (London: Routledge and Kegan Paul, 1951), 148–49.

23. Émile Mâle, *Rome et ses vieilles églises* (Paris: Flammarion, 1942), p.105.

24. Mâle, *L'art religieux du XIIIe siècle*, p.397.

25. André Michel, *La sculpture romane: la sculpture en France* (*Histoire de l'art*, Vol. I [Paris: A. Colin, 1905–29]), Part II, pp.592–94.

26. Saint Bernard, "Apologie de la vie et moeurs des religieux," in *Traitez doctrinaux de S. Bernard*, transl. from the Latin into French by Dom Antoine de S. Gabriel (Paris, 1675), pp.72–73.

27. *Ibid.*, p.67.

28. Guillaume, Abbé de Saint-Thierry, et al., "Vie de Saint Bernard," in F.-P.-G. Guizot, *Collection des mémoires relatifs à l'histoire de France*, X (Paris: Dépot Central de la Librairie, 1824), 173.

29. Saint Bernard, "Apologie," p.70.

30. Louise Lefrançois-Pillion, *Les sculpteurs français du XIIe siècle* (Paris, 1931), pp.13–14.

31. Saint Bernard, "Apologie," pp.70–71.

32. A. Kingsley Porter, *Romanesque Sculpture of the Pilgrimage Roads*, I (Boston: M. Jones, 1923), 77.

33. Guillaume, Abbé de Saint-Thierry, et al., pp.172, 326.

34. A.-M. Armand, *Saint Bernard et le renouveau de l'iconographie au XIIe siècle* (Paris: Jouve, 1944), p.26.

35. *Saint Bernard et l'art des cisterciens.* Catalogue of exhibition at Museum of Dijon (Dijon: Darantière, 1953), Plate 63.

36. Émile Mâle, *L'art religieux du XIIe siècle en France* (Paris: Armand Colin, 1922), p.358.

37. Joan Evans, *Life in Medieval France* (London: Phaidon Press, 1957), p.63.

38. Marcel Aubert et La Marquise Jacquelin de Maillé, *L'architecture cistercienne en France* (Paris: Les Éditions d'Art et d'Histoire, 1943), p.32.

39. Abbé E. Vacandard, *Saint Bernard et l'art chrétien* (Rouen: E. Cagniard, 1886), p.12.

40. Guillaume, Abbé de Saint-Thierry, et al., p.242.

41. Saint Bernard, "Apologie," p.73.

42. Marcel Aubert, in catalogue, *Saint Bernard et l'art des cisterciens*, Preface, p.16.

43. Guillaume, Abbé de Saint-Thierry, et al., p.313.

44. Aubert, catalogue, p.15.

45. Victor Mortet et Paul Deschamps, *Recueil de textes relatifs à l'histoire de l'architecture et à la condition des architectes en France au moyen-âge, XIIe–XIIIe siècles*, II (Paris: A. Picard, 1929), Document CIV, 214.

46. Meyer Schapiro, "From Mozarabic to Romanesque in Silos," *Art Bulletin*, XXI (1939), 369.

47. Evans, p.58.

48. Achille Luchaire, *Histoire des institutions monarchiques de la France sous les Capétiens, 987–1180*, I (Paris: Imprimerie Nationale, 1883), 286–87.

49. Erwin Panofsky, *Abbot Suger on the Abbey Church of St.-Denis and Its Art Treasures* (Princeton: Princeton University Press, 1946), Introduction, p.32.

50. Abbot Suger, "Vie de Louis-le-Gros," in Guizot, *Collection de mémoires*, VIII, 148.

51. Panofsky, Introduction, p.33.

52. Suger, pp.147–48.

53. Suger, "On What Was Done under his Administration," in Panofsky, pp.65–67.

54. Suger, "The Other Little Book on the Consecration of the Church of St.-Denis," in Panofsky, p.107.

55. Suger, "On What Was Done," p.59.

56. Panofsky, Introduction, p.24.

57. Suger, "The Other Little Book," p.101.

58. Suger, "On What Was Done," p.73.

59. Suger, "The Other Little Book," p.115.

60. Porter, p.223.

61. Aubert, catalogue, p.15.

CHAPTER IX

1. Theophilus Presbyter, *The Various Arts*, transl. from the Latin into English with introduction and notes by C. R. Dodwell (London: T. Nelson, 1961), preface to Second Book.

2. *Journal de Paris* (July, 1837).

3. A.-N. Didron, "Documents sur les artistes du moyen-âge," *Annales Archéologiques, par Didron*, I (July, 1844), 77–82.

4. Fernand de Mély, *Les primitifs français et leurs signatures—les sculpteurs* (Paris: Aux Bureaux de "L'Ami des monuments des arts," 1908); and *The Canterbury Psalter*, with Introduction by M. R. James (London: Percy, Lund, Humphries & Co., 1935).

5. Eugène Viollet-le-Duc, *Dictionnaire raisonné de l'architecture française du XIe au XVIe siècle*, VIII (Paris: A. Morel, 1866), under "Sculpture," 136.

6. Joan Evans, *Art in Medieval France, 987–1498* (London: Oxford University Press, 1948), p.15.

7. L. F. Salzman, *Building in England down to 1540* (Oxford: Clarendon Press, 1952), p.1.

8. R. E. Swartwout, *The Monastic Craftsman* (Cambridge, England: W. Heffer and Sons, 1932), pp.70, 80, 83, 101, *passim*.

9. Theophilus Presbyter, preface to First Book.

10. Jules Quicherat, "Notice sur l'album de Villard de Honnecourt, architecte du XIIIe siècle," *Mélanges d'Archéologie et d'Histoire. Archéologie du Moyen-Âge* (Paris: Alphonse Picard, 1886), p.239.

11. Hans R. Hahnloser, *Villard de Honnecourt* (Wien: A. Schroll, 1935), p.237.

12. *Ibid.*, pp.225 ff.

13. Quicherat, p.251.

14. Jean Gimpel, *Les bâtisseurs de cathédrales* (Paris: Éditions du Seuil, 1958), p.110.

15. Émile Mâle, *L'art religieux du XIIIe siècle en France* (Paris: Armand Colin, 1925), pp.400–1.

16. Viollet-le-Duc, under "Sculpture," p.142.

17. Rudolf Berliner, "The Freedom of Medieval Art," *Gazette des Beaux-Arts* (July, 1945), 278, footnote.

18. George Zarnecki et Denis Grivot, *Gislebertus, sculpteur d'Autun* (Paris: Éditions Trianon, 1960), p.67.

19. *Ibid.*, p.160.

20. Émile Mâle, *L'art religieux du XIIe siècle en France* (Paris: Armand Colin, 1922), pp.77, 97.

21. Victor Mortet, *Recueil de textes relatifs à l'histoire de l'architecture et à la condition des architectes en France au moyen-âge, XIe–XIIe siècles* (Paris: A. Picard et Fils, 1911), Document LXXXVII, pp.264–65.

22. Victor Mortet et Paul Deschamps, *Recueil de textes relatifs à l'histoire de l'architecture et à la condition des architectes en France au moyen-âge, XIIe–XIIIe siècles*, II (Paris: A. Picard, 1929), pp.lxii–lxiii.

23. E. Lefèvre-Pontalis, "Répertoire des architectes, maçons, sculpteurs, charpentiers et ouvriers français au XIe et au XIIe siècle," *Bulletin Monumental*, LXXV (1911), 441.

24. Didron, II (1845), 247.

25. Marcel Aubert, "La construction au moyen-âge," *Bulletin Monumental* (1961), 306.

26. Jules Quicherat, "Notice sur plusieurs registres de l'oeuvre de la cathédrale de Troyes," *Mélanges d'Archéologie et d'Histoire. Archéologie du Moyen-Âge* (Paris: Alphonse Picard, 1886), pp.192 ff.

27. Étienne Martin Saint-Léon, *Histoire des corporations des métiers* (Paris: PUF, 1941), pp.127–28, 173.

28. Didron, I (1844), 118–19.

29. Aubert, pp.37–38.

30. Pierre du Colombier, *Les chantiers des cathédrales* (Paris: A. et J. Picard, 1953), pp.32–33.

31. *Ibid.*, p.32.

32. Salzman, p.42.

33. *Ibid.*

34. René de Lespinasse et François Bonnardot, *Les métiers et corporations de la ville de Paris, XIIIe siècle. Le Livre des métiers d'Étienne Boileau* (Paris: Imprimerie Nationale, 1879–97), p.v.

35. *Ibid.*, p.iv.

36. Hippolyte Boyer, "Histoire des corporations et confréries d'arts et métiers de Bourges," *Mémoires de la Société Historique, Littéraire et Scientifique du Cher* (1937–38), 19.

37. De Lespinasse et Bonnardot, pp.cxli–cxlii and footnote.

38. Lefèvre-Pontalis, pp.423–24.

39. Salzman, p.24.

40. Gimpel, pp.73–74; and Martin Saint-Léon, p. 160.

41. Salzman, p.47.

42. Aubert, pp.83, 90, 93.

43. Louis Demaison, "Les architectes de la cathédrale de Reims," *Bulletin Archéologique du Comité des Travaux Historiques et Scientifiques* (1894), 24.

44. Erwin Panofsky, *Gothic Architecture and Scholasticism* (Latrobe, Pa.: The Archabbey Press, 1951), p.26.

45. Gimpel, pp.132–33.

46. Quicherat, "Notice sur plusieurs registres . . . de Troyes," pp.192 ff.

47. Du Colombier, pp.15 ff.

48. Lefèvre-Pontalis, p.436; Du Colombier, p.14.

49. Quicherat, "Notice sur plusieurs registres . . . de Troyes."

50. R.-C. de Lasteyrie du Saillant, *L'architecture religieuse en France à l'époque romane* (Paris: Auguste Picard, 1928), p.289.

51. Victor Mortet, *Maurice de Sully, évêque de Paris (1160–1196). Étude sur l'administration épiscopale pendant la seconde moitié du XIIe siècle* (Nogent-le-Rotrou: Daupeley-Gouverneur, 1890). pp.108–9.

52. *Ibid.*, p.109.

53. Otto von Simson, *The Gothic Cathedral* (New York: Pantheon Books, 1956), p.172.

54. C. R. Cheney, "Church-Building in the Middle Ages," *Bulletin of the John Rylands Library*, XXXIV (1951–52), 36.

55. Aubert, pp.241–59.

56. Marcel Aubert et La Marquise Jacquelin de Maillé, *L'architecture cistercienne en France* (2nd ed.; Paris: Les Éditions d'Art et d'Histoire, 1947), pp.103–4.

57. Aubert, "La construction au moyen-âge," p.256.

58. *Ibid.*, p.245.

59. *Petri Cantoris Verbum abbreviatum*, in J.-P. Migne (ed.), *Patrologia latina* (1853), t. CCV, Chap. LXXXVI, col. 257.

60. Aubert, "La construction au moyen-âge," p.245.

61. Von Simson, p.179.

62. Aimé Champollion-Figeac, *Droits et usages concernant les travaux de construction, publics et privés, sous la troisième race des rois de France* (Paris: A. Leleux, 1860), p.301.

63. *Ibid.*, p.335.

64. Viollet-le-Duc, in *Dictionnaire*, V (Paris: B. Bance, 1861), 161 ff., lists almost 1,000 old churches in France, the greatest number of them built during the twelfth and thirteenth centuries, as still existing at his time, despite the destruction of at least that many more.

65. Louis Réau, *Les monuments détruits de l'art français*, I (Paris: Hachette, 1959), 295.

66. Robert Branner, *Burgundian Gothic Architecture* (London: A. Zwemmer, 1960), p.103.

67. M. J. Bulteau, quoted by Von Simson, p.168.

68. Joan Evans, *The Romanesque Architecture of the Order of Cluny* (Cambridge, England: The University Press, 1938), pp.7–9; and review by K. J. Conant, in *Art Bulletin*, XXII (1940), 276 ff.

69. Maurice Bouvier-Ajam, *Histoire du travail en France* (Paris: Librairie Générale de Droit et de Jurisprudence, 1957), p.242; and Ferdinand Lot, *Conjectures démographiques sur la France au IXe siècle* (Paris, 1921), p.25.

70. Henri Sée, *Histoire économique de la France—le moyen-âge et l'ancien régime*, I (Paris: A. Colin, 1939), 17.

71. Archibald R. Lewis, "The Closing of the Medieval Frontier, 1250–1350," *Speculum*, XXXIII (1958), 475–83.

72. Du Colombier, p.7.

73. Aubert, "La construction au moyen-âge," pp.256 ff.

74. R. S. Lopez, "Économie et architecture médiévale," *Annales: Économies, Sociétés, Civilisations*, VII (1952), 434.

75. *Ibid.*, p.437.

76. Robert Branner, "Historical Aspects of the Reconstruction of Reims Cathedral, 1210–1241," *Speculum*, XXXVI (1961), 32, footnote.

77. Ferdinand Lot et Robert Fawtier, *Le premier budget de la monarchie française: le compte général de 1202–1203* (Paris: Honoré Champion, 1932), p.139.

78. Von Simson, p.171, footnotes.

79. Abbé M. J. Bulteau, *Monographie de la cathédrale de Chartres*, I (Chartres: R. Selleret, 1887), 118.

80. Lefèvre-Pontalis, p.439.

81. Quicherat, "Notice sur plusieurs registres . . . de Troyes," pp.192 ff.

82. *Ibid.*

83. Marcel Laurent, "Godefroid de Claire et la croix de Suger à l'abbaye de Saint-Denis," *Revue Archéologique*, XIX (1924), 79–87.

84. Hahnloser, p.260.

85. Theophilus Presbyter, preface to First Book.

86. Salzman, p.25.

87. Emma Medding-Alp, "Zur Baugeschichte von St.-Denis," *Zeitschrift für Kunstgeschichte*, V (1936).

88. Paul Deschamps, "La sculpture romane," in *Nouvelle histoire universelle de l'art*, I (Paris, 1932), 301 ff.

89. Paul Deschamps, *La sculpture française á l'époque romane* (Paris: Les Éditions du Chène, 1947), pp.15, 21.

INDEX

Abailard, Peter. *See* Abélard, Pierre

Abélard, Pierre, scholastic philosopher: established classes away from Notre-Dame, 6; condemned by Church for his ideas, 6; relationship with Héloïse, 61–62; a modern forerunner, 90; befriended Jews, 147; condemned by St. Bernard for intellectual inquisitiveness, 175

Abraham, Pol, scholar, 23–24

Albi cathedral, 119–20, 163–64

Albigensian art: funerary steles, 133; recent finding of book-cover ends, 133; its primitiveness, 134, 136; false Catholic images, used in reply to cult of images, 136; signs of developing sophistication, 136

Albigensian heresy: Church used Aristotle's works in fighting, 7; influenced Albi cathedral structure, 120; continued after Montségur's fall, 120; influence on other southern churches, 120–21; its Manichean inspiration, 122; widespread in France, 122; a revulsion to clerical immorality, 122; the "crusade" against it, 124–25; Church reply to it through art, 125–31, 137, 138; military resistance ended after Montségur, 133; iconoclastic tendencies of, 135–36; followers destroyed Carcassonne monastery, 136; anti-Semitism in "crusade" against, 146; sparked Cistercians' drive for clerical reform, 176–77; mentioned, 138

Aliénor (Eleanor) d'Aquitaine, queen of France and England, 56

Amiens, cathedral and city: improved attitude toward women illustrated at, 50; improved relationship of sexes illustrated at, 53; burghers mentioned at Bouvines, 69; sculpture of dye merchants, 85, 94; where Master of Naumburg got his training, 96; relief of Vice of Ingratitude, 102; lancet illustrating Church's land-settlement program, 106–7; sculpture illustrating "Truce of God" movement, 108; art illustrating folk humor, 115; mentioned, 208

"Amour courtois," court love poetry: role as originator of cult of Mary denied, 47; influenced language of St. Bernard and Hugues de Saint-Victor, 47; influenced cult of Mary in

certain details, 59; reflected woman's improved social status, 59; new interpretation of, 59–60; Eduard Wechssler's theory of, 60

Antelami, Benedetto, Italian sculptor, 104, 111

Anti-Semitism. *See* Jews

Anti-Semitism in art: the conical hat, 131, 140, 149, 156; at Beaulieu-sur-Dordogne, 139–44; in the Bury St. Edmunds cross, 144; the Jewish stereotype in art, 148–49; Church *vs.* Synagogue, 149; in manuscript art, 149, 153; its intensity reflects real life situation, 149, 150; Christ roles illustrating, 150; "good Jews" *vs.* "bad Jews," 150–51; patristic source of Jewish stereotype, 153; in the Christ story, 155; Jewish blacksmith's wife, 155; the Jew and the Devil, 155, 156; the Jew as usurer, 155–56; Jews in the martyrdom of saints, 156; the Jew as heretic, 156; conversion stories, 157, 158–59; responsibility of medieval art in fostering anti-Semitism today, 162. *See also* Jews

Aquinas, St. Thomas, theologian: his effort to integrate Aristotelianism with Catholicism, 7; his teachings banned at Paris, Oxford, 7; held that Jews would be judged on Judgment Day, 142; mentioned, 4

Aquitaine. *See* Aliénor (Eleanor) d'

Aragon, Isabelle d', princess of France, 94

Architects, medieval: their social-economic status changed greatly from twelfth to thirteenth century, 199; depicted in lancet at Saint-Germer-de-Fly, 199; often got tombal plaques, 199–200; effigies of, 200. *See also* under individual names

Aristotle, Greek philosopher: his works banned by Church, then praised, 7; portrayed as victim of woman's wiles, 45; on Chartres' west portal, 99; mentioned, 188

Arles, cathedral and city: Jews of, 148; destruction of Alyscamps at, 169; sculpture on cathedral façade, 188

Art, topical references in: "Life of the Students" reliefs, 3–16; punishment of attacks on scholars, 17–18; social factor largely neglected by historians, 22–23; Louis VII in warning to a foe, 32; reliefs reflecting feudal conflicts at Souillac, 33; fear of Saracens, 35;

Art (*continued*)
runaway slaves brought back, 36; dangers of medieval travel, 36; violence of medieval life reflected in art, 64; devils identified with Church's enemies, 66, 67; workers being paid in coin, 111. *See also* Albigensian heresy; Crusades, iconography of

Artists, medieval: self-portraits of, 93–94, 183, 185, 186; supposed anonymity, 183–84, 185; supposed humility, 185; most frequently laymen, 185; their "freedom" of expression, 187–88, 194–95; rapid development of technic, 188, 208; originality of, 194; steadily improving social status, 195, 197–200; conditions of work, 197–98; class-consciousness, 198; special privileges, 198–99; intense exchange of ideas among, 206–7; traveled widely, 206–7. *See also* Gislebertus and under individual names

Aubert, Marcel, scholar: works on Notre-Dame de Paris, 4; refers to conflict at Paris University, 5; defends Viollet-le-Duc, 23

Augustine, St., 144

Autun, Honorius (or Honoré) d', encyclopedist, 47, 155

Autun, cathedral and city: in controversy over Mary Magdalene's remains, 28; Compostela pilgrim in tympanum, 31; misogynous art at, 42; sculpture plastered over, then uncovered, 167–68; Eve "lost," rediscovered, 168; Gislebertus, sculptor at, 188–94

Auxerre cathedral, 164

Avenas, church at, 32

Avignon: occupancy by the popes, 41; canons in dispute for artists' services, 206. *See also* Villeneuve-les-Avignon

Bayeux Tapestry: its motivation, 36, 37; used at cathedral commemorative services, 36–37; shows William carrying pope's banner, 37; role of Bishop Odo in, 37–38; its reflections of medieval life, 38; dated by Lefebvre des Noëttes, 38; sexual love scene in border, 55; scenes from described as true to life today, 103

Beauvais, city, 67, 69

Beaulieu-sur-Dordogne, abbey church at: Judgment Day scene, 139; interpretations of its sculpture reviewed, 139–40; new interpretation of sculpture offered, 140–44

Bernard, St., abbot of Clairvaux: his misogynous attitude, 42; his description of Mary, 46; literary style influenced by "amour cour-
tois," 47; preached Second Crusade at Vézelay, 65; his idea of Jews' fate on Judgment Day, 142–43; defended Jews against attacks, 142, 148; believed in eventual conversion of Jews, 158; campaign against church art "excesses," 172, 203; his asceticism, 174; called "beauty-hating," 175; flayed "monsters" in art, 175; his anti-intellectualism, 175; his reception of Innocent II, 176; iconoclastic tendency, 176; his pressure on other orders continued by disciples after his death, 176–77; supported Church's temporal claims, 178–79; Abbot Suger's reply to his Spartan ideas, 179; his influence on art compared with that of Suger, 181–82

Bible of the Poor, 112, 153

Blanche of Castile, queen of France: sent her archers against Paris students, 8; friendly to burghers, 69; mentioned, 158

Bloch, Marc, scholar, 64

Blumenkranz, Bernhard, scholar: book on Jew in Christian manuscript art discussed, 149; article on Church *vs.* Synagogue discussed, 149

Bogomils, heretics, 134, 136

Boileau, Étienne, Paris provost, 198

Bourges cathedral: improved attitude toward women illustrated at, 50; guild-donated lancets at, 75; Saint-Ursin relief, a reply to heresy, 125; art featuring the priesthood as reply to heresy, 131; great amount of stained-glass at, 206; mentioned, 11

Bouvines, battle of, 69

Braine, Henri de, archbishop of Reims, 71

Bruxelles, Henry de, sculptor, 206

Bruyes, Pierre de, heretic: burned at stake at Saint-Gilles, 128; combatted by Peter the Venerable, 130–31; his agitation impeded building of Saint-Gilles church, 134–35

Building in Middle Ages: among most extensive in history, 200; often exceeded finances, 200; slowed by transport, 200–1; speed depended on available funds, 201–2; methods of raising funds for, 202–4; voluntary labor comparatively infrequent, 203; indulgences used to raise funds for, 204; estimated number of churches built, 204; engaged large proportion of France's wealth, 204–5; may have strained economy at times, 205; shortage of skilled workmen, 206; little use of impressed labor in France, 206; swift development of technics, 208; use of sketches in, 208

Bulla Parens Scientiarum, Paris University's Magna Carta, 8, 9

Burghers: clamored for the commune, 42; effect of burgher-Church strife on church-building, 64, 67–68, 71–72; in battle of Bouvines, 69; supported rulers in conflict with barons near Paris, 69; as donors to church art, 69–70; helped rebuild Amiens cathedral after fire, 70; active role in rebuilding Chartres, 70–71; not donors of twelfth-century glass, 72; important donors of thirteenth-century glass, 72–82; merchants' wives and daughters in Renaissance art, 79–80; individual burghers as window donors, 82; guildhall at Reims, 90; penchant for heresy, 122; their earnings estimated from Paris 1292 tax list, 199. *See also* Communes

Burghers in art: Hosea's reformed harlot puts on bourgeois hat, 50; castigated in Vice of Avarice, parable of Lazarus and Dives, 67; portrayed in sculpture, 69, 85–87, 90, 94; in stained-glass "signatures," 74, 76–79; individual burgher donors' portraits in glass, 82; entire windows given over to work scenes, 82–83; a "Passion Play" series at Strasbourg, 83–85; a lost lancet of Strasbourg "Stadtrat," 85; in processional art at Paris, 85; bourgeois woman illustrating Vice of Ingratitude, 102; mentioned, 99, 110

Byzantine architecture and art, 3, 98

Cambridge University, 8

Canterbury cathedral, England: building of, 201–2; archbishop donated window to Chartres, 204; Guillaume de Sens brought new material-handling equipment to, 207

Castanet, Bernard de, bishop of Albi, 120

Castelnau, Pierre de, papal legate, 124

Cathars. *See* Albigensian heresy

Catherine, comtesse de Chartres, 59

Chansons de geste: role in popularizing Compostela pilgrimage, 30; show Charlemagne marrying off Crusade widows, 59; labor dispute described in, 198

Chanson de la croisade albigeoise, epic poem, 58, 124, 132

Charlemagne, emperor of the West: described as Compostela pilgrim, 30; depicted in medieval art, 5, 31, 33; described as marrying off Crusade widows, 59; sculpture primitive during his period, 208

Chartres, cathedral and city: cult of Virgin's Tunic at, 26; royalty and nobility in art of, 32; pilgrimage to, fostered by art, 48; improved attitude toward women illustrated at, 50, 53; humanization of art illustrated at, 53; sculptures of "The Active Life," 57, 100; Comtesse Catherine took husband's place after his death in Crusades, 59; excellent burgher-church relationship, 71; twelfth-century windows donated by churchmen, 72; many thirteenth-century windows donated by burghers, 72–82; donor "signatures," 74–79, 207; individual burgher a donor of two windows, 82; floral decoration at, 91–92; developed portraiture in façade statues, 98; seen as "cornerstone" of Gothic, 98; west portal sculpture, 99; merchants' and artisans' lancets, 99; sculptures of "The Contemplative Life," 100; humane treatment of Cain at, 102; window donated by Simon de Montfort, 124; story of Job, a reply to heresy, 126; destruction of roodscreen at, 167; destruction of stained-glass at, 167; "miraculously" preserved during Revolution, 169; its Genesis window, 194; slowness of carting stone to, 200; its rebuilding after 1194 fire, 203–4; rebuilding aided by Richard the Lion-Hearted and archbishop of Canterbury, 204; city had 10,000 inhabitants in thirteenth century, 205; estimated cost of building it in nineteenth century, 205–6; great amount of sculpture and stained-glass at, 206; sculptors' window at, 207; mentioned, 11, 111, 172, 186, 208

Chartreuse-du-Val-de-Bénédiction, monastery, 41, 60

Church form, influences on: controversy over primary inspiration of Gothic form, 23–24; anomalies in, explained, 24–25; dictated by defense needs, 25; reason for Cluny's tunnel vaulting, 25; altered by cult of relics, 25, 26; as dictated by topography, 25–26

Church reform: Gregory VII's campaign, 45, 122, 172; Cistercians' role in, 45; Peter Damian, 46; St. Bernard's role in, 172, 174, 203

Church interests stressed in art: confirmation of bequests, 33–34, 35; money-coining rights, 35; rights of justice, 35; land claims, 35

Church's land-settlement program: and sudden popularity of Labors of the Months, 105, 109–10; numbers of lay brothers hired, 106; Church's attitude toward slavery, 106; illustrated in a lancet, 106–7; Church's relations with its serfs, 107; feudal violence and the,

Church's land-settlement program (*continued*) 108; peasant revolts, 108–9; possible relation to of Lazarus and Dives illustrations in churches, 109–10

Church *vs*. Synagogue: as sermon and liturgical drama, 143–44; in Bury St. Edmunds cross, 144; in manuscript art, 149; in monumental art, 149, 150

Cistercians, order: prohibited contact with women, 44; role in reform movement, 45, 122, 172; devotion for Mary, 45; Raoul, monk, persecutor of Jews, 148; intellectual pursuits limited, 175; restrictions in art and architecture, 175, 176; castigated Cluniac luxury, 176; fight on luxury associated with heresy, 176; their iconoclasm, 177; gave Villard de Honnecourt an assignment, 186, 207; borrowed heavily to build, 203; mentioned, 9, 172, 175, 176, 177, 181. *See also* Bernard, St.; Clairvaux abbey

Claire, Godefroid de, artist, 207

Clairvaux abbey: a sermon by St. Bernard at, 42; books in library, 175; a mammoth agricultural community, 175; its church called "dismal," 175–76; reception of Innocent II, 176, 179

Clovis, king of Franks: 5, 31, 106–7

Cluny, order: fostered Compostela pilgrimage, 29; built churches along Compostela roads, 30; cult of Mary as "Mother of Mercy," 47; number of units in France, 204; mentioned, 30, 130, 175

Cluny abbey: its tunnel vaulting explained, 25; sculptures of crafts practiced by its monks, 100; art "excesses" castigated by St. Bernard, 174; mentioned, 147, 192, 208

Coincy, Gautier de, poet, 47

Communes: burghers clamored for, 42; opposition to, of churchmen, 42, 64–66, 67–68; effect of communal strife on church-building, 64, 67–68, 71–72; communal strife at Laon, 68; Philippe-Auguste friendly toward, 68–69; mentioned at Bouvines, 69; Reims townsmen loaned money to Auxerre commune, 71; "communal" rising of peasants described, 108–9; communal charters exchanged for church-building donations, 203. *See also* Burghers

Conical hat, 131, 140, 149, 156

Conques, abbey church at, 172

Constantinople: as source of holy relics, 28, 31; center of "quarrel of images," 170–71; Byzantium defended by Leo III against Mos-lems, 171; mentioned, 148

Conteville, Odo de, bishop of Bayeux: William the Conqueror's brother, 37; his role in the Tapestry, 37–38; may have ordered the Tapestry made, 38

Crusades: holy relics acquired during, 26; among rare historical events treated in art, 31; Crusade to reclaim Spain, 36; relief representing the Albigensian "crusade," 58, 132; women's social status influenced by, 58; Second Crusade preached at Vézelay, 65; death of Louis IX on last Crusade, 94; tombal memorial of Isabelle d'Aragon, who died on return from last Crusade, 94; growth of anti-Semitism during, 147–48, 156, 158; mentioned, 14, 59, 68, 178

Damian, Peter, Church reformer, 46

Daurade, La, church at Toulouse, 126, 169

De Altercatione Ecclesiae et Synagogae, polemic, 143–44

Destruction of monuments: in Paris, 163; by Huguenots, 163–64; during Revolution, 163, 168–69; during nineteenth century, 169–70; Toulouse's three cloisters, 169; Cluny abbey, 170; Saumur's old quarter, 170; by Baron Haussmann, 170. *See also* Iconoclasm

Devil in art: on Notre-Dame roodscreen, 18, 66; in Theophilus story, 33, 155; with women, 42; retires into background in later Temptation scenes, 53; swarms at Vézelay, 64; prevalence at cloisters, illustrated, 66; identified with church enemies, 66, 67; at Dives' deathbed, 67; realism in portrayal, 93; in Judgment Day scenes, 117; Job and the Devil, 126; with those rejecting Sacraments, 131; absent from Beaulieu Judgment Day, 139; with Nero and Jews, 156; in art of Autun, 192; at Last Supper at Selles-sur-Cher, 194

Didron, Adolphe-Napoléon, scholar, 3, 184

Dominicans, order: founded Toulouse University, 7; in conflict over control of Paris University, 9–10; built churches adapted to preaching to large audiences, 121; Carcassonne monastery destroyed by heretics, 136; in Paris debate between Christians and Jews, 162

"Eadwine," English scribe, 185

Ecumenical Councils: at Lateran (1215), 13, 148; Vatican II, 162; at Nicea (787), 170, 171–72

Ely cathedral, England, 36

Fabliaux, 85, 112
Feudalism in art, 31, 33
For-l'Évêque, Paris bishop's secular court, 20–21
Foulque, artist-serf, 111, 195
Francis, St., of Assisi, 91
Franciscans, order, 8–9, 122

Garlande, Jean de, author, 15
Gislebertus, sculptor of Autun cathedral, 188–94
Glaber, Raoul, monk and author, 40n, 157, 162
Grands-Augustins, Paris convent, 17
Grève, Philippe de, chancellor of Notre-Dame, 6, 7
Grodecki, Louis, scholar: describes royal theme at Sainte-Chapelle, 31–32; role of stained-glass in development of Gothic, 69–70; tells how Sainte-Chapelle's glass was preserved, 169n
Grosseteste, Robert, scientist-philosopher, 90–91
Guilds: at Paris, 5, 15, 69; the guild lancet "signature," 72, 74, 79; guild lancets at Chartres, Bourges, illustrated, 72, 75, 76–79; defeat Strasbourg bishop's cavalry, 84; in lost lancet at Strasbourg, 85; guild hall at Reims, 90; other workers' organizations, 198; guild statutes, 198
Guillaume III, comte de Nevers, 65–66, 67

Hastings, battle of, 37, 38
Hauser, Arnold, author, 90
Haussmann, Baron, Paris prefect and city-planner, 170
Héloïse. *See* Abélard, Pierre
Heresy: of eleventh and early twelfth centuries, 121; Waldenses, 122; burghers' penchant for, 122; Pierre de Bruys, 128, 134; Bogomils, 136; Jews accused of, 156; Byzantine image-destroyers proclaimed heretics, 171. *See also* Albigensian heresy
Heresy, Church's iconographic reply to: liturgical changes carried into art, 125; reassertions of Eucharist, 125, 129–30, 131; reply to Dualism, 126; in Transfiguration, Majesty, and Crucifixion scenes, 128; doubts of divinity of Mary, 128–29; featuring the priesthood, 131; mentioned, 126, 128, 138, 150
Hildegarde of Bingen, abbess, 153

Honnecourt, Villard de, architect: drawing of a lion, 93; compared with Theophilus Presbyter, 185; wanted to be "remembered," 186; Sketchbook described, 186–87; worked for Cistercians, 207
Hoving, Thomas, scholar, 144

Iconoclasm: at Saint-Gilles, 134, 135; of Albigensians, 135–36; by Protestants, 135, 163–64; Jews accused of, 156; during French Revolution, 163, 168, 169, 170; in Sweden, 166n; during Enlightenment, 166–67; destruction of stained-glass, 167; by king's architect, 167; at Autun, 167–68; at Toulouse's cloisters, 169; at Cluny, 170; during Byzantine "quarrel of images," 170–72; perennial anti-image trend within Church, 172; of St. Bernard and Cistercians, 172, 174, 176, 177; mentioned, 167
Iconography, changes in: St. James, 30; St. Peter, 32–33; Temptation scenes, 53; sexual relationship humanized, illustrated, 53; leading male Vice, 67; Synagogue's image, 149–50. *See also* Albigensian heresy; Mary, iconography of; Woman, iconography of
Images, cult of, 136, 170–72

Jalabert, Denise, scholar, 91–92
Jews: in feudal courts, 20; in disputations with Christians, 131, 159–62; their fate on Judgment Day, 142; befriended by St. Bernard, 142, 148; during Crusades, 142, 147–49; archbishop Agobard and, 143; efforts to convert, 144, 157–58; Innocent III's anti-Semitism, 146, 148; under Charlemagne, 146–47; at Montpellier medical school, 147; befriended by Abélard, 147; attacks on social-economic position of, 147, 148, 156; crimes laid to, 156; accused of heresy, 156; "responsibility" for Christ's death, 162; at Vatican II, 162; and Abbot Suger, 179. *See also* Anti-Semitism in art
Justice, rights of, 18, 19–20

Labors of the Months: theological concept of "redemption through work," 100; few dogmatic restrictions in, 103; national differences in, 103–4, 105; reflect differences in climate, 104–5; associated with zodiac, 105; associated with Church's agricultural problems, 105; and burgher-donated art contrasted, 110–11; December as depiction of Eucha-

Labors of the Months (*continued*)
rist, 125; mentioned, 79, 85, 102, 103, 111, 125
Landsberg, Herrade de, abbess, 39
Laon, cathedral and city: commune at, 67; architect's self-portrait, 93; oxen on towers, 100; folk humor in art, 115; drawn by Villard de Honnecourt, 186
Lasteyrie, Robert de, scholar, 24, 25
Lefebvre des Noëttes, Richard, commandant, 38–40, 200
Le Mans cathedral: burgher donors at, 74, 76; anti-Semitism in art at, 155, 159; bishop borrowed artist-monk to work on, 206
Lenoir, Alexandre, art guardian, 17
Leo III, Byzantine emperor, 171
Le Puy, city: Compostela pilgrims from, 30; Moorish influence in architecture, 30; pilgrim art in hospice, 31; "Truce of God" movement launched at, 108; mentioned, 120
Libergier, Hugues, architect, 200
Louis VI, king of France, 68, 178, 179
Louis VII, king of France, 32, 65, 179
Louis VIII, king of France, 69
Louis IX, king of France: role in controversy over Vézelay's relics, 28; built Sainte-Chapelle, 31, 201; depicted in art, 32, 96; praised burghers, 69; his death on last Crusade, 94; his anti-Semitism, 148, 158, 161–62; mentioned, 8, 14, 198
Louis, St. *See* Louis IX, king of France
Luke, bishop of Tuy, 136, 187–88, 194
Lyon, cathedral and city: improved attitude to women illustrated at, 53; sensitive handling of sexual love at, 55; Philippe-Auguste encouraged commune at, 68; communal strife curtailed donorship, 71

Magnus, Albertus, St., theologian, 7
Mâle, Émile, scholar: on Verneilh, 5, 10; on Paris University, 5; on Notre-Dame's "Porte Rouge," 24; holds historical references in art are rare, 31; describes changes in Virgin's image, 47–48; says some stories only for popular appeal, 112; says medieval artist was docile, 187, 190; on Selles-sur-Cher sculpture, 194
Marxists, 66, 170
Mary, cult of: late in coming to West, 46; as "Mother of Mercy," 47; and the Year Thousand, 47; as influenced by "amour courtois," 47, 59; fostered by prayers, poetry, hymns, drama, art, 47; its influence on iconography,

47–50; Jean de Meung's reply to, 62; important source of church-building funds, 202, 204
Mary, iconography of: influenced by notions of royalty, 31; in Theophilus legend, 33; conditioned by French queen's high position, 33; as the anti-Eve, 46; greatly enriched by her cult, 47–48; her humanization, 48–50; in Reims draper's relief, 87; intercedes for sinners, 113, 191; in Jesse Tree scenes, 115; as answer to heretics, 128–29; false images of, 136; anti-Semitism in, 136; mentioned, 3, 188, 192, 194
Materialistic philosophy, 90–91
Mérimée, Prosper, author and art guardian, 164–66, 169
Mervilliers, church at, 33–34
Meung, Jean de, poet, 9, 60–61, 62
Moissac, church of Saint-Pierre: feudal relations in tympanum, 31; façade sculpture described, 67, 183; portraiture at, 98; during Revolution, 169; mentioned, 208
Montfort, Comte Simon de, 58, 124–25, 132
Montreuil, Pierre de, architect, 200
Mont-Saint-Michel, abbey, 177
Montségur, Catharist stronghold, 120, 133
Moslems: direct and indirect influence on Christian art and architecture, 25, 30; in Christian art, 35–36; at Montpellier medical school, 147; fall of Jerusalem to, 148; halted at Byzantium, 171; destroyed monastery, 204; mentioned, 147

Narbonne, city, 146, 159
Notre-Dame de Paris, cathedral: the eight reliefs, 3–4, 4n, 10, 11–16, 19, 22; chapter of, 15, 18–19; artisans' booths at, 15; rood-screen devil at, 18, 66, 66n; mystical interpretations regarding, 24; statues of Louis IX and wife at, 32, 96; relationship of sexes in art of, 53; burghers' donations to, 67; façade sculpture, 99; a sermon at, 107; folk humor illustrated at, 115; anti-Semitic art at, 158–59; iconoclasm at, 167, 168; destruction of buildings around, 170; sources of building funds, 202–3; amount of sculpture at, 206; mentioned, 4, 11, 13, 16, 169, 208
Notre-Dame-du-Port, church at Clermont-Ferrand, 42, 69, 103

Oloron-Sainte-Marie, church of Notre-Dame, 35, 85
Oxford University, 7, 8

Paris, city, the royal provost, 8, 16, 198; buildings at, mentioned, 16, 17, 147; For-l'Évêque, 20, 21; Sainte-Chapelle, 31–32, 169, 201; trades practiced by women, 57; rulers defended by burghers, 69; prostitutes of, 76; burghers' processional art, 85; a Paris lady's tombstone, 94; its population, 106; public debates between Christians and Jews, 159, 161–62; Talmuds burned at, 162; destruction of monuments at, 163, 168, 170; Saint-Germain-des-Près, 169, 200; its Jews, 179; statutes of guilds, 198; poll-tax listings, 199; mentioned, 11, 12, 16, 19, 21, 167, 168. *See also* Notre-Dame de Paris

Paris bishops: conflict with University, 5–10, 18; banned Thomas Aquinas' doctrine, 7; granted charter in 1222, 12; in dealings with students, 15, 16; rights curtailed by royal encroachment, 16; conflicts with chapter, 18–19; one of them in For-lÉvêque sculpture, 20; mentioned, 6, 11, 13, 21. *See also* Sully, Maurice de

Paris, University of: Bonaventura and Thomas Aquinas students at, 4; conflict between masters and bishops for control of, 5–10; banned Thomas Aquinas' doctrine, 7; controversy over curriculum, 6; Albertus Magnus taught at, 7; student excesses described, 7; police violence against students, 7; masters' and students' privileges, violated, 7, 16–18; granted *Bulla Parens Scientiarum*, 8; role of Guillaume de Saint-Amour, 9

Parthenay, church of, 188

Peter the Venerable, abbot of Cluny, 63, 67, 130–131, 147

Petits-Augustins, Paris convent, 17

Philippe II (Auguste), king of France: his charter of 1200, 7; his charter of 1222, 12, 17, 21; in relief at For-l'Évêque, 21; intervened in quarrel at Chartres, 59; friendly to communes, 68; at Bouvines, 69; and Albigensian "crusade," 124; expelled Jews, 147; earnings of, 205

Philippe III (le Hardi), king of France, 94, 148

Poitiers, city, 156, 171

"Poor Men of Lyon," heresy, 122

Popes: role in Paris University controversies, 6, 8, 9; in dispute between Saint-Germain-des-Près and bishop, 18; in dispute over Mary Magdalene's remains, 28, 64; laid claim to Spain, 28; in dispute between Saint-Sernin and Cluny, 29; changes in St. Peter's iconography increased papal authority, 32–33; at Avignon, 41; Gregory VII's clerical reform, 45, 122, 172; conceded suzerain's rights to Queen Aliénor, 56; role in Vézelay communal strife, 65; actions regarding Jews, 142, 146, 147, 148, 157; Innocent II's visit to Clairvaux, Saint-Denis, 176, 179; in fundraising quests for church-building, 180, 203–204; mentioned, 33, 178. *See also* Rome (in sense of Church, papacy); Rome, city

Popular impact on church art, 77, 112–14, 115–16, 117–18

Portraiture, development of: through artists' self-portraits, 93–94; in funerary art, 94; in burgher portraits, 94; in portraits of royalty, 94; in portraits of Christ, Mary, and Apostles, 96–99; influenced by Byzantine art, 98

Prefigurations of Christ and Mary, 144–46

Presbyter, Theophilus, monk and artist, 183–84, 185–86, 207

Protestants, 134–35, 137, 163–64

Provost of Paris, royal official, 8, 16, 198

Realism in art: responsive to social-economic factors, 91, 99; in floral decoration, 91–92; in depiction of devils, 93; in animal art, 93; in portraiture, 93–94; artists began working from nature, 99; in Gislebertus, 191

Reims, cathedral and city: World War I bombing of, 23; French kings portrayed at, 31; communal strife at, 67; strife curtailed donations, 71–72; reliefs of the guilty draper, 85–87; "House of Musicians," 90; a guildhall at, 90; a Communion scene at, 131; church of Saint-Nicaise, 200, 205; four architects and an archbishop depicted in labyrinth, 200; amount of art at, 206; mentioned, 186, 208

Relics, cult of: at Saint-Denis, 26, 180; inspired pilgrimages, 26; at Chartres, 26, 70–71; multiplied number of chapels, 26–28; controversy over Mary Magdalene's remains, 28, 64; art depicting miracles performed by relics, 28; St. James' remains, 28, 29; those at Saint-Gilles vaunted, 30; depicted in a lancet, 32; source of church-building funds, 202

Revolution, French: and the destruction of monuments, 163, 168, 200; iconoclasm during, 168, 169; statement of didactic purpose of painting, 170

Rome (in sense of Church, papacy): Thomas Aquinas' work on Aristotle has blessings of, 7; role in Albigensian "crusade," 124; in "quarrel of images," 171; in struggles with German emperor, 179; mentioned, 45

Rome, city: delegations of masters go to, in Paris University controversy, 6, 8, 9; heresy strong at, 122; mentioned, 33, 45, 125, 136

Rouen, cathedral and city: individual burgher donated a lancet at, 82; anti-Semitic art at, 149; Jews converted at, 157; archbishop mentioned, 177

Royalty in art: at For-l'Évêque, 21; Mâle's view of infrequent occurrences, 31; Clovis, 31, 106–7; Charlemagne, 31, 33; at Reims, 31; at Sainte-Chapelle, 31–32; portraits of Louis IX, 32, 96; at Strasbourg, 32, 83; at Chartres, 32, 207; at church of Avenas, 32; in Bayeux Tapestry, 36–38; Isabelle d'Aragon, 94; its idealization in art, 94; "kings of France" at Notre-Dame, 168

Rutebeuf, trouvère, 9

Sabouret, Victor, engineer, 23–24

Saint-Amour, Guillaume de, Paris University master, 9

Saint-Benoît-sur-Loire, abbey church, 28, 35, 36

Sainte-Chapelle, Paris: royalty in its art, 31–32; during Revolution and after, 169, 169n; required six years to build, 201

Saint-Denis abbey: tomb of Isabelle d'Aragon at, 94; façade statues, 98; Innocent II's reception at, 179; during threatened invasion, 179; art of, 180; popes are donors to, 180; rebuilt by Suger, 180–81, 201; pioneer of Gothic churches, 181; artistic ideas brought to, 181, 207; Godefroid de Claire at, 207; church soon needed bulwarking, 208; mentioned, 181. *See also* Suger, abbot of Saint-Denis

Saint-Étienne, church at Toulouse, 55, 148, 169

Saint-Georges-de-Boscherville, church, 35

Saint-Germer-de-Fly, church, 199

Saint-Germain-des-Prés, abbey at Paris, 18, 169, 200

Saint-Gilles, church and city: its relics vaunted, 30; a dead worker depicted, 102; Albigensian "crusade" began here, 124; art reflecting the heresy at, 128; center of cross-burning heresy, 128, 134–35; heresy impeded church's construction, 134–35; anti-Semitic art at, 150–51, 155; mutilation by Protestants, 163; its screw-staircase studied by architects, 207; mentioned, 208

Saint-Martin-d'Ainay, church at Lyon, 46

Saint-Martin de Tours, church, 25–26

Saint-Nazaire, church at Carcassonne, 58, 132

Saint-Nicaise, church at Reims, 200, 205

Saint-Remi, church at Reims, 174

Saint-Savin-sur-Gartempe, church, 164, 194

Saint-Sernin, church at Toulouse: claimed to have St. James' relics, 29; opposed, then supported Compostela pilgrimage, 29; cloister destroyed, 169; its early apse sculpture, 208

Saint-Trophime, church at Arles, 53

Salzman, L. F., scholar: holds most medieval builders were laymen, 185; describes class-consciousness of medieval workers, 198; holds medieval building often "unscientific and uneconomic," 208

San Domingo da Silos, abbey and saint, 36, 177

Santiago da Compostela, pilgrimage: its multiple motivation, 28–29; its influence on architecture and art, 28, 30–31; fostered by Cluny, 29, 30; opposed by Toulouse cathedral, 29; popularized by epics, 30; had its own guidebook, 30; an early group of pilgrims to, from Le Puy, 30; Compostela pilgrims in art, 31

Schapiro, Meyer, scholar: on portrayal of feudal tensions in Theophilus legend, 33; on leading male and female Vices in medieval art, 42; suggests how shift in class relations influenced iconography, 67

Seignelay, Guillaume de, bishop of Paris, 21

Selles-sur-Cher, church at, 194

Semur-en-Auxois, church of Notre-Dame, 82–83

Sens, Guillaume de, architect, 201–2, 207

"Signatures" (donor work-scenes): at Chartres, 74–79, 207; at Bourges, 75; at Le Mans, 76; at Semur-en-Auxois, 82–83

Sorbon, Robert de, educator, 12, 15–16

Souillac, church at, 33, 98

Souvigny, church of Saint-Pierre, 35

Stained-glass windows: their role in development of Gothic style, 24, 69; French royalty at Sainte-Chapelle, 31–32; first use on monumental scale, 70; high cost of, 70; no burgher-donors of, at Lyon, Reims, 71–72; burgher-donors of, 72, 74, 76; donor "signatures," 74–79, 82–83, 207; twelfth-century donors of, chiefly churchmen, 75; one offered by Paris prostitutes, 76; individual burgher-donors, 82; "Passion-Play" series at Strasbourg, 83–85, 90; Strasbourg lancet of "Stadtrat," 85; Cain humanely treated at Tours, 102; land-settlement illustrated, 106–7; a reply to heresy in, 131; the "mystic mill," 145; anti-Semitism in, 159; destruction of, 167; Goethe's attitude toward, 167; how

Sainte-Chapelle's glass was preserved, 169n; banned by Cistercians, 176; an architect depicted, 199; amount of at Chartres, Bourges, Reims, 206; sculptors depicted, 207; praised by Theophilus Presbyter, 207. *See also* Chartres cathedral

Strasbourg cathedral: royalty and nobility in art of, 32; reversal of role of Eve at, 53; "Passion-Play"lancets,83–85; burghers took over cathedral "fabrique," 84–85; lost lancet of "Stadtrat," 85; panel of Doubting Thomas, 90; anti-Semitic art at, 155

Suger, abbot of Saint-Denis: active role in rebuilding his church, 26, 177–78, 180–81, 201, 208; commissioned the "mystic mill," 145; boyhood friend of Louis VI, regent of Louis VII, 179; his nationalism, 179; reception of Innocent II, 179; his sacramental view of art, 179; described abbey's new art, 180; anagogical view of light, 180; his pioneer use of monumental stained-glass, 181; tore out old roodscreen, 181; influence on art compared with that of St. Bernard, 181–82; not originator of typological symbolism, 207

Sully, Maurice de, bishop of Paris: conflict with Saint-Germain-des-Près, 18; compared merchant to the Devil, 67; his sermons, 67, 107; was offered window by prostitutes, 76; received confiscated synagogue from Philippe-Auguste, 147; accepted money from usurer for building fund, 203; mentioned, 203

Tavant, church at, 194

Tempier, Étienne, Paris bishop, 7, 15

Thibaut II, comte de Champagne, 176, 180

Tithes, 13–15, 30

Torigini, Robert de, abbot of Mont-Saint-Michel, 177

Toulouse, city: University at, 7, 8; church of Saint-Sernin, 29; its bishop loyal to Cluny, 29; Simon de Montfort's death at, 58; Jacobins church, 121; in Albigensian "crusade," 124; church of Saint-Étienne, 148; its three medieval cloisters destroyed, 169. *See also* Saint-Sernin; Daurade, La

Toulouse, Comte de, 124

Tours cathedral, 53, 82, 102

Troyes, Chrétien de, poet, 58

Troyes cathedral: lancet in reply to heresy,131; slowness of carting stone to, 201; building of, protracted by lack of funds, 202; changed artists for its roodscreen, 206

"Truce of God" movement, 108

Tudela, Benjamin da, traveler and diarist, 146, 148

Verneilh, Comte Félix de, scholar, 3–4, 5, 10, 12

Vézelay, abbey and city: in controversy over its relics, 28; relief of scene of justice at, 35; anti-woman art at, 42; pro-woman art at, 50; violence in art of, 63–64; Peter the Venerable at, 63; communal conflicts delayed church construction, 64–65; its relics authenticated by pope, 64; conflict with Comte de Nevers, 65–66, 67; devils in art of, 66; description of devils there by Peter the Venerable, 67; relief of honey-gathering scene at, 104; burghers bury their own dead, 122n; relief of the "mystic mill" at 145; its art "excesses" condemned by St. Bernard, 174; mentioned, 114, 188

Villeneuve-les-Avignon, city, 41, 45, 60

Viollet-le-Duc, Eugène, architect and author: in controversy over Gothic style, 23–24; on development of floral decoration, 92; on Church *vs.* Synagogue sculpture, 149; holds clerics fostered idea of medieval artist's anonymity, 185; holds that medieval artist could express himself freely, 187; estimated what building Chartres would cost in his day, 205; on swift development of medieval technic, 208

Wace, Robert, poet, 37, 46, 108–9

Waldo, Peter, founder of Waldenses, 122

Webster, James C., author, 104–5

White, Lynn, Jr., scholar: holds medieval artists inaccurate in depicting world about them, 39; describes development of materialistic viewpoint in Middle Ages, 90–92; describes symbolic viewpoint in Middle Ages, 91

William the Conqueror, king of England, 36, 37

Woman, clerical attitude toward: pejorative view illustrated at Villeneuve-les-Avignon, 41, 45; "Daughters of Eve," 42, 46, 62; in other monastic-influenced art, 42; as exemplified by liturgical drama, 42–44; shaped by Church's need to reform clergy, 44, 45; paradox of Church's pejorative view of woman and the glorification of Mary, 45, 46; Mary as the anti-Eve, 46; was opposed to her acquisition of new social rights, 55–56; mentioned, 59, 140

Woman in art: Paris harlots in Prodigal Son
scenes, 11, 114; in scenes with Paris students,
11–15; Old Testament women in art, 32; female royalty and nobility portrayed, 32, 96;
in obscene posture with a goat, 41, 60; in
Hell and/or associated with the Devil, 42; always represents Vice of Unchastity, 42; Eve
kicked by Adam after Original Sin, 42; she
beguiles even Aristotle and Virgil, 45; Mary
the Egyptian pays for her passage "in trade,"
46; feminization of Mary humanizes handling of other women, illustrated, 50; griev-
ing mothers, 53; change in Original Sin—
shared guilt, 53; relationship with and depiction of man humanized, illustrated, 53;
Tempter and the Foolish Virgin, 53; sex in
Bayeux Tapestry, 55; subtle handling of sexual love, illustrated, 55; iconographic changes
held to be effect of altered social status, 55;
women at work, 57, 100; role of art in humanizing attitude toward woman, 62; merchants' wives and daughters in Renaissance
art, 79–80; bourgeois women as donors, 82;
in Reims draper's relief, 86; in tombal art,
94, 100; "The Contemplative Life," 100; a
bourgeois woman illustrating Vice of Ingratitude, 102; ordinary woman saw self
reflected in sinner-saints, 114; Theospita, a
loyal wife, 114; in rigid depictions of Virtues, 115; in Communion scene, 129–30;
absent from Beaulieu Judgment Day, 140;
the Jewish blacksmith's wife, 155; the Autun
Eve, 168, 191–92; in Autun Vice of Unchastity scene, 192; God shown mistrustful
of Eve during her creation, 194

Woman's social status: Church's historic role
in improving, 45; improvement in, seen as
cause of change in her artistic representation,
55; acquired right of inheritance, 55; improvement in, opposed by seigniors, churchmen, 55–56; an important concession by Innocent III, 56; equality of sexes in middle
class, 57; improvement hastened by Crusades, 58–60; as mirrored in "amour courtois," 59–60; Pierre de Montreuil's wife got
her own inscribed tombstone, 200

"Year Thousand": end of world expected at,
40; surge of church-building when world was
spared, described by Raoul Glaber, 40n; rise
of cult of Mary attributed to fears of, 47;
fears of, encouraged many gifts to Church,
105